POSITIVE DISCIPLINE
PARENTING TOOLS

POSITIVE DISCIPLINE PARENTING TOOLS

THE 49 MOST EFFECTIVE METHODS
TO STOP POWER STRUGGLES,
BUILD COMMUNICATION, AND RAISE
EMPOWERED, CAPABLE KIDS

JANE NELSEN, ED.D., MARY NELSEN TAMBORSKI, M.A., AND BRAD AINGE

HARMONY

BOOKS · NEW YORK

Copyright © 2016 by Jane Nelsen, Mary Nelsen Tamborski, and Brad Ainge

Published in the United States by Harmony Books, an imprint of the Crown
Publishing Group, a division of Penguin Random House LLC, New York.
crownpublishing.com

Harmony Books is a registered trademark, and the Circle colophon is a trademark of
Penguin Random House LLC.

Library of Congress Cataloging-in-Publication Data is available upon request.

ISBN 978-1-101-90534-0
eBook ISBN 978-1-101-90535-7

Printed in the United States of America

Illustrations by Paula Gray and Diane Bleck, Discovery Doodles LLC
Cover design by Jenny Carrow
Cover photograph by vgajic/E+/Getty Images

10 9 8 7 6 5 4 3 2 1

First Edition

To Mary and Brad. What fun to have two of my children join me in creating this book.

—Jane

To Mark, my husband, who provides endless love and support; and to my three boys, Greyson, Reid, and Parker, who remind me daily how challenging and how rewarding parenting can be.

—Mary

To my three children, Kelsie, Gibson, and Emma, about whom I have more to say in the acknowledgments.

—Brad

CONTENTS

CONTENTS

POSITIVE DISCIPLINE PARENTING TOOLS

INTRODUCTION

HOW IS POSITIVE DISCIPLINE DIFFERENT?

Parenting-style research has focused for several decades now on identifying what parenting practices are most effective. Alfred Adler, a
Viennese medical doctor and one of the first to create the field of psychiatry along with Freud in the late 1800s, believed that the primary
goal of all people is to belong and to feel significant, and that people
make all kinds of mistakes in their efforts to overcome a feeling of
inferiority (feeling not good enough). Those "mistakes" often are identified as misbehavior. Adler believed that "misbehavior" was based on
beliefs such as "I will feel good enough only if I get lots of attention,"
or "only if I am the boss," or "if I hurt others as I feel hurt," or "if I
give up and assume that I am inadequate." These beliefs form what
Adler called "private logic," and he taught that the only way to change
behavior is to help an individual change those beliefs.

Unlike B. F. Skinner, who believed that the best way to change behavior is from the outside-in (external motivators), through punishment
and rewards (an approach now called behaviorism), Adler believed the
best way to change behavior is from the inside-out (internal motivators), through encouragement that helps a person experience the deep
need to belong as a social being. His was a philosophy of treating
everyone with dignity and respect. He saw patients face-to-face instead

of having them lie on a couch (as did Freud) and taking a position of superiority to the patient.

Rudolf Dreikurs, a protégé and colleague of Adler, continued teaching the Adlerian philosophy after the death of Adler in 1937, and took this philosophy of equality, dignity, and respect for all people to parents and teachers, instead of confining it to the psychiatric office for psychoanalysis. Dreikurs referred to this philosophy as "democratic" (freedom with order), as distinguished from "authoritarian" (order with no freedom) and "anarchic" (freedom without order). He used this three-dimensional model to examine how parents influence their children.

Diana Baumrind, a psychologist working at the University of California, Berkeley, used the term "authoritative," which we'll use more often throughout the book, to describe what Dreikurs called "democratic." Dreikurs identified the "democratic" parenting style as most beneficial, and he advocated for this responsive yet firm approach to leadership at home as well as in schools. Both Adler and Dreikurs recognized the need for respectful discipline designed to teach problem solving and other important life skills.

Diana Baumrind's longitudinal research on parenting style has spanned several decades.[1-4] Her work also supports Positive Discipline's parenting model, which focuses on the practical application of the same methods Baumrind and others identify as influential in child and adolescent development. Baumrind systematically examined how parenting impacts the social and psychological adjustment, academic success, and general well-being of children and adolescents. Baumrind found that adolescents whose parents were democratic or authoritative performed better academically, were more emotionally and socially stable, and used alcohol and drugs substantially less than adolescents from either permissive or authoritarian family environments. Baumrind summarized her own research by stating: "Adolescents from authoritative and democratic families showed by far the most social competence, maturity and optimism." They also scored the highest on verbal and mathematical achievement tests.[5]

The majority of discipline models practiced in homes and school today are based on punishments and rewards. Positive Discipline is based on the Adlerian model of eliminating all punishment and rewards in favor of encouragement that addresses the basic needs of children to belong and feel significant, and our task is to help children find belonging and significance in socially useful ways. We begin by understanding and addressing mistaken beliefs about how to achieve belonging and significance, and then we teach skills to achieve belonging and significance in socially useful ways.

A child's behavior, like the tip of the iceberg below, is what you see. However, the hidden base of the iceberg (much larger than the tip) represents the *belief* behind the behavior, and the child's deepest need for belonging and significance. Most parenting programs address only the behavior. Positive Discipline addresses both the behavior and the belief behind the behavior.

When children misbehave, they usually have a *mistaken belief* about how to gain a sense of belonging. The belief generates what parents call misbehavior. Most parents react to the behavior with some kind of punishment (blame, shame, or pain). This only confirms a child's belief that he or she doesn't belong, creating a vicious cycle.

Alfred Adler and Rudolf Dreikurs taught that a misbehaving child is a discouraged child. The discouragement comes from the belief "I don't belong." In most cases, this is shocking to parents. They wonder, "How can my child believe she doesn't belong? How could she not know how much I love her? This doesn't make sense."

Aha! You have now entered the realm of one of life's greatest mysteries. How and why do children create their beliefs—especially when they don't make sense to us? This is why it is so important to get into the child's world to understand the child's "private logic." We all have our unique way of perceiving the world, yet sometimes parents forget that their children perceive the world differently than they do. In this book, you will learn to understand the beliefs your children form as they interact with the world, and the tools you can use to empower your children to adopt more encouraging beliefs. First we would like to challenge some mistaken beliefs adults have.

Some parents have thought that Positive Discipline implies a positive way to use punishment. Actually, we don't believe in punishment at all. In addition, we don't believe in praise, punitive time-out, taking away privileges, or rewards. The forty-nine Positive Discipline tools in this book help show how many discipline methods there are that do not include rewards or punishment. Research shows that punishment and rewards are not effective in the long term and in fact negatively impact things such as self-regulation, intrinsic motivation, and the quality of family relationships.[6] We even discourage the use of logical consequences—at least most of the time—because many parents try to disguise punishment by calling it a "logical consequence." Following is a list of beliefs that are likely to be created by punishment.

THE 4 R'S OF PUNISHMENT
1. Resentment: "This is unfair. I can't trust adults."
2. Rebellion: "I'll do just the opposite to prove I don't have to do it their way."
3. Revenge: "They are winning now, but I'll get even."
4. Retreat:
   • Sneakiness: "I won't get caught next time."
   • Reduced self-esteem: "I am a bad person."

Some people think this leaves only one alternative—permissiveness, which can be just as damaging as punishment. Permissiveness invites children to develop the belief that "Love means I should be able to do whatever I want," or "I need you to take care of me because I'm not capable of responsibility," or even "I'm depressed because you don't cater to my every demand."

Baumrind's findings also illustrate how the permissive parent style can be harmful because few demands are made on children. In addition, the lack of structure and routine coupled with overindulgence is less than effective. Furthermore, her findings show that authoritarian parents who are autocratic and highly directive because they value immediate obedience are also ineffective in the long term. It is evident in the research that neither permissive parenting nor authoritarian parenting provides what children need for long-term social and emotional growth and for academic success.

"So," you may ask, "if not punishment and not permissiveness, then what?"

The answer is **encouragement**. Positive Discipline is an encouragement model. Since a misbehaving child is also a discouraged child, Dreikurs taught that a child needs encouragement the way a plant needs water. All of the tools we share with you are encouraging to children, as well as to parents. They are designed to increase a sense of belonging and significance, and thus they focus on the belief behind the behavior. To be more specific, they meet all five of the criteria we've listed as essential to Positive Discipline.

FIVE CRITERIA FOR POSITIVE DISCIPLINE
1. Helps children feel a sense of connection, belonging, and significance
2. Is kind and firm at the same time
3. Is effective in the long term
4. Teaches valuable social and life skills for good character, fostering respect, concern for others, problem solving, and cooperation
5. Invites children to discover how capable they are, and how to use their power constructively

Even though the Positive Discipline tools are designed to meet these criteria, it is essential to understand that they are based on the Adlerian principles discussed above. They are not effective if used simply like a script. When you understand the principles upon which a tool is based, and add your heart and wisdom, you won't sound as if you are reading a script. Instead, you will find your own unique way, and your own words, to apply these tools.

It helps to be very clear about what you hope to achieve with children. Parents play a crucial role in the development of a child's personality and greatly influence children's overall well-being.[7] Different parenting styles have been linked to a variety of specific developmental outcomes related to social and emotional well-being as well as academic achievement. Numerous studies show a direct correlation between parenting style and levels of self-regulation, overall life satisfaction, grades, alcohol use, aggression, and oppositional behavior.[2, 8, 9–12] Each of the Positive Discipline tools in this book is designed to help parents practically apply what is well identified in the research as most beneficial for family relationships and child development. This approach supports what Adlerians have said for so long: that parenting style is a family leadership variable influencing family dynamic, which in turn impacts children's perceptions, level of adjustment, and developmental outcomes over time.

WHAT DO YOU WANT FOR YOUR CHILDREN?

When embarking upon the journey into Positive Discipline, it helps to have a destination in mind, and a road map to help you get there. Creating a list of characteristics and life skills you hope to have your children develop can serve as your road map.

Imagine your child as an adult who has come home for a visit. What kind of person would you hope to spend time with? What characteristics and life skills do you hope he or she has? Take time to create your list. Does it look similar to the following?

- Problem-solving skills
- Responsibility
- Cooperation
- Self-discipline, self-control
- Communication skills

- Resilience
- Self-confidence
- Courage
- Courtesy, patience
- Open-mindedness

- Sense of humor
- Compassion
- Respect for self and others
- Empathy
- Integrity
- Enthusiasm for life
- Interest in learning
- Honesty
- Belief in personal capability
- Social consciousness
- Self-motivation

Add any characteristics to your list that you feel have been left off. Keep your list handy and refer to it often to verify that the Positive Discipline tools in this book are helping you to reach your destination.

Now create a list of the *challenges* you may be having with your child or children. You will be learning tools to deal with every one of them.

The following is a compilation of challenges brainstormed by hundreds of parents. You may find it comforting to know you are not alone.

CHALLENGES

- Not listening
- Back talk
- Lack of motivation
- Entitled attitude
- Materialism
- Being strong-willed
- Defiance
- Neglecting chores/work
- Media addictions, constant texting
- Tantrums, whining
- Cheating
- Fighting
- Biting
- Aggression
- Lying
- Stealing
- Homework problems
- Morning hassles, bedtime hassles
- Foul language
- Interrupting

Add any behaviors that are challenging to you. You'll find it encouraging to experience that the Positive Discipline tools you will be learning not only change negative behavior but also encourage the development of the characteristics and life skills you want for your children.

GETTING INTO YOUR CHILD'S WORLD

During our Positive Discipline workshops and classes, we teach through experiential activities in which parents have the opportunity to role-play parents and children. This provides them with the opportunity to get into the child's world to gain a sense of what works and what doesn't work.

After each activity, the adult who role-played as the child is taken to two lists (similar to those above) that are prominently displayed on a wall, and asked, "As the child, were you learning anything on this list of characteristics and life skills?"

After experiencing an ineffective parenting method, the "child" always says, "No."

We then point out the list of challenges and ask if he or she is feeling motivated to engage in any of these behaviors. The "child" usually points out several misbehaviors that he or she feels motivated to do. This helps parents understand how they may have a part in creating the misbehaviors they complain about. They experience what it is like to be a child who responds to disrespectful parenting methods with more misbehavior, and why the child acts that way.

After the "child" experiences a Positive Discipline tool during a role-play, he or she is always able to identify several of the characteristics and life skills he or she is learning. This kind of experiential learning has a greater impact on parents than any other kind of learning.

After introducing the Two Lists activity, we love to start with the Motivational Curiosity Questions activity to deal with the challenge of "not listening." In the section "Curiosity Questions (Motivational)" in Chapter 5, you too can experience the profound awareness that comes from getting into the child's world through role-playing.

Will all of these activities and tools turn you into a perfect parent? No. Sorry, there is no such thing as a perfect parent. (You will learn more about this in Chapter 3, on mistakes.)

Will your children feel a sense of belonging, significance, and a strong belief in their personal capability? Yes.

Does this mean they will be perfect and never misbehave? No! It is part of their developmental process to *individuate*—to test the boundaries as they discover who they are and how to use their personal power. In fact, when you provide a safe place for them to individuate, they may feel it is safer to rebel (which is just another word for "individuate"). All the more reason to use parenting tools that focus on problem-solving skills instead of methods that increase power struggles and revenge cycles.

IS POSITIVE DISCIPLINE MANIPULATIVE?

A participant in one of our workshops commented that she thought one of the Positive Discipline tools sounded manipulative. In fact, all Positive Discipline tools are manipulative. Perhaps the word "guidance" sounds better than "manipulation." Don't we all want our children to develop the characteristics and life skills we hope they will have?

The key is what the "manipulation" looks like. Is it respectful and empowering, or disrespectful and discouraging? Positive Discipline tools are all designed to be empowering and encouraging, and there is a very important key to make sure that they are: as mentioned above, **every tool must be based on foundational principles.**

A principle can be used in many ways. For example, when you use the principles of math, there are many ways to get to 4: $2 + 2$, $3 + 1$, $8 - 2 - 2$, and so on. When a Positive Discipline tool is based on one or more principles and you add your heart and wisdom, the tool can be used in many different ways. For example, when you ground curiosity questions on some basic principles (such as connection before correction, understanding the belief behind the behavior, kindness and firmness) and then add your heart and wisdom, your curiosity questions will fit the situation and be encouraging and empowering. However, if you use curiosity questions like a script, they will sound false, and they will be manipulative in a negative way. If you try to use any Positive Discipline tool without understanding the principle behind it, your children will often respond negatively.

When your children test the limits, you will have Positive Discipline tools to help them learn socially acceptable behaviors that increase their sense of capability, belonging, and significance. Sometimes the seeds you are sowing take a while to bloom. You know you're doing a great job when your friends and neighbors tell you how great your kids are, and you wonder if they are thinking of someone else's kids. It's because they feel safe to "individuate" with you, and then use the skills they learn from you when they're on their own.

In this book you will hear the effectiveness of these Positive Discipline tools from many parents all over the world who share their success stories. We will start with our own.

SUCCESS STORY FROM DR. JANE NELSEN

I wrote my first Positive Discipline book in 1981. At the time I was just learning these parenting methods based on the work of Alfred Adler and Rudolf Dreikurs. Even though I agreed with their basic philosophy of giving up all punishment and treating children with dignity and respect, changing old habits was not easy. Still, as I used the tools, I learned and improved (as much from mistakes as from successes), and my joy in parenting increased tenfold. I wanted to share what I was learning with anyone who would listen.

Little did I know that I would someday be traveling all over the world! Positive Discipline has grown so much over the past thirty-five years, and it warms my heart to hear so many testimonials and success stories.

However, nothing can quite compare with the feeling I have when my own children have success using Positive Discipline with my grandchildren. You can only imagine the joy I feel to be writing this book with two of my children, Brad (my fifthborn) and Mary (my seventhborn). We have been writing blogs about these tools for several years and find that parents enjoy hearing the real story of implementing Positive Discipline—both successes and failures. It is such a relief for parents to learn that perfection is not part of the process.

SUCCESS STORY FROM MARY NELSEN TAMBORSKI

As a young girl, I remember sitting at the back of the room and selling books at my mom's lectures on Positive Discipline. I would listen to the parents compliment her for her presentation. Many thanked her for changing their lives. I never really understood the impact she had on these parents until I became one myself.

My mom recently asked me, "How often would you say that you practice Positive Discipline?"

I said, "At least 80 percent of the time."

She laughed and said, "Wow, that's really good, I could only do about 70 percent, and I wrote the books."

I came to some possible conclusions: (1) maybe I'm not being realistic with that 80 percent, (2) maybe being the author's daughter gave me a 10 percent advantage, or (3) maybe I truly and deeply understand the benefits of practicing the Positive Discipline parenting model after being raised with it.

I've always known how fortunate I was to be raised by the author of the Positive Discipline series, but only when I used family meetings with my college roommates did I realize how it helped my parents and siblings live harmoniously and remain friends for life.

I have now been teaching Positive Discipline since my second son was born, a little over seven years ago. It's humbling to share my knowledge and personal experience through parenting workshops and coaching. I can only imagine how proud my mom is, and I can say without a doubt that she is my biggest fan. It brings us both so much joy to work together, whether it's facilitating, presenting, or writing a book. I am honored and blessed to be working with my mother—my best friend.

SUCCESS STORY FROM SINGLE DAD BRAD

Becoming a full-time single father was quite a shock for me at first! Like most dads, I was much better at being a relief pitcher. I would come home from work, play with the kids, and maybe read them a book before bed. I also enjoyed coaching Little League teams and helping with the other extracurricular activities. But like most of the fathers I knew, I would start to crumble if I was left home alone with the kids for more than an hour.

So when I first started parenting on my own, I was completely overwhelmed! Television became a thing of the past. My golf game began to suffer, and folding laundry became my new hobby. And then about a month into this new adventure I went through what I call single parent boot camp—when the flu hit our household with a vengeance. But of course my kids didn't get the flu bug at the same time. Instead they each got the flu about one week apart. So for three solid weeks I was nursing kids back to health, changing sheets, and cleaning up puke. And then just when I thought the nightmare was over, *I* got the flu!

Suddenly I gained a new perspective on single parenting. Being a full-time single parent is hard, but when you try to handle that job with the flu, you realize that it could be much, much worse. So from that day forward I tried to have an attitude of gratitude.

Parenting is the most rewarding job in the world. It can also be the most challenging. That is why I embarked on a yearlong adventure of implementing one Positive Discipline tool per week. This experiment gave me new perspective on my relationship with my children and how I could improve my parenting skills.

Don't be too hard on yourself. The danger of starting something new is that sometimes we raise our expectations too high and become frustrated when not everything is perfect. A couple of times when I first started using these tools, I found myself expecting perfection from my children, and my frustration with them made things worse. But when I changed my attitude and focused on improvement, not perfection, the atmosphere in our home got much better.

Every family is different and every child is different. It is important to find what works for you and what feels right to you. Use your intuition and have fun!

CHAPTER ONE

THE BASICS

BREAK THE CODE

Children decide amongst themselves which role they intend
to play in the family and parents reinforce their decision.

—*Rudolf Dreikurs*

You will be most effective with your children if you understand the
"belief behind their behavior."

USE THE MISTAKEN GOAL CHART:

1. Choose a behavior challenge.
2. Identify the feelings you have and how you react.
3. Identify the child's reaction when you tell him or her to stop.
4. Use the chart to identify what belief may be behind your child's behavior.
5. Try the suggestions in the last column of the chart to encourage behavior change.

In the Introduction we introduced the iceberg analogy to demonstrate how Positive Discipline deals with both the *behavior* and the *belief behind the behavior*. In this chapter we introduce the Mistaken Goal Chart and four more icebergs illustrating four categories of beliefs that lead to what Rudolf Dreikurs called mistaken goals. He called them mistaken goals because the behavior is based on mistaken beliefs about how to achieve the primary goals of belonging and significance. These mistaken beliefs are undue attention, misguided power, revenge, and assumed inadequacy.

For *undue attention*, the belief is "I belong only when you pay constant attention to me, and/or give me special service." The coded message that provides clues for encouragement is "Notice me. Involve me usefully."

For *misguided power,* the belief is "I belong only when I'm the boss, or at least when I don't let you boss me around." The coded message that provides clues for encouragement is "Let me help. Give me choices."

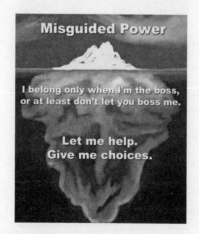

For *revenge,* the belief is "I don't belong, and that hurts, so I'll get even by hurting others." The coded message that provides clues for encouragement is "I'm hurting. Validate my feelings."

For *assumed inadequacy,* the belief is "I give up. Leave me alone." The coded message that provides clues for encouragement is "Don't give up on me. Show me a small step."

Often Dreikurs was asked why he kept putting children in these boxes. He said, "I don't keep putting them there; I keep finding them there."

It is understandable that parents often react to misbehavior. How you feel in reaction to your child's behavior is your first clue in breaking the code to your child's behavior.

When a child's goal is misguided power, some parents may say they feel helpless to "make" the child do what he or she is supposed to do. At a deeper level, these parents may be feeling challenged or defeated because they aren't winning the power struggle. Many parents today still struggle with shifting from autocratic rule ("because I said so" parenting) to democratic (authoritative) leadership ("let's solve this together"). Positive Discipline tools are designed to help parents across cultures shift away from inferior/superior relationships and toward a model that teaches respect and dignity for each individual while focusing on teaching important life skills for finding solutions to life's problems.

Check out the Mistaken Goal Detective Clue Form below to help you navigate the Mistaken Goal Chart on pages 18–21. It will help you "break the code" to your child's behavior, along with offering you clues for encouragement—ways to inspire your child to choose more empowering beliefs and behaviors.

MISTAKEN GOAL DETECTIVE CLUE FORM

1. Think of a recent challenge you had with your child. Write it down. Describe what occurred as though you are writing a script: what did your child do, how did you react, and then what happened?

2. What were you feeling when you were in the middle of this challenge? (Choose a feeling from Column 2 of the Mistaken Goal Chart.) Write it down.

3. Now move your finger to the right across the row over to Column 3 of the Mistaken Goal Chart to see if the action you took in response to that feeling comes close to one of these typical responses. If your action is described in a different row instead, double-check to see if there is a feeling in another row in Column 2 that better represents how you were feeling at a deeper level. (We often say we are feeling "annoyed" when, at a deeper level, we are feeling challenged or hurt; we often say we feel "hopeless" or "helpless" when we really feel challenged or

MISTAKEN GOAL CHART

1. THE CHILD'S GOAL IS:	2. IF THE PARENT/ TEACHER FEELS:	3. AND TENDS TO REACT BY:	4. AND IF THE CHILD'S RESPONSE IS:	5. THE BELIEF BEHIND THE CHILD'S BEHAVIOR IS:
Undue attention (to keep others busy or get special service)	Annoyed Irritated Worried Guilty	Reminding Coaxing Doing things for the child that the child could do for him- or herself	Stops temporarily, but later resumes the same or another disturbing behavior Stops when given one-on-one attention	"I count [belong] only when I'm being noticed or getting special service." "I'm important only when I'm keeping you busy with me."
Misguided power (to be the boss)	Angry Challenged Threatened Defeated	Fighting Giving in Thinking, "You can't get away with it" or "I'll make you" Wanting to be right	Intensifies the behavior Defiant compliance Feels he or she has won when the parent or teacher is upset Passive power	"I belong only when I'm the boss, in control, or proving no one can boss me." "You can't make me."

6.	7.	8.
HOW ADULTS MAY CONTRIBUTE TO THE PROBLEM:	**THE CHILD'S CODED MESSAGES:**	**PARENT/TEACHER PROACTIVE AND EMPOWERING RESPONSES INCLUDE:**
"I don't have faith in you to deal with disappointment." "I feel guilty if you aren't happy."	"Notice me. Involve me usefully."	Redirect by involving child in a useful task to gain useful attention. Tell your child you care, and then say what you will do: "I love you and _____" (for example, "I care about you and will spend time with you later"). Avoid special services. Say it only once and then act. Have faith in the child's ability to deal with his or her feelings (don't fix the problem or rescue the child). Plan special time. Set up routines. Engage the child in problem solving. Use family or class meetings. Ignore (touch without words). Set up nonverbal signals.
"I'm in control and you must do what I say." "I believe that telling you what to do, and lecturing or punishing you when you don't do it, is the best way to motivate you to do better."	"Let me help. Give me choices."	Acknowledge that you can't make the child do something, and redirect to positive power by asking for help. Offer a limited choice. Don't fight and don't give in. Withdraw from conflict and calm down. Be firm and kind. Act, don't talk. Decide what you will do. Let routines be the boss. Develop mutual respect. Get help from the child to set a few reasonable limits. Practice follow-through. Use family or class meetings.

1.	2.	3.	4.	5.
THE CHILD'S GOAL IS:	**IF THE PARENT/ TEACHER FEELS:**	**AND TENDS TO REACT BY:**	**AND IF THE CHILD'S RESPONSE IS:**	**THE BELIEF BEHIND THE CHILD'S BEHAVIOR IS:**
Revenge (to get even)	Hurt Disappointed Disbelieving Disgusted	Retaliating Getting even Thinking, "How could you do this to me?" Taking the child's behavior personally	Retaliates Hurts others Damages property Gets even Intensifies Escalates the same behavior or chooses another weapon	"I don't think I belong, so I'll hurt others in the way I feel hurt." "I can't be liked or loved."
Assumed Inadequacy (to give up and be left alone)	Despairing Hopeless Helpless Inadequate	Giving up Doing the task for the child Helping too much Showing a lack of faith in the child	Retreats further Passive No improvement No response Avoids trying	"I don't believe I can belong, so I'll convince others not to expect anything of me." "I am helpless and unable; It's no use trying because I won't do it right."

6. HOW ADULTS MAY CONTRIBUTE TO THE PROBLEM:	7. THE CHILD'S CODED MESSAGES:	8. PARENT/TEACHER PROACTIVE AND EMPOWERING RESPONSES INCLUDE:
"I give advice (without listening to you) because I think I'm helping." "I worry more about what the neighbors think than what you need."	"I'm hurting. Validate my feelings."	Validate the child's hurt feelings (you might have to guess what they are). Don't take the child's behavior personally. Step out of the revenge cycle by avoiding punishment and retaliation. Suggest Positive Time-Out for both of you, then focus on solutions. Use reflective listening. Share your feelings using an "I" message. Apologize and make amends. Encourage strengths. Put kids in the same boat. Use family and class meetings.
"I expect you to live up to my high expectations." "I thought it was my job to do things for you."	"Don't give up on me. Show me a small step."	Break tasks down into small steps. Make the task easier until the child experiences success. Set up opportunities for success. Take time for training. Teach skills and show how, but don't do the task for the child. Stop all criticism. Encourage any positive attempt, no matter how small. Show faith in the child's abilities. Focus on the child's assets. Don't pity the child. Don't give up. Enjoy the child. Build on the child's interests. Use family or class meetings.

defeated in a power struggle.) How you react is a clue to your deeper feelings.

4. Now move your finger to the right across the row to Column 4. Do any of these descriptions come close to what the child did in response to your reaction?

5. Once you've identified what the child did in response to your reaction, move your finger left across the row to Column 1. It is likely that this is your child's mistaken goal. Write it down.

6. Now move your finger to the right across the row to Column 5. You have just discovered what your child's discouraging belief may be. Write it down.

7. Move your finger over to Column 6. Does this come close to a belief you have that may contribute to your child's behavior? (Remember, this is not about blame—only awareness.) While you are learning skills to encourage your child, you will also change your belief. Try it now. Write down a belief that would be more encouraging to your child. You'll find clues in the last two columns.

8. Move your finger to the right, over to Column 7, where you will find the coded message about what your child needs in order to feel encouraged.

9. Move once more to the right, to the last column, to find some ideas you could try the next time you encounter this challenging behavior. (You can also use your own wisdom to think of something you could do or say that would speak to the coded message in Column 7.) Write down your plan.

10. How did it go? Record in your journal exactly what happened. You want to revisit your success stories for future encouragement. If your plan wasn't successful, try another tool. (See "Connection Before Correction," later in this chapter, and make sure you first make a connection before making a correction.)

You will notice that the Mistaken Goal Chart includes a column called "How adults may contribute to the problem." Helping parents become aware of how they contribute to misbehavior can be very touchy. For this reason, we will say over and over that it is not about blame or shame, but awareness.

Identifying the belief behind the behavior and the mistaken goal is not always easy, because children may use the same behaviors to achieve any of the four mistaken goals. For example, children may refuse to do their homework in order to gain attention ("Look at me, look at me"), to show power ("You can't make me"), to seek revenge ("It hurts that my grades are more important to you than I am, so I will hurt you back"), or to express their sense of inadequacy ("I really can't"). Parents have different feelings in each case. Effective intervention and encouragement will be different for each goal, so it is important that you use your reaction feeling as a clue to understand your child's goal.

Note that we talk about "encouragement." It does not matter whether the child's beliefs are based on facts or on her perception of the situation. Behavior is based on what children *believe* is true, not what is true. Behavior changes when parents understand the belief and use encouragement (Positive Discipline tools) to help children find constructive ways to find belonging and significance.

SUCCESS STORY FROM KOREA

I have a 7-year-old girl and an 11-year-old boy. My daughter always wants to stay with me. Whenever I helped my son with his homework, she would stand in front of the door and ask me to come out and help her. Since I already spend so much time with her, I couldn't understand why and used to scold her for her demanding so much attention.

I was feeling irritated, and worried about her constant whining.

I told her, "I need to help your brother solve difficult problems, so don't stand in front of the door. Go to your room and play with your toys." She would go to her room for a little while, but later she would resume the same behavior, calling me again for any of several reasons: "Read me a book," "Play a game with me," "Stay with me till I fall asleep."

When I studied the Mistaken Goal Chart, I could see that her mistaken goal was undue attention. Her belief was "I feel significant only when I'm being noticed or getting special service." Her coded message was "Notice me. Involve me usefully."

I decided to redirect my daughter when she tried to gain my attention. The next time she called me when I was working with my son, I said with kindness and firmness, "I love you and will spend time with you later."

She seemed satisfied and stayed in her room, drawing. Later I asked her what she wanted to do with me. She wanted to play the piano, so we played together. After that, the number of times she called me while I was working with her brother decreased.

—Seonghwan Kim, Certified Positive Discipline Educator

SUCCESS STORY FROM PRINCE GEORGE, BRITISH COLUMBIA, CANADA

My child kept taking ingredients off the counter while I was preparing dinner. I had just learned about the Mistaken Goal Chart. I felt irritated, so I realized his mistaken goal was undue attention.

Before learning about the mistaken goals, I would keep reminding him that dinner would be ready soon and that he should wait to eat. He seemed to think it was funny and would take more food when I told him to wait.

It seemed true that his belief could be "I belong only when you pay attention to me" and that his annoying behavior was intended to gain my attention.

I decided to try something related to the coded message "Notice me. Involve me usefully." I cleared a space on the counter, prepared a bowl with some carrots in it, and asked him if he would like to sit with me while I prepared dinner. He ate a few carrots, chatted with me, and then went and played.

What a difference for both of us when I learned to provide ways for him to experience attention in useful ways!

—Sarah Munt, Certified Positive Discipline Parent Educator

TOOL TIPS

1. Make a copy of the Mistaken Goal Chart and several copies of the Mistaken Goal Detective Clue Form.

2. Practice using the Mistaken Goal Detective Clue Form until you are ready to become a full-fledged behavior detective.

3. When *you* "misbehave," use the Mistaken Goal Detective Clue Form to see if you can discover the belief behind your behavior—and how to encourage yourself.

4. Teach the mistaken goals to your children to help them understand themselves, and use family meetings regularly to practice encouragement and problem solving.

TAKE TIME FOR TRAINING

A mother who constantly reminds and does things for a child
unnecessarily not only takes a child's responsibility away from
him but also becomes dependent on him for her feeling of
importance as a mother.

—*Rudolf Dreikurs*

Training is an important part of teaching children life skills. Don't
expect children to know what to do without step-by-step training.
For example, their standards of cleanliness differ wildly from yours, so
you can't simply tell your child to clean his room and expect him to
clean it to your satisfaction.

1. Explain the task in a kind way as you perform it, while your child
   watches.
2. Do the task together.
3. Have your child do it by herself while you supervise.
4. When she feels ready, let her perform the task on her own.

Jane

Parents often don't take time for training because life is hectic or
because they don't fully understand how important it is for children
to contribute and how essential it is that they learn the skills that will
allow them to contribute. Too many parents think children should be
allowed to be children and that they can learn skills later. They do
not realize that children develop beliefs about their capabilities during
early childhood.

The following question from Tamee on the Positive Discipline Social

Network (used by permission) provides an excellent opportunity for me to explain how to take time for training.

This morning my 5-year-old put a bunch of dirty dishes from the sink into the dishwasher. It made me happy to see her doing this. Afterward I told her that was very helpful.

Then she said, "Since I did that for you, would you bring all my breakfast things to the table?"

I didn't really think that was a good idea, since it would make doing dishes seem like something to do to get something in return. I said, "I'm willing to bring the gallon of milk out and pour it. You can do the rest."

She started crying, saying it wasn't fair that I didn't do half of her breakfast things. It became a fit and she said, "Fine! I'll just do it all myself!" which led to her feeling sorry for herself, having to pour the big heavy gallon all by herself and blaming me for it. Help!

I asked Tamee if her daughter was used to getting rewards from someone else. Tamee shared that her ex-husband and ex-mother-in-law used rewards all the time. It wasn't a difficult guess to make, because her daughter's behavior was typical of the long-term results of rewards.

My suggestion for Tamee was to let her daughter have her feelings without trying to rescue her or talk her out of them, and then later take time for training by brainstorming together to create a list of things they could do for other people without expecting anything in return. This is a good example of seeing challenges as opportunities for teaching skills.

You can make time for training fun by turning it into a game. "Let's find at least one thing to do for each other every day as a surprise, and see how long it takes the other person to find out what it was." This could be expanded at dinnertime discussions by sharing, "What did you do for someone else today without expecting anything back?"

We need to take time for training in many areas, such as manners and problem solving, instead of expecting children to learn from our lectures. Children may resist the training you provide in your home (it is part of their individuation process—always testing how to use their power in a safe place), but your friends and neighbors will notice and tell you what a great kid you have. Get over your shock and keep taking time for training, even when it seems like it isn't working.

Many parents have a difficult time giving up rewards. As one father wrote:

I'm totally on board with the idea of encouragement and avoiding punishment, but I'm struggling with effective ways to encourage my 6- and 9-year-old kids to take care of their contributions and family responsibilities without frequent reminders. Last year we had a reward program, which allowed them to easily earn enough "points" within a week to earn a small reward from the prize bin. It worked pretty well, but it was also easy to take away points, which I now see as a form of punishment. In attending a Positive Discipline class and reading the book, I learned that the problem with rewards programs is that they do not help children learn to be responsible, because the parent is the one responsible for monitoring their behavior, and children don't learn to use their own good judgment. Unfortunately, with no incentive, there appears to be a lack of any motivation to do anything they don't want to do. (And who wants to do chores?) I believe their responsibilities and contributions are age-appropriate; they include things like cleaning up their spot at the table, emptying the dishwasher, helping to set the table at dinner, picking up toys, and so on. Things actually seem to have slid backwards. For instance, the 9-year-old used to be pretty good about cleaning up her spot at the table, but now seems to leave it more often than not. With the reward system, things were getting better over time, but without it, the kids have to be reminded for almost everything.

We have had several family meetings and discussed the problem, but most of the ideas really just involve different ways to remind the kids (which still results in the parent being responsible, instead of the child). I am seriously considering returning to a rewards program. A friend mentioned not taking away points, to leave the punishment aspects out of it. But I'm not sure that's teaching the kids how to use their own good judgment.

I told this father that he had described a challenge that goes on in just about every family, whether or not they are implementing Positive Discipline, and I made the following points:

1. If kids were responsible, they wouldn't need parents for the eighteen years it takes them to learn. Responsibility isn't learned from one lecture or from using Positive Discipline tools one or two times. It takes years of repetition.
2. Rewards work, if you want the long-term effects of raising children who will do things for external rewards instead of the inner feeling of capability and contribution.
3. Kids are very responsible about doing things that are high on their priority list. Chores aren't on their priority list—until they have kids of their own to nag.
4. Even though chores are not on their priority list, they still need to do them. Figuring out how to accomplish that using Positive Discipline methods provides many opportunities to teach your kids skills and attitudes that will serve them for the rest of their lives.
5. What if reminding was just part of your job as a parent? If you accepted it as your job, you could incorporate other skills that would increase responsibility and capability in the long term. The first step is to change your attitude and to accept this challenge as an opportunity to teach your children.
6. Think of your kids as dishes. Dishes never stay washed—you have to keep washing them over and over. As a parent, you'll find yourself having to "retrain" yourself and your kids using these tools.
7. Keep getting them involved in agreements. The process of creating agreements is a great skill that needs constant practice. With your new attitude, one way to remind is to ask, kindly and firmly, "What was our agreement?"

8. Keep having family meetings. One woman complained that the solution her kids came up with lasted for just one week. I asked her if she had found anything else that worked for a whole week. She had to admit that she hadn't, so I suggested she keep having the meetings. It took my own kids about two years before they came up with a plan that worked for six months.

9. Create a routine where everyone does chores at the same time, followed by doing something fun together.

10. Use the many other Positive Discipline tools to teach your children to feel responsible and capable—eventually.

Brad

In today's Internet age, taking time for training has become a lot easier. My kids know so much more than I do because they have grown up with Google. I find myself asking them how to do things because they know how to utilize the Internet as a resource.

We need to remember that skills that were important when we were children may not be necessary for our kids. So many things have been automatized and can be done differently now. Of course, technology can also make things harder for parents, because kids think that there's an easy solution when that's not always the case. So taking time to train your child in social, emotional, and problem-solving skills is more important than ever. Next time you want to train your children to do something, ask them if they have ideas about how to do it better. You might be surprised at what they know.

Mary

Taking time for training may be one of the more important tools, but I often forget that my children need to be trained over and over.

My husband has always disliked it when I remind him that we need to take time for training. He replies, "Honey, they're not dogs." So I've needed to alter my language by reminding my husband and myself that with almost every task, chore, job, manner, or behavior we want our children to learn, we need to show, teach, demonstrate, model, and educate. They don't learn overnight, which I need to remember for myself.

Training my boys to clean their rooms is a good example. I can't count how many times I've threatened, bribed, made a game out of it, begged, nagged, and then usually ended up cleaning it by myself while resenting them and every toy we've ever given them. I always wish that they could just appreciate a clean room the way I do.

The last time I took the time to train my boys on how to clean their rooms, I noticed that I was using all kinds of Positive Discipline tools: asking instead of telling, encouraging them instead of praising them, validating their feelings, saying "I love you and it is time to clean your room," and a sense of humor, just to name a few. In the end, this was the best experience we've had with cleaning their rooms. I asked them when we were done how it felt to have a clean room, and reminded them how much I appreciated their help. I also went on to say that I had full faith in them to clean it next time by themselves.

Then I had to train them not to interrupt me when I'm on the phone. This is one of my most frustrating moments as a mom. Unfortunately, I think I've "trained" my kids to have no manners, consideration, or respect when I'm on the phone, because for so many years I wouldn't talk on the phone when they were awake or around. Of course the time came when I had to speak with someone on the phone with them in the room. I knew my kids were being loud and annoying when the lady asked, "Would you like to call me back at a better time?" I needed to leave the room to finish our conversation.

I immediately realized this was nobody's fault except my own. Instead of being upset with them, I was humbled to know that this was my opportunity once again to take time for training, this time about how to behave when I'm on the phone. I agreed to be respectful by keeping my conversations short, and they agreed to return the respect by staying quiet. We then went on to role-play it. The next couple of conversations were short, and the kids were quiet.

Just as kids need continued training in academics (reading, writing, math, and so on), I'm sure their training in cleaning and manners will be an ongoing process.

My daughter, Claire, and I love to cook. It's our favorite way to spend time together and one of the best examples of taking time for training.

Since she was 18 months old, Claire has been adding to her skills in the kitchen through hands-on practice, doing as many tasks as she could independently. Before she was 2 years old, she could handle very simple steps, such as scooping flour or pouring milk. As she got older, I'd show her how to knead a ball of pastry dough, then give her a piece of dough to knead on her own. Sure, sometimes it got messy, and I would frequently find food in strange places (like between her toes). But it's been so worth it to see my daughter become a confident, independent young chef.

Over time, Claire practiced more complex tasks and gained an understanding of how recipes work. One weeknight when she was nearly 5, we decided to create a quick, easy dinner recipe, Mini Corn Dog Muffins. These are mini corn muffins with little cocktail hot dogs baked inside. I knew there would be many ways for Claire to participate independently in the process, including measuring dry ingredients, cutting the mini hot dogs in half (with a child-safe knife), and stirring the ingredients in a mixing bowl.

After the muffins went into the oven, I began talking to Claire about cleaning up, because it was a school night, with chores and bath time and bedtime to consider. But Claire had other plans. She had a grand idea for a recipe she wanted to create completely on her own—something she had never done before. She noticed we had several leftover cocktail hot dogs, and she announced she was going to cook them. Struggling against the voice in my head listing everything on the evening to-do list, I asked, "What do you want to make?" She explained how she wanted to make a sauce and cook the hot dogs in the oven. Seeing her determination, I laughed and sat down to keep her company. She was ready to put her training to the test!

Claire mixed the hot dogs with salt, pepper, water, and dried seaweed flakes. Yes, seaweed! (Hey, I was just thankful she was incorporating a vegetable.) Then we heated the hot dog mixture in the oven.

It was a greasy, slimy concoction, and Claire was just thrilled! She gobbled up the seaweed dogs, exclaiming, "These are heavenly!" The look on her face in the photo I took says it all. She made her entire dinner from scratch, all by herself, and she was bursting with pride.

Looking back at Claire's request to cook the hot dogs, I could have easily shut her down, given everything we had to do that evening. I'm grateful I saw an opportunity there instead.

Those seaweed dogs were a turning point for Claire. Her creation involved planning, organizing, and following through. She showed me she was ready to take her training to the next level. She was advancing her skills, both in the kitchen *and* in life. I'd been training her how to cook, but I suddenly realized she'd been training me too. As adults, we often forget how much fun it can be to try something new, without caring about the outcome. Over the years, Claire has taught me that one of the most important ingredients in life is an open mind!

—Amy Knobler, Certified Positive Discipline Parent Educator

Mini Corn Dog Muffins

MAKES ABOUT 24 MUFFINS

1 package store-bought cornbread or corn muffin mix*

1 package cocktail-size hot dogs

One or two mini muffin pans, greased

Condiments for serving

* Read the directions on the package of corn muffin mix to see if you need milk, eggs, or any other ingredients in order to prepare the muffin batter. Make sure you have those ingredients on hand. Alternatively, feel free to use your own favorite corn bread recipe if you prefer to bake from scratch.

1. Preheat the oven and prepare the muffin batter according to the package directions. Encourage your child to help you read the directions, pour the liquid ingredients, and whisk the batter.

2. Cut each little hot dog in half. Even young children can help with this step, using a child-safe knife, with adult supervision.

3. Ask your child to place a piece of hot dog in each muffin tin. Use a small scoop to pour muffin batter over each hot dog, filling each tin nearly to the top. Kids can help with this too.

4. Bake the muffins according to package directions. Allow to cool slightly. Serve the muffins with condiments such as mustard, ketchup, or barbecue sauce.

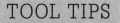

TOOL TIPS

1. Kids need skills, and skills need to be taught.

2. Put on your detective hat. Watch for behavior challenge patterns.

3. When you find a pattern, figure out the skills needed to handle the challenge—for both you and your child.

4. Find a calm time to teach the skill to your child. Include role-playing for practice.

5. Don't expect perfection. Practice invites improvement.

6. Avoid rewards. Rewards cover up the inner good feeling of accomplishment that helps children develop a strong sense of capability.

KIND AND FIRM

Firmness refers to your behavior in a conflict situation: domination means forcing your decision on the child.

—*Rudolf Dreikurs*

Firmness and kindness should always go hand in hand to avoid extremes of either. Begin by validating feelings and/or showing understanding. Offer a choice when possible. Here are some examples:

1. I know you don't want to brush your teeth, *and* we can do it together.
2. You want to keep playing, *and* it is time for bed. Do you want one story or two?
3. I love you, *and* the answer is no.

Jane

Some parents are kind but not firm. Others are firm but not kind. Many parents vacillate between the two, being too kind until they can't stand their kids and their attitude of entitlement, and then being too firm until they can't stand themselves and their own tyrannical behavior.

All Positive Discipline tools emphasize the importance of kindness and firmness at the same time.

Opposites Attract: When One Parent
Is Kind and the Other Is Firm

Have you noticed how often two people with opposing philosophies about kindness and firmness get married? One has a tendency to be too lenient. The other has a tendency to be too strict. Then the lenient parent thinks he or she needs to be more lenient to make up for the stricter, "mean" parent. The strict parent thinks he or she needs to be stricter to make up for the more lenient, "wishy-washy" parent. So they get further and further apart and fight about who is right and who is wrong. In truth, they are both ineffective. The trick is to be kind and firm at the same time. They should work together as a team and learn from each other.

Rudolf Dreikurs taught that kindness shows respect for the child. Firmness shows respect for ourselves and for the needs of the situation. Authoritarian methods usually lack kindness. Permissive methods lack firmness. Authoritative methods are kind and firm. Researchers Sigrud Adalbjarnardottir and Leifur Hafsteinsson reported that adolescents who characterized their parents as authoritative were more protected against substance abuse.[15] Research also shows that adolescents whose mothers were characteristically authoritative reported lower levels of depression.[16] And a team of researchers found that authoritative parenting was related to higher self-esteem and life satisfaction.[11] Historically, in the twentieth century there was a shift away from autocratic (or authoritarian) parenting, which is characterized by a high level of adult control. Authoritarian parenting places little to no emphasis on teaching important life skills such as collaboration, problem solving, and effective communication.

The shift away from autocratic rule toward a more democratic or authoritative approach has been documented in research across many cultures.[12] For example, in China parents are consistently identified as more authoritative. In fact, in China autocratic parenting has been negatively associated with high academic achievement. However, in another Chinese study examining preschool-age children and their parents, authoritative parenting (characterized by democratic leadership) was found to have a positive influence on the development of social and emotional skills and social competence in young children.[13]

To better understand this shift in family leadership styles, we need to look at the history of permissive parenting as well. As early as the 1950s, and continuing on into the 1960s and 1970s, there was a shift in many cultures away from parent as "dictator." However, the pendulum swung far in the opposite direction, and a permissive pattern emerged.[14] This permissive parenting style was overly kind, lacking any firmness at all. With permissiveness there is an increased tendency to overly indulge children, which has a long-term harmful effect.

To sum up, the negative effects of both autocratic and permissive parenting have been documented in the professional literature again and again, while researchers consistently identify more positive outcomes when a balanced, kind *and* firm approach is used.

Many parents struggle with this concept. They may not feel like being kind when a child has pushed their buttons, so they go to the extreme of using only firmness. Others want to avoid the harshness of standing firm and go to the extreme of permissiveness. It takes awareness and skills to be kind and firm at the same time. One of my favorite examples of being kind and firm at the same time is to say "I love you, and the answer is no." Notice the importance of the "and"! Following are more examples:

VALIDATE FEELINGS. I know you don't want to stop playing, *and* it is time for dinner.

SHOW UNDERSTANDING. I know you would rather watch TV than do your homework, *and* homework needs to be done first.

REDIRECTION. You don't want to brush your teeth, *and* I don't want to pay dentist bills. I'll race you to the bathroom.

FOLLOW THROUGH ON AN EARLIER AGREEMENT. I know you don't want to unload the dishwasher now, *and* what was our agreement? (Kindly and quietly wait for the answer.)

PROVIDE A CHOICE. You don't want to go to bed, *and* it is bedtime. Is it your turn to pick a book or mine?

VALIDATE FEELINGS, GIVE A CHOICE, AND THEN FOLLOW THROUGH BY DECIDING WHAT YOU WILL DO. I know you want to keep playing video games, *and* your time is up. You can turn it off now, or I will.

At times the energy of firmness needs to be a little stronger, while still being respectful. Notice that there is no "piggybacking" (adding lectures of blame and shame) in the statements above.

Kind Is Not Always Nice

Some parents think these firm statements are not nice or kind. One of the biggest mistakes some parents make when they decide to use Positive Discipline is to become too permissive because they don't want to be punitive. They mistakenly believe they are being kind when they please their children, or when they rescue them and protect them from all disappointment.

Being kind means respecting yourself and your child. It is not respectful to pamper children. You're essentially stunting their emotional growth by preventing them from developing their "disappointment muscles."

Neither punishment nor permissiveness has positive long-term effects. We can look to nature for a good example. The mother bird knows instinctively when it is time to push her baby bird from the nest so it will learn to fly. If we didn't know better, we might think this is not very kind of the mother bird. If the baby bird could talk, it might be saying, "No. I don't want to leave the nest. Don't be so mean. That's not fair." However, we know the baby bird wouldn't learn to fly if the mother bird did not provide that important push. What seems kind in the moment may be unkind in the long term. It would be unkind for the mother bird to allow her baby to be handicapped for life by pampering it.

Many mistakes are made in the name of kindness, such as:

Pleasing

Rescuing

Overprotecting

Pampering (providing everything the child wants)

Micromanaging

Giving too many choices

Making sure children never suffer

You may be surprised to see "making sure children never suffer" as a mistake parents make in the name of kindness. It is important that parents do not "make" children suffer, but sometimes it is most helpful to "allow" them to suffer with support. For example, suppose a child suffers because she can't have the toy she wants. Allowing her to suffer through this experience (after validating her feelings) can help her develop resiliency. She learns that she can survive the ups and downs of life, which leads to a sense of capability and competency.

So many parents can't stand to see their children suffer. They say, "I just want my child to be happy." Making sure your child is always happy now is a good way to ensure suffering in her future. She will become angry or depressed when the people in her life are not interested in making sure she is always happy—especially at their own expense.

Have faith that your children can learn and grow from suffering, especially in a supportive environment. Understand that being kind does not always mean being nice in the short term. True kindness and firmness together provide an environment in which children can develop the wings they need to soar through life.

Mary

When Reid was 2 years old, he discovered gum through his older brother. Naturally Reid wanted what his brother had, and insisted on having gum before breakfast.

I explained that 2-year-olds can't have gum. Finally, I taught him how to just lick it, and this kept him entertained for about thirty minutes. Little did I know that experience would invite future power struggles about having more gum.

About a week later, before the coffee had even finished brewing, Reid said, "I want gum."

I told him he couldn't have gum.

He countered, "I'll just lick it."

I said, "No, you can't have gum."

He said, "I'll just lick it."

After going back and forth for several minutes, I remembered about being kind and firm. I knelt down to his level, eye to eye, and said, "Reid, I love you, *and* the answer is no."

Reid said, "Okay, Mom, I'll have cereal."

It worked! Those few simple words can be so powerful and effective.

Brad

Personally, I haven't completely mastered being kind and firm at the same time. However, I've finally realized that the fewer words I use, the easier it is to be kind and firm. It's like that old adage: "If you don't have anything nice to say, don't say anything at all." So instead of a lecture, I might just say no.

"No" can be both kind and firm, depending on how you say it and as long as you don't add any extra angry words. "Yes" can also be kind and firm, as in "Yes, I will take you to your friend's house as soon as your room is cleaned."

SUCCESS STORY FROM SAN DIEGO, CALIFORNIA

When our children were younger, my husband and I had attended a talk based on Positive Discipline where they discussed being firm and kind and following through. This information made an impact on us, and we tried to always be firm and kind during the many family meetings we have had.

When the girls would ask for ice cream on a Monday, when at our meeting we had discussed having dessert only on the weekend, we would simply ask, "What do you think?"

We often dealt with strong emotions, especially with my oldest, who would cry out, "Please say yes, Mom."

Kindly and firmly, my answer was always the same: "Remember what we decided during our family meeting."

On my birthday a few years ago, I received a card from my daughter that said, "You are the best mom and thank you for raising me the way you did. I always knew that you would keep your word and back me up no matter what."

I was touched and humbled to have received such a warm note. She later called and said, "Mom, thank you for teaching me how to do my laundry, complete my forms, and teaching me to cook. I used to think that you were so mean, but now I feel very capable at school."

—Yogi Patel, Certified Positive Discipline Trainer

TOOL TIPS

1. Consider the long-term effects of discipline methods.

2. Control your own behavior before expecting your children to control theirs.

3. Be aware that all the Positive Discipline tools are based on kindness and firmness.

4. Learn and practice as many Positive Discipline tools as you can. It is impossible to give up old habits until you have new tools.

CONNECTION BEFORE CORRECTION

Love is not an emotion. It is a relationship.

—Rudolf Dreikurs

Create closeness and trust instead of distance and hostility by communicating a message of love.

1. " I love you, and the answer is no."
2. "You are more important to me than your grades. What do your grades mean to you?"
3. "I love you and have faith that we can find a respectful solution."

Jane

The one Positive Discipline tool I wish I had used more consistently is connection before correction. Too often I thought focusing on the correction was the best way to be a good mother—not knowing that my correction couldn't be effective if I didn't first make a connection. Extensive research has shown that we cannot influence children in a positive way until we create a connection with them. Alfred Adler knew this when he emphasized the importance of using encouragement to fulfill the basic need to belong.

Punishment does not create a connection, nor does lecturing, nagging, scolding, blaming, or shaming. So what kind of encouragement does?

SPEND SPECIAL TIME WITH YOUR CHILDREN. What could create a greater
connection for your child than to know you enjoy spending time with
him or her?

VALIDATE YOUR CHILD'S FEELINGS. Don't we all feel connected when we
feel understood?

FOCUS ON COMING UP WITH SOLUTIONS WITH YOUR CHILDREN. You
will hear the word *with* many times—because it is a golden bridge to
connection.

HUGS. There are times when all of us need nothing more than a hug.

Once the connection is made, children are then open to respectful
correction. However, it is important to understand that the Positive
Discipline way of correction is very different from conventional correction. The biggest difference is that conventional correction usually
involves punishment. Punitive time-out, grounding, and taking away
privileges are the most common punishments. **In other words, conventional correction consists of adults doing something *to* children.
Positive Discipline correction respectfully involves children whenever
possible, finding solutions *with* them.**

Sometimes we have to stop dealing with the misbehavior and first
heal the relationship through an abundance of connection. One way to
start is to stop whatever you are doing and say, "Do you know I really
love you?" One father of a teenager was shocked when his son's eyes
filled with tears as he replied, "How would I know that?"

When children feel a connection, they feel belonging and significance. Often that is enough for the correction to follow—for the misbehavior to stop. As you learn about the many Positive Discipline tools,
notice that they are all designed to create a connection before correction.

Mary

Of all the Positive Discipline tools, connection before correction is my
favorite! This seems to be the tool that I use the most. In fact, I have

used it so often that it is also my children's favorite. If I forget, often they are the first to remember the importance of connection and come to me with arms open wide for a big hug.

They have even learned to remind me to take a few deep breaths when I'm upset. I was flabbergasted when my oldest child, who was three at the time, said "Mommy, calm down and take some deep breaths."

He was absolutely right. I was embarrassed and grateful at the same time—embarrassed because my 3-year-old caught my misbehavior before I did, and grateful because he actually learned what I had taught him.

Brad

Ever since my son became a teenager he has become more defiant, which I'm sure is a common problem a lot of parents have with their teenagers. It seems like he tries to contradict me at every turn and even tries to sabotage my efforts to create a more harmonious family environment. This also shows in his relationship with his sister. There is a lot of sibling rivalry, and it looks like he takes out a lot of his anger on her.

My reaction has often been to react to him with anger, which creates more distance and causes him to dig in his heels and become even more defiant. Before I knew it, we were in a full-blown power struggle.

We talk about how a misbehaving child is a discouraged child. The reason children feel discouraged is that they don't think they belong. Whether that is true or not, that is what they believe. One possible solution is spending special time together, which is so simple and yet so powerful in helping children feel belonging, significance, and connection. The catch-22 is that a misbehaving child is also an annoying child, and the last thing you want to do is spend more time with the child who is annoying you.

But I decided to trust the process. So during our next family meeting I scheduled a time for Gibson and me to go play golf. That week we got to spend a couple of hours on the golf course together.

After that special time together there was an immediate change of attitudes. My son began to be much more cooperative. The next day he did his chores without being reminded and without any complaining. Even his relationship with his little sister improved. He is still an older brother, so he can't give up teasing his sister completely, but the teasing seems to be more fun-loving instead of angry.

Creating connection with our children is such a powerful tool. Once we reestablish connection, everything else seems to fall into place.

SUCCESS STORY FROM MONTANA

Picture this challenging moment: I'm walking to the car with a 1-year-old at 5:00 p.m. I lift him toward the car seat and am met with a blood-curdling scream in my ear, a hip thrust forward, and kicking legs. One of his legs kicks me in the side of my stomach. I am frustrated!

I'm tired from a long day, and I just want to get home to eat dinner and enjoy the help of my husband. Everything in me wants to scold my child and tell him his behavior is unacceptable. I want to say, "You *will* get your bottom in that car seat because there is no other option."

Instead, I pause to connect before I correct. I pull him away from the car seat and back onto my hip so I can put a hand on his back. I say something like, "Whoa, whoa, whoa. Hold on a moment. I can tell you don't want to go home. You were having so much fun in our music class, weren't you? That was such a fun time! It's hard to leave places that are so fun, huh?" With each word and stroke of his back, I feel his body relax incrementally, appreciating the validation.

Then I continue with correction. "But wait. Let's look. Look at the other kids getting into their cars. The class is done. No one is staying here. We are all headed home to see mommies and daddies and have dinner. And we get to come back next week for music again. Let's go home and see Daddy!" He nods, and I lift him toward the car seat with no resistance at all. We buckle up and head on our way. Really, only two minutes were lost in the time it took to connect before correction of his behavior. And it was well worth it.

—Flora McCormick, Certified Positive Discipline Parent Educator

TOOL TIPS

1. Remember that kids *do* better when they *feel* better—and so do you.

2. Remember that you are the adult, and that modeling is the best teacher.

3. Remember to calm down, touch your heart (to connect with yourself), and then connect with your child.

4. Remember that connection is often enough to correct the problem. Nothing more need be said or done.

5. When you forget all of the above and blow it, apologize. Apologizing is a great way to connect, because it brings out a child's instinct to forgive.

ENCOURAGEMENT

A child needs encouragement like a plant needs water.

–Rudolf Dreikurs

A misbehaving child is a discouraged child. When children feel encouraged, misbehavior disappears.

1. Encourage by creating a connection before correction.
2. Every suggestion in this book of Positive Discipline tools is designed to help children feel encouraged and to develop valuable social and life skills that will help them feel capable.

Jane

Rudolf Dreikurs taught that a child needs encouragement in the same way that a plant needs water. In other words, encouragement is essential. Children may not die without encouragement, but they will certainly wither. Since encouragement is so crucial, it's important for parents to know exactly what encouragement means and how to do it.

Let's start with what encouragement is not. Encouragement is not cheering, clapping, and commenting on everything your child does. Parents talk too much. Sometimes it is an attempt to be encouraging, and sometimes the talking is just plain old lecturing. Parents seem to think they have to make a comment on everything a child does, especially in today's world.

Imagine you are a 2-year-old child and you have just poured your own milk from a small measuring cup into a small cup without spilling anything. What are you feeling? When I get into that role, I'm feeling proud of myself—and very capable.

Stay in the role and imagine that your mother starts clapping and cheering. The most popular cheer is, "You did it!" You'll still feel proud, but the underlying belief that it's even more important to please your mother is beginning to take root. Instead of that inner sense of pride, you are learning to depend more on what others think.

Clapping and cheering is a form of praise (see "Encouragement Versus Praise" in Chapter 6), and the danger is that children do like it. They don't understand the subtle beginnings of the need to please and the fear that they might not. Other children may rebel because they feel that is the only way to hang on to their sense of self. All of these feelings and decisions are occurring at a subconscious level.

Cheering, clapping, and commenting on everything a child does are subtle ways of making your child's accomplishments more about you than about him or her. It actually robs your child of the ability to maintain his or her sense of personal satisfaction and feelings of capability.

Encouragement is helping your children develop courage—courage to grow and develop into the people they want to be, to feel capable, to be resilient, to enjoy life, and to be happy, contributing members of society. And, as Dreikurs said, children need to have the courage to be imperfect—that is, they need to feel free to make mistakes and to learn from them.

In a recent workshop a mom wanted help regarding her 5-year-old, who has temper tantrums when she doesn't immediately get what she wants. I had her sit in a chair next to me and told her to role-play her daughter having a tantrum while I role-played the mom sending out energetic support. All I did was sit there and watch her with a compassionate look on my face. It was fun to process with her later how she was aware of what I was doing even though she was in the middle of her tantrum. She shared that she felt loved and supported—even though she was a little frustrated that her tantrum didn't work in the sense of getting her what she wanted right away.

I pointed out that when children feel confused because their behavior isn't working, they are ready to go shopping for a new behavior. So even though a Positive Discipline tool doesn't seem to be encouraging changed behavior, it may be effective in the long term once the child decides to shop for another behavior.

Think of adults who encouraged you when you were a child. What did they do or say? This will give you the best clues about how to encourage your children. You will find several examples of encouragement in the stories below.

Brad

I can remember a time when I was about 7 or 8 years old and I wanted to build a doghouse for my dog, but I had absolutely no idea where to start. So my dad spent an entire Saturday working with me on the project. He didn't do it for me, but he was by my side every step of the way. That was the first time I had ever even hammered a nail into a piece of wood, so I'm sure it took a great deal of patience from my father. But he let me bend a lot of nails before I finally got the hang of it. By the time I was finished, I was so proud of my accomplishment that I spent the night with my dog in that new doghouse.

It's not always easy to give our children encouragement. I think that is why it is more meaningful than praise. "Good boy" and "You're so awesome" won't get a doghouse built. "Keep trying—it's not easy to hammer a nail straight" will get the job done and instill a feeling of capability in a child.

Mary

When my son Greyson started kindergarten, I was very discouraged by the color card punishment system the school used. On the first day of orientation, they recommended that if our child did not get a green card, which signified good behavior all day, they should be "punished with a consequence at home."

I rolled my eyes and thought, "Not in our home." We don't believe in punishment, and we definitely don't believe in making children pay for their mistakes or for acting like 5-year-olds. I also believed that if I brought both the teacher and the principal a copy of my mom's book *Positive Discipline in the Classroom,* they might change the system they've been using for more than thirty years. Oops—there I went again with my magical thinking.

Everything changed when Greyson got his first red card (the worst card you can get). I honestly can't even remember what it was for, but I can remember how I felt when the teacher pulled me aside at pickup to explain the situation. I felt like I'd just gotten a red card in parenting.

Silly, I know. And if you had told me that first day of school that I would've taken this system personally, I would have told you "Not me. I know better." But when I was listening to the teacher with what felt like my tail between my legs, I couldn't help but feel that my child's behavior was a reflection of my parenting. When I told Mom about this later, she warned me, "If you're going to send Greyson to a school with this system, then you can't feed into it." And she reminded me that it's not what they do at school but how we handle it at home that counts, and to focus on solutions with him.

Greyson has provided me with several opportunities to practice. In the beginning, I did a lot of talking (telling, really) to Greyson about how he should behave. I volunteered in his classroom twice a month so I could see exactly what it takes for a child to get a yellow or red card (such as talking to a classmate at the wrong time). Several times I saw other students get a card and I wasn't even sure what they had done.

I'm embarrassed to say that I did not stick with the original plan to not get hooked by this system. I started punishing at home—taking away privileges, not allowing him to go to Legoland (more painful for me than for him), lecturing, and threatening. Recently, after feeling completely discouraged with both my son and myself, I started asking him curiosity questions. For example, "How do you think your teacher feels when she's trying to teach and you keep interrupting?" Or "Now that you know it's not okay to play ninja on the carpet at school, where is it that you can play?"

After a long three-week vacation from school, I thought for sure it would be a challenging week. I was pleasantly surprised when he came running to give me a hug at pickup and was excited to say, "I got a green card." He was so happy and proud! He confirmed this when I tucked him into bed that night and he shared that his happiest part of his day was getting his green card. I was happy because he was happy, but in the same breath I felt like my son was already being sucked into the system of thinking he is "good" when he gets a green card and that he is "bad" when he gets any other color.

It was only three days later that everything started going south. He got a yellow card, but his teacher told me that she'd wanted to give him a red card . . . yikes! She explained that he'd been extra wiggly during circle time and that he'd needed to be reminded several times to listen. I asked him in front of his teacher, "What would help you to listen to your teacher?" And then I suggested, "What if you came up with your own code word and a silent signal that would be just between you and your teacher?" They both liked that idea!

I waited until that night when I was tucking him in and asked him the same question again. Greyson came up with the code word "zip," and then he showed me the silent signal of him zipping his lips closed. He loved this idea and told me he was excited to tell his teacher the next morning.

The next day at pickup my fingers were crossed. Sure enough, it had worked! His teacher told me that their code word and signal had worked well all day. I was pleased to share with her that when the child comes up with the solution, he will usually follow it. I believe that Greyson felt encouraged to follow through with their agreement.

It definitely felt better to encourage my son and to focus on finding solutions and problem solving. It felt completely discouraging to fall into the trap of punishment and consequences. I was glad I remembered to use encouragement to help my child form a different belief that fueled a different behavior. I hope I can remember to stay out of the discouragement trap.

I want to share an encouraging moment from recent life. Our week started with a particularly upsetting episode for my 3½-year-old daughter. She was at preschool and apparently came down with a spontaneous case of the rotavirus that is spreading around the school like wildfire. She had an accident that required a change of clothes and cot cover . . . you get the picture. So I got the call at noon to come pick her up. She was upset, but she recovered.

Two days later, it was time for her to go to school again. The first thing she said to me at seven o'clock that morning was, "I'm still sick. I can't go to school."

I listened to her and asked a few questions but went on with the morning routine, even as she continued to insist she didn't want to go to school. The whining increased. I started to tense up, thinking, "We don't have time for this. She's too young to be saying she doesn't like school. Why can't we just have *one* morning go smoothly?"

And then (and I think this is only because I had been sick in bed myself the previous day, grading graduate students' homework on Adlerian parenting and Positive Discipline), I paused and said to myself, "I bet I can figure out what is going on here."

So I made a guess. I said to her, "I know what happened on Monday was so upsetting and you were so surprised by that. I bet it felt a little scary."

She instantly began to cry (real tears, not the crocodile kind) and nodded, saying, "Yes, and I'm so scared it's going to happen again."

She immediately let me hug her and hold her, and I reassured her that her body was all better now and that it would not happen again. The rest of the morning was fine, and we got in the car and made it to school on time. No more tears.

That afternoon I told her she must be feeling so proud of herself for being so brave, but really I was thinking, "Yay for me! I guessed right! I slowed down long enough to listen to her. I didn't get mad! I validated her feelings. I didn't let the tension of hurried mornings get in the way of hearing her very real and valid fear." She must have felt encouraged, because she changed her behavior.

After this experience, I thought back to a topic brought up in a recent parenting class. A parent expressed some respectful doubt that we could "guess" at the beliefs and fears behind a behavior. My example above is not necessarily a mistaken goal, and I know that it is not always appropriate or possible to do goal disclosure with our own children. However, orienting myself to the origin of her (at the time very annoying) behavior and combining that with some curiosity and calming-down time for myself proved to be highly effective.

—Monica Holiday, Certified Positive Discipline Trainer

SUCCESS STORY FROM PERU

One afternoon my son, Ignacio, appeared with a grin on his face, but he looked preoccupied. When I asked him if everything was okay, he said yes. However, he was not convincing enough. I knew something was wrong.

A couple of hours later I accidentally discovered that he had failed an exam. I immediately knew that this was the cause of his discomfort. Before, I would have yelled at him and grounded him.

This time, though, I stopped myself from reacting and decided to try a Positive Discipline tool. First I took a positive time-out for myself and took a deep breath. After I calmed down I sat down with him and asked some curiosity questions and listened without interrupting. That's when I realized that the reason for his behavior was that he was afraid to tell the truth. I felt so sad to discover that my son couldn't trust me.

I decided to work on his confidence. I started by telling him that I'd found the test by accident, and I asked if there was something that he wanted to share with me because I wanted to help him solve this problem. I assured him that he could trust me and that I could help him find a solution.

I held his hand and tried to encourage him by telling him that I had faith in him and that I was sure that he could do better on exams in the future. I also encouraged him to think of some solutions and told him it was my job to support his decisions. It felt so good when he hugged me. I knew my encouragement had gotten through to him.

—Susana O'Connor, participant in Gina Graham and
Mariella Vega's Positive Discipline class

SUCCESS STORY FROM XIAMEN, CHINA

I seem to forget how much encouragement I used with Niuniu, because it's my habit to encourage. When he was very little, he used to ask me before each performance, "Mom, what do I do when I am wrong?"

I calmly said, "Making mistakes is normal. You are a human being, not a machine. Only the machine is unlikely to go wrong. I know you want to convey to the audience what your inner thoughts on music are. You know what to do."

He agreed with me. After a few shows, he said he particularly enjoyed communicating with the audiences while he was on the stage.

After we came to the United States, Niuniu's father was the one who drove him to and from school. I also had a driver's license, but I hadn't done much driving. One morning Niuniu's dad got sick and told me he couldn't drive Niuniu to school. Niuniu's dad is a very strong and reliable person and would never say he wouldn't drive if he could, but it was raining cats and dogs outside. What could I do?

Niuniu would definitely be late for school if he walked. He was also feeling overwhelmed. He looked at me and said, "What can I do, Mom? I have a math test first thing today."

I thought for a little, then said, "I could drive you. But do you dare to go with me in my car?"

He didn't know how worried I felt, and so he cried out, "Of course, no problem. Let's go!" So we drove. I didn't even know how to use the wipers, but Niuniu said, "All right, take it easy, I'll help you!"

We got to school safely, with ten minutes before class started. I said to him, "Take your umbrella and go to your class."

Then I left and drove slowly back home. At noon I returned to school and picked him up. There was a very steep slope near the door of their school. Niuniu kept on encouraging me, saying, "Look at the way you drive downhill! You drive so well!"

I realized that he was encouraging me the way I used to encourage him. He knew that it was hard for me to drive for the first time. I felt so happy when he showed his encouragement!

After I'd driven with him several times, he began encouraging me to improve my skills. "Mom," he'd tell me, "if you can't parallel-park the car, pull it into the garage." Or "Don't drive too fast when you come to a sharp turn, because the car will go into a little drift." With my son's encouragement, I felt confident driving.

—Zhili Shi, Certified Positive Discipline Parent Educator, co-author with Jane Nelsen of the *Positive Discipline for Piano Moms Workbook*

TOOL TIPS

1. Think about the long-term results of your approach. Does it encourage internal or external motivation? Internal motivation is important for the long term.

2. Are you promoting self-evaluation or dependence on the evaluation of others?

3. Are you inviting your child to think or telling him what to think?

4. Are you allowing your child to figure things out for herself and engaging her in problem solving, or are you rescuing her and fixing things for her?

5. Are you considering what your child might be thinking, feeling, and deciding in response to what you do or say, or do you avoid getting into your child's world?

6. Are you helping your child feel capable or dependent?

WINNING COOPERATION

Competition is neither "natural" nor mandatory. It makes the realization of equality impossible. The less competitive a person is, the better he can stand competition. The competitive person can stand competition only if he wins.

—Rudolf Dreikurs

Children feel encouraged when you understand and respect their point of view.

1. Express understanding for the child's thoughts and feelings.
2. Show empathy without condoning challenging behavior.
3. Share a time when you have felt or behaved similarly.
4. Share your thoughts and feelings. Children listen to you after they feel listened to.
5. Focus on solutions together.

Jane

Rudolf Dreikurs taught the importance of "winning children over," instead of "winning over children." Winning over children invites rebellion or giving up. Winning children over invites cooperation.

Trying to win over children is hard. It takes constant effort. You have to be very vigilant to police your children's actions so that you can implement your control tactics—usually punishment and rewards. You have to catch children being "good" so you can reward them and catch them being "bad" so you can mete out punishment. It never ends—and what happens when you are not around? If you are very good at being in control over your children, what have they learned? Have they learned self-discipline, respect for self and others, responsibility, problem-solving skills, cooperation?

Trying to gain control over children is disrespectful and greatly decreases your chances of winning cooperation. Controlling methods invite distance, hostility, rebellion, revenge, sneakiness to avoid getting caught, or, worst of all, a child's developing belief that "I am a bad person." On the other hand, respectful methods invite closeness, trust, and cooperation.

It can be so difficult for parents to think they are not doing their job if they don't engage in a lecture or some kind of consequence (usually a poorly disguised punishment). This will take you right back to the resistance or full-blown rebellion you will experience by trying to gain control over children instead of winning them over. Winning your children over does not mean giving them what they want so that they like you and are more likely to do what you want them to do. Winning your child over means you have created a desire for cooperation based on a feeling of mutual respect.

One of the best ways to win children over is to do things *with* them instead of *to* or *for* them. Doing things with them means respectfully involving them in finding solutions that work for everyone. In the process your children will learn thinking skills, problem-solving skills, respect for self and others, self-discipline, responsibility, listening skills, and motivation to follow through on the solution they have helped create. The list could go on and on. What better way to achieve a connection? Once you have achieved a connection you have created an atmosphere where you can focus on a solution together. You have won cooperation.

Brad

My son has always been a very good student. School has always come easy for him, and he ended up graduating at the top of his high school class and winning an academic scholarship to college. My daughter, on the other hand, really has to work hard to get good grades. Lately she has been struggling in her math class. I noticed a couple of F's showing up on her assignments, so we had to come up with a solution.

The first thing I did to win her cooperation was to express my understanding about how difficult math can be. Then I shared my experience with calculus in college. The first day of my calculus class, the instructor turned his back to the class and started writing on the chalkboard. Chalk was flying as he quickly demonstrated functions, derivatives, and complex equations. I leaned over to the person next to me and asked, "Is this the first day of class? Did I miss something?"

After class I approached the teacher and asked him the same questions. He replied, "This is a college calculus class. You are expected to have read and studied the first two chapters." This was news to me, and I realized that I was never going to pass this class without some help. I immediately went to the math lab and did my homework with the help of the teacher's aides. I spent every day that semester in the math lab trying to understand the concepts of calculus, and with the help of those wonderful tutors, I was able to earn an A in calculus.

Emma loved this story. I asked Emma if it might help her to do her homework in the math lab at her school. She agreed to try it and started going to school early or staying late to do her homework. Eventually she was able to catch up and turn in her missing assignments—just like her dad.

Mary

Before my husband, Mark, and I got married we came up with the 3 C's to a successful marriage: communication, compromise, and compassion. Since becoming parents we've agreed that there was a C that we were missing: cooperation. We believe that anytime something is going wrong in our relationship or with one of our children, one of the 4 C's is missing.

The winning cooperation tool teaches that children feel encouraged when we parents understand and respect their point of view. For example, my boys love to play baseball, and they want to play every day. However, I am constantly overwhelmed with laundry, dishes, and picking up the house. Instead of feeling resentful, which then usually turns into anger, I waited for my golden opportunity, knowing they would eventually ask to play baseball. When they asked, I said I would love to as soon as I finished doing my chores around the house. I had already formulated a plan to say, "Why don't you help me and then we can play?" But before I could say it, my oldest son, Greyson, who was 6 at the time, said, "We can help you unload the dishwasher, and we'll put away our laundry." Those few sentences made me feel that we had just met all four C's, and everyone was happy.

Before I thought of a way to win their cooperation, I would provide them with a long lecture, followed with a guilt trip. Still, they would persuade me to play baseball with them, and I would feel exhausted and resentful. But now I was able to acknowledge them for being helpful, compassionate, and patient problem solvers. It was so much more fun to have them help with the chores and more rewarding for all of us to play baseball after.

Another example of winning cooperation: My boys were feeling mad because they couldn't have soda. I don't drink soda myself, because I know how bad it is. I wish it wasn't, because I love it! Greyson started in with, "It's not fair that you don't let us have soda. My friend always gets soda. Why can't we have it?"

Instead of lecturing him and feeling annoyed that he was asking yet again, I expressed understanding and showed him empathy by sharing how I never had soda when I was a kid, and how I always wanted it too. Then we made a fun game out of it by taking turns saying all the things we wished were good for us but are not.

He said, "I wish I could have candy for dinner."

I backed him up by saying, "I wish I could have ice cream for dinner."

He said, "I wish sugar was good for you."

I followed by saying, "I wish that chewing gum and hard candy were good for my teeth."

It was much more fun for both of us to be joking, laughing, and making a game out of it instead of a lecture, guilt trip, and annoyance. Winning cooperation is win-win for everyone.

SUCCESS STORY FROM DEER PARK, NEW YORK

One day I got frustrated and raised my voice at my 2-year-old son. Like any other parent would, I felt awful for doing so. I realized that I was winning at the expense of my child. I immediately remembered the 3 R's of recovery from mistakes, which would win him over.

As I was following the 3 R's, I felt empowered and competent, rather than frustrated and helpless. "I'm sorry that I yelled at you," I said. "It was wrong of me. It was disrespectful, and I'm sorry if I hurt your feelings. What can we do next time I tell you to stop?"

I gave my son some choices of things that he could do and that I could do as well the next time we had a similar challenge. After that I hugged him really tight and turned it into a tickle. I told him to tell me when he wanted me to stop, being mindful not to hurt him. Then he got a chance to tickle me.

I remembered that children listen to you when they feel listened to. It worked very well!

—Dimitrios Giouzepis, Certified Positive Discipline Parent Educator

TOOL TIPS

1. It is essential to give up your need to win over your child so you can win your child over.

2. Winning cooperation can involve a combination of Positive Discipline tools.

3. Make a connection (create closeness and trust) before correction through winning cooperation.

CHAPTER TWO

PARENTAL GUIDANCE

FAMILY MEETINGS

Communication in the contemporary American family has not broken down; it exists, but not always for beneficial purposes.

—Rudolf Dreikurs

Children learn social and life skills during weekly family meetings. The format for the family meeting is as follows:

1. Compliments and appreciations
2. Evaluation of past solutions
3. Agenda items to be solved
4. Calendar (events, meal planning)
5. Fun activity and dessert

Jane

If I had to choose my favorite Positive Discipline tool, it would have to be family meetings because children learn and practice so many valuable social and life skills: resiliency, social interest (contribution), mutual respect, how to learn from their mistakes, listening skills, brainstorming skills, problem-solving skills, the value of cooling off before solving a problem, concern for others, cooperation, accountability, and how to have fun together as a family. Where else can you get so much for such a small investment of time?

The quote by Dreikurs at the beginning of this section indicates a need to improve communication in families for the beneficial purpose of encouragement. Family meetings will not be effective if parents try to use them as another platform to lecture and control. Yes, we know how difficult this is. Somehow we parents think we aren't doing our jobs unless we are talking, talking, talking. Parents need to talk less and listen more. They need to be sure to get their children involved in brainstorming solutions and choosing the ones they think will work best. The more your kids feel involved in the process, the more likely they are to follow through on decisions they help come up with.

It is most effective to have family meetings once a week and to stick to a maximum of twenty to thirty minutes, even if everything on the agenda has not been covered. Items that you don't get to can be "tabled" until the next meeting. This gives everyone time to absorb what was discussed during the meeting, to try the agreed-upon solution, and to practice working things out for themselves in between meetings.

My children loved family meetings when they were between the ages of 4 and 12 or so. Then they started complaining, as typical teens do, about "stupid family meetings." I asked them to humor me, and told them we could shorten the time from thirty minutes to fifteen. One day Mary, one of the complainers, spent the night at a friend's house. The next day she announced, "That family is so screwed up. They should be having family meetings."

When Mary went off to college, she initiated regular "family meetings" with her roommates and said they would not have survived without them. Keep a family meeting album, which can be as much fun as a photo album. You and your family will chuckle as you look back at past challenges you solved together. You can find an example of a family meeting album at www.positivediscipline.com.

10 STEPS FOR EFFECTIVE FAMILY MEETINGS
  1. **Introduction.** "We will read these steps until we all know them. Who would like to start with number two?" (If children are old enough, they can take turns reading the steps.)
  2. **Compliments or appreciations.** "Each of us will share one thing we appreciate about each member of the family. I will start. I would like to compliment _____ for _____." Give

each family member a compliment, and then have everyone else do the same.

3. **Family meeting agenda.** "The agenda will be placed on the refrigerator so everyone can write down problems during the week. You'll notice that leaving dishes in the sink is on the agenda for us to practice problem solving."

4. **Talking stick.** "This item will be passed around to help everyone remember that only one person can talk at a time, and that everyone gets a turn."

5. **Brainstorming.** "Brainstorming means thinking of as many solutions as we can. While brainstorming, all ideas are okay (even funny ideas) without discussion."

6. **Focus on solutions.** "Let's practice with the problem on the agenda. Who would like to be our scribe and write down every suggestion?" (If your children aren't old enough, you can take this job.)

7. **Encourage the kids to go first.** "Who would like to start with some wild and crazy ideas?" (If no one speaks up, you might need to get them started with some wild ideas and some practical ones by saying, "What about throwing dirty dishes in the garbage? What if each of us takes one day of the week?" But first allow for silence.) If someone objects to an idea, say, "For now we are just brainstorming for solutions. All ideas will be written down."

8. **Use the 3 R's and an H to assess proposed solutions.** Encouraging solutions must be (1) related, (2) reasonable, (3) respectful, and (4) helpful. "Who can see any solutions we need to eliminate because they are not related, reasonable, respectful, or helpful? Our scribe can cross them off after we discuss why."

9. **Choosing the solution.** "Do we want to narrow the ideas down to one solution or try more than one? We can evaluate how the solution or solutions worked during our next meeting, in one week."

10. **Fun activity.** "We will take turns choosing an activity for the end of each family meeting. For tonight I've chosen charades. Who will volunteer to decide the fun activity for next week?"

Remember, learning skills such as cooperation takes time. Avoid skipping weekly family meetings, and be consistent.

Brad

We had always held family meetings on a fairly regular basis, but the structure was a bit unorganized. We would just look at the calendar for the upcoming week and then plan our meals. I decided to download a family meeting album from www.positivediscipline.com for a fresh start, and when I did, I realized that we were missing some valuable steps.

Going by the rules, we started our family meeting with compliments. I complimented both the kids and then asked if anyone else had any compliments. My daughter said she did, and it went something like this:

> EMMA: I would like to compliment Gibson for not calling me names this week.
>
> GIBSON: What are you talking about, Emma? I just called you a name ten minutes ago.
>
> EMMA: I meant before that.
>
> GIBSON: Whatever, Emma.

I'm not sure if that exchange counts as a compliment, but maybe that is as close as you can get in the teenager world.

I also decided to post a family meeting agenda so we could add items during the week. One morning the kids were having an argument about using the iPod Touch. I asked Gibson to put it on the family meeting agenda. He wasn't too thrilled about that idea, but he did it anyway. Things definitely were a little more peaceful around the house after he did—sometimes simply putting an item on the agenda is enough to defuse the problem.

Here are the items on our family meeting agenda for that week:

1. iPod Touch (the kids had been arguing about sharing and the fact that it was always dirty and needed to be charged)

2. Water bottles (Dad was frustrated that the kids would take one drink from a water bottle and then leave it on the counter; we were wasting a lot of water)
3. Name-calling (Emma was concerned about all the name-calling between her and Gibson)

Emma acted as the scribe and was writing down all of the minutes for the meeting.

After compliments we began to focus on solutions for the challenges on the agenda. We first brainstormed solutions for the iPod Touch. Here are the ideas we came up with:

1. Emma would clean her hands before using it.
2. Gibson would let Emma have a proper turn.
3. Whoever uses it cleans it.
4. Everybody plugs it in after using it.
5. Gibson has to understand that Emma does *not* pick her nose.
6. Have Emma sell her iPod Nano and buy her own iPod Touch.
7. Get rid of the iPod Touch.
8. Have a two-hour limit.

The solutions the kids chose were numbers 3 and 4. We decided that if someone didn't follow the rules, they would lose the privilege of using the iPod Touch for the rest of the week. And guess what? There wasn't a single argument about the iPod Touch that week. Emma was very conscientious about cleaning and plugging in the iPod Touch, and Gibson never complained.

The last item on the list of challenges was name-calling. We came up with the following solutions:

1. Gibson would stop trying to annoy Emma.
2. When you want to call someone a name, say "I love you" instead.
3. Emma would try to be patient.
4. Emma would use her stress ball when she was feeling frustrated.

The solution Emma chose was to use her stress ball. And Gibson decided he would say "I love you" when he felt like calling Emma a name.

You may be thinking, "Come on! There is no way a teenager agreed to say 'I love you.' " But a couple of days later, I actually heard Gibson say "I love you" to Emma when he was annoyed. And then later in the week, Emma came up to me and said, "Hey, Dad, guess how many days it has been since me and Gibson had a fight? Five days!"

I'll admit that I had my doubts about solving our problems with a family meeting, but I am now a convert.

Mary

Five years ago we had our first family meeting with Greyson, who was then 4, Reid, who was 2, my husband, Mark, and me. We all gave and received compliments or appreciations. Reid was not old enough to give compliments, but he grinned each time he received one.

Mark struggled with the idea of compliments and said, "This is so *Brady Bunch*!" He wondered, "Why do we have to give compliments? Can't we just go to the agenda item?"

I gave him the stink eye and mouthed, "Just trust me." Grudgingly he did. Later he understood that giving and receiving compliments helps set the stage for encouragement and cooperation.

The item on the agenda was our son, Greyson, wanting to wear his baseball pants every single day. Greyson loves baseball. At that point he wanted to be a San Diego Padre when he grew up, so he wanted to look like a baseball player every single day. Unfortunately, his pants were white and he was a 4-year-old boy; so keeping them clean was impossible. I considered purchasing five pairs, but decided instead to see if we could find another solution during a family meeting.

We started by letting Greyson know that we admired his passion for acting and dressing the part of a baseball player, but that Mommy was struggling to keep his baseball pants clean. We asked him if we could focus on solutions and come up with some different ideas on how he could wear baseball pants.

He had just recently finished creating his routine chart, and suggested making a chart for that too. The chart read as follows: "Monday baseball pants, Tuesday jeans, Wednesday baseball pants, Thursday jeans, Friday baseball pants, Saturday baseball pants, Sunday baseball pants."

I had to admire his creative thinking and agreed it was a solution that could work. So we agreed to follow through with his plan. The next day he asked, "Mom, what day is it?" When I said it was Tuesday, Greyson replied, "Awww, that means I have to wear jeans." He was disappointed, but he followed through with his solution and reluctantly went upstairs to put on his jeans.

My husband was shocked by our son's attitude and willingness to follow through with his agreement, and he told me, "I can hardly wait to have our next family meeting."

SUCCESS STORY FROM UPPER SADDLE RIVER, NEW JERSEY

Positive Discipline has changed my life in many ways and equipped me with powerful tools to connect better with my 6-year-old son, husband, friends, and others. One tool I find especially powerful is family meetings.

I was full of apprehensions about introducing family meetings in my family. Prior to our first family meeting, it was hard for me to imagine how my family of three could sit down to discuss any family matters or even to consciously compliment each other. However, our first family meeting turned out to be a complete eye-opener for both my husband and me.

The idea of sitting in a meeting with Mommy and Daddy was very empowering and encouraging for my son—so much so that he felt very comfortable opening up and sharing his feelings with us during the meeting. He told us that he felt pressured and frustrated because we were constantly lecturing him about what to do and how to do it, and not allowing him to make his own decisions.

I could not believe what I learned from my own child during our first family meeting. The meeting left the three of us in tears as we felt a strange connection that was new to us.

—Nisha Maggon, Certified Positive Discipline Parent Educator

SUCCESS STORY FROM LIMA, PERU

Once I was familiar with the various Positive Discipline tools, I decided to use them and see how they worked. One of the tools I felt I needed to try most urgently was the family meetings.

I am a mother of two boys: the oldest is 6 years old, and the youngest is 4 years old. This academic year we needed to change our routine since our two boys had to arrive at school earlier. So we had a major challenge in front of us: how could we facilitate things for our children in order for them to get ready on time while, at the same time, having a peaceful start to the day? Before Positive Discipline arrived in my life, this would have seemed like *Mission: Impossible*. Now I believe that magic is possible, thanks to Positive Discipline.

My husband, my children, and I agreed to have a family meeting. For me, the first big change occurred in the way we presented the family problem we needed to solve. For our children, the fact that "we all had a problem"—which was how we could do things in the morning in order for them to get to school on time—was a new experience. We were so used to putting the responsibility entirely on our children. We even blamed them for the things they did wrong. So this way of starting the meeting was a transforming experience for all of us.

The part they liked the most was brainstorming. In particular, our oldest boy was astonished to be asked for ways of solving the problem and felt very excited to give his opinions.

It was easy for the four of us to set an agreement, and we all liked the notion that we, as a family, are a team that needs to work together at keeping up our commitments and being responsible for them. For us, this family meeting experience was a powerful one, and from that day onward our mornings have been usually nice, smooth, and happy, and our two children arrive at school on time.

I definitely recommend Positive Discipline both as a philosophy of human relationships and child rearing and as a set of useful tools for parents and families.

—Joan Hartley, participant in Gina Graham and
Mariella Vega's Positive Discipline class

TOOL TIPS

1. Remember the long-term purpose of family meetings: to teach valuable life skills.

2. Have all family members sit around a table (not during a mealtime) or in another comfortable space where they can all see each other.

3. Post an agenda beforehand where family members can write their concerns or problems.

4. Start with compliments to set the tone.

5. Focus on solutions, not blame.

VALIDATE FEELINGS

When a child makes a mistake or fails to accomplish a certain goal, we must avoid any word or action which indicates that we consider him a failure.

—*Rudolf Dreikurs*

1. Allow children to have their feelings so they can learn they are capable of dealing with them.
2. Don't fix, rescue, or try to talk children out of their feelings.
3. Validate their feelings: "I can see you are really angry [or upset, or sad]."
4. Then keep your mouth shut and have faith that your children can work it through.

Jane

Billy is sad because his friend doesn't want to play with him. Billy's mom tries to comfort him by saying, "Don't feel sad, Billy. You have other friends, and I love you."

Susan is angry because she doesn't want to pick up her toys. Susan's dad tries to squelch Susan's anger by getting angry at her: "Don't act like such a spoiled brat. Do you expect me to do everything? Can't you be more responsible?"

Tammie hates her baby brother and wants to hit him. Tammie's mother tries to deny Tammie's feelings: "No, you don't hate your baby brother. You love him."

No wonder many adults have trouble expressing their feelings. As children they were not allowed to feel what they felt. Next time you feel like fixing, squelching, or denying your child's feelings, instead try to just validate them through a question or a statement, such as "How are you feeling about that?" or "I can see that makes you very mad" or "Little brothers can be so annoying." This allows children to discover that they can work through their feelings and learn from them.

Avoid overvalidating. I have seen some parents validate, and validate, and validate. They think that lots of validation will fix the problem and help their children feel better. One of the hardest things a parent can do is watch their children suffer, but it is important to allow your children to feel what they feel so they can learn how capable they are.

Teach Children the Difference Between What They Feel and What They Do

Feelings give us valuable information about who we are and what is important to us. Children need to learn that it is okay to feel whatever they feel. We can then teach them that what they *do* is a different matter. Feeling angry doesn't mean it is okay to avoid chores or hit someone. Feeling sad isn't a permanent condition but an important life experience. How can children understand the difference between feelings and actions when we discount their feelings?

Validating a child's feelings is one of the best ways to create a connection. Once children have their feelings validated and have an opportunity to calm down, they are usually open to considering a new belief and a new behavior. As we will point out often, children do better when they feel better.

Billy's mom could say, "I know how much that hurts. I felt the same way when my friends didn't want to play with me."

Susan's dad could say, "That's how I feel sometimes when I have to go to work. The toys still have to be picked up. I'll bet you can come up with some good ideas about how to get it done quickly."

Tammie's mom could say, "I can see that you are very upset with your baby brother right now. I can't let you hit him, but you can draw a picture about how you feel."

We help children understand the difference between feelings and actions when we start early to teach children that feelings are okay. When your child says, "I'm hungry," don't say, "No, you aren't. You just ate twenty minutes ago." Say instead, "I'm sorry you are hungry. I just cleaned up from lunch and I'm not willing to fix any more food right now. You can either wait until dinner or you can choose something from the healthy snack shelf." This is respectful of the child's feelings and needs and your own.

Brad

As a single dad, I need this reminder because feelings are not my strong suit. Oftentimes the mom is the parent that provides emotional support. Dads usually jump in with something profound, like "Rub some dirt on it."

I know there have been many times when I have actually told my children to stop having their feelings: "Stop being so dramatic." "That's nothing to be upset about." "Stop that right now! There's no reason to be angry!"

But if we sincerely validate our children's feelings, I think they feel empowered. They may not even know why they are angry, upset, or sad. I know I've had days like that. Sometimes that's just how you feel.

Each week as we introduced a new Positive Discipline tool, I taped a description of the tool to the refrigerator. One day my son was having a bit of a meltdown about something and I was doing my usual thing of trying to talk him out of his feelings. Then my daughter walked over and tapped me on the shoulder. Without saying a word she pointed to the "Validate Feelings" reminder I'd posted on the refrigerator. That was exactly the nudge I needed. I stopped trying to talk Gibson out of his feelings, and that seemed to defuse the situation. Then Emma asked Gibson if he would like a hug.

Sometimes it takes the wisdom of a child to give us perspective. That is why I am so glad that I have been involving my children in the process. We can learn and grow together.

Mary

The validating feelings tool provides daily, if not hourly, opportunities for me to practice this skill with my two boys. Recently I've made the extra effort to come up with new ways to validate their feelings in our conversations, often saying, "You're so mad," "You didn't like that," or "I can see how that really hurt your feelings," and finally, "I can see that you're really upset. Let me know when you're ready for a hug or to try again."

I can also validate my child's feelings by following up with a story of how I can relate to them. My oldest son, Greyson, loves when I tell him stories about when I was growing up.

When I validate my children's feelings, it prevents me from thinking I need to fix the problem. I know that I feel validated when my friends or husband say, "I can relate to what you're saying and completely understand how you feel." Even if that doesn't solve the problem, it helps me feel better.

My mom taught me a valuable lesson when my oldest was 18 months old and was just starting daycare. It was so difficult and painful for me to leave my son there crying and pleading for me to stay or begging me to take him with me—absolutely heartbreaking! I called my mom from the parking lot, crying and feeling like the worst mother ever.

My mom reassured me that every emotion and feeling Greyson was having was normal and developmentally appropriate. She reminded me that we had been very careful to find a good child development center at San Diego State University, and that Greyson spent enough time with me to feel securely attached. Strengthening his "disappointment muscles" was a very important part of his development.

I instantly felt better. As a mother, all I want for my kids is for them to be happy and healthy, but it wasn't until I spoke to my mom that I also realized how important it was to have Greyson develop his "disappointment muscles"—even if it meant he was temporarily unhappy. I have to say that both my sons have developed more self-confidence and capability because of their time away from me three days a week than they might have without this experience.

SUCCESS STORY FROM BOZEMAN, MONTANA

I don't know about your child, but mine cries often over very small things. If he could talk, he would likely be saying things like, "I don't want to sit there," "I hate putting my coat on," "I don't want to get in the car," or "I'm not sitting in this high chair!"

Since he can't talk, he screams or cries. Today he was crying and flinging his body to the ground when I was trying to get his shoes on. I stopped and thought of his crying as a way to communicate his feelings, and I was able to validate him even though his frustrations seemed small to me.

I said, "Oh boy. You are frustrated that we are getting shoes on right now. You do not like putting shoes on. It's okay to be frustrated. Take a minute to just be frustrated about that. I'm here. I'll give you a hug. I don't like doing things sometimes too."

I paused the process of putting shoes on to just connect with a hug (another great Positive Discipline tool). My calmness and validation softened his frustration until finally he became more willing to accept my help. In a moment of screaming, two minutes can feel like forever, but it's not that long at all when you think of the lifelong benefit you are giving your child in helping them understand and manage their emotions.

—Flora McCormick, Certified Positive Discipline Parent Educator

SUCCESS STORY FROM MONROE, WASHINGTON

My son is 9 years old and he is full of big emotions. Disappointment, anger, frustration, and embarrassment—it can send him into the pit of despair, and he is known to drag anyone who is around him into the pit.

What shows up for him is a physical meltdown, literally. He looks toward the sky with a face full of anguish, and then his body seems to melt into the earth. This is usually coupled with wailing as he voices his dismay at the current situation. It's really easy to be dragged into his emotions when he falls apart. It triggers a physical reaction from me: tightness in my chest and belly, rigidity in my jaw. This is not where I find my most effective parenting skills.

Last night was a great example. We were looking for something to watch as a family. As I scrolled through the options on Netflix, I mentioned, "I don't want to watch any movies with snowboarding monkeys, or where an animal is the main character." I was trying to be funny, while also setting a boundary about what we could choose from. Well, my boy did not feel the humor—he freaked out, way more than what the situation called for.

I could feel the tension creeping into my body, and knew that I would need to pay attention to my breathing and to stay relaxed so that I could connect with him.

"Wow, you are really feeling full of emotion," I said.

"I am!" he wailed from the floor.

"I was trying to be funny with the monkey comment," I said.

"It wasn't funny," he told me, still from the floor.

"All right, well, it seems like you are letting the emotion that showed up take you for a ride," I said.

This is something we talk about a lot—the emotional freight train that we may find ourselves on, along with the always available choice of getting off the train.

It was at this point that I noticed him shift from being stuck in the emotion to being open to move on. This is how it is with my boy. The validation creates a connection that allows him to make a choice, based on previous training, to emerge out of the emotion of the experience and to resurface, able to think clearly and logically about problem solving and solutions. I used a combination of validating feelings, connection before correction, and time for training.

Connecting before correcting is essential for my relationship with my son. It keeps our relationship strong, it helps him feel seen, and it allows him space to move on.

—Casey O'Roarty, Certified Positive Discipline Trainer

TOOL TIPS

1. Acknowledge your own feelings and that it's painful to watch your children suffer.

2. Think long-term. How much better is it for your children to learn that they can handle their own emotions?

3. Allowing children to "suffer" doesn't mean you're abandoning them. Acknowledging their feelings provides a safe environment for them to learn from the ups and downs of life.

DECIDE WHAT YOU WILL DO

The greatest stimulation for the development of the child is exposing him to experiences which seem to be beyond his reach but are not.

—Rudolf Dreikurs

Decide what you will do, instead of engaging in power struggles.

1. Plan what you will do and notify in advance:
   - "When the table is set I will serve dinner."
   - "I will help with homework on Tues. and Thursday, but not last minute."
   - "When chores are done I will drive you to your friend's house."
2. Follow through on your plan with kindness and firmness.

Jane

By now, we are sure, you have discovered how many tools work well together, or work better after another tool has been used. We had a difficult time deciding which tool should come first, and it is almost impossible to decide which one is more important. The tools in their entirety are like an intricate puzzle, and the picture is not complete without all of the pieces. To some it is easier to find the outline pieces first, but others like to work on pieces that have the same color or pattern. The Positive Discipline tools don't have outline edges or patterns, but you will need to group some of them together for greater effectiveness. You'll notice that sometimes, even when we are focusing on one tool, we refer to another. Some tools could be called foundational or representational of basic principles because they are required as part of every other tool.

Focusing on solutions is a foundational Positive Discipline tool, with another foundation tool being to involve children in the problem-solving process whenever possible. However, there are times when it is appropriate to make decisions without the involvement of the kids, as illustrated in the following story of the Jones and Smith families.

The Jones family is very excited. They have just finished planning a day at the beach. Seven-year-old Jason and 5-year-old Jenny have promised that they won't fight. Mr. Jones has warned, "If you do, we'll turn around and come back."

"We won't, we won't," promise Jason and Jenny again.

The Jones family hasn't gone two miles when a loud wail is heard from the backseat: "Jason hit me."

Mrs. Jones says, "What did we tell you kids about fighting?"

Jason says, defending himself, "Well, she touched me."

Mr. Jones threatens, "You two had better cut it out, or we are going home."

The children cry out it unison, "Nooooooo! We'll be good."

And they are—for about ten minutes. Then another wail is heard: "He took my red crayon."

Jason replies, "Well, she was hogging it. It's my turn."

Mr. Jones says, "Do you want me to turn around and go home?"

"Nooooooo. We'll be good."

And so the story goes. Throughout the day Jason and Jenny fight, and Mr. and Mrs. Jones make threats. At the end of the day, Mr. and Mrs. Jones are angry and threaten never to take the kids anywhere again. Jason and Jenny feel bad that they have made their parents so miserable. They are beginning to believe they really are bad kids—and they keep living up to their reputation.

Now let's visit the Smith family. They have just planned their trip to the zoo during their weekly family meeting. Part of the planning included a discussion about limits and solutions. Mr. and Mrs. Smith have told Susan and Sam how miserable they feel when their children fight. The kids promise they won't. Mr. Smith said, "I appreciate that, and I think we should come up with a plan for what will happen if you forget." The kids keep insisting they won't fight. Mr. and Mrs. Smith know their children have good intentions, and they are also very familiar with the pattern of good intentions gone awry. So they have decided what they will do and they will follow through.

Mrs. Smith says, "Well, then, is it okay with you if we stop the car if you do forget? We don't think it is safe to drive when you are fighting, so we'll just pull over to the side of the road and wait for you to stop. You can let us know when you are ready for us to drive again. How do you feel about that solution?" Both kids agree with innocent enthusiasm.

Typically, it doesn't take them long to forget their promise, and a fight begins. Mrs. Smith quickly and quietly pulls off to the side of the road. She and Mr. Smith take out magazines and start reading. Each child starts blaming the other while protesting his or her own innocence. Mr. and Mrs. Smith ignore them and just keep reading. It doesn't take long for Susan to catch on that Mom and Dad must mean what they said. Susan says, "Okay, we are ready to keep driving."

Mr. Smith says, "We'll wait until we hear it from both of you."

Sam says, "But she hit me!"

Mom and Dad just keep reading. Susan hits Sam as she says, "Tell them you are ready."

Sam cries, "She hit me again."

Mom and Dad just keep reading.

Susan realizes that hitting Sam won't help, so she tries to reason with him. "We'll have to sit here forever if you don't say you are ready." Susan follows her parents' lead and starts to color.

Sam holds out for about three more minutes before saying, "I'm ready for you to start driving."

Mom says, "Thank you very much. I appreciate your cooperation."

About thirty minutes later another fight starts. Mom starts to pull over to the side of the road. Both kids cry out in unison, "We'll stop. We're ready to keep driving."

There is no more fighting for the rest of the day, and the Smiths enjoy a wonderful day at the zoo.

What is the difference between the Jones family and the Smith family? Are Jason and Jenny really "bad" kids?" No. The difference is that the Smith family is helping their children learn cooperation and problem-solving skills, while the Jones family is helping their children learn manipulation skills. Mr. and Mrs. Smith demonstrate that they say what they mean and mean what they say by using kind and firm follow-through. Mr. and Mrs. Jones don't. They use angry threats. This has a temporary effect, but it doesn't take long for the kids to start fighting again.

Mr. and Mrs. Smith stop using words and instead follow through with kind and firm action. It takes a little longer for the kids to catch on, but once they do, it has a longer-lasting effect. Because they are kids, they just have to test the waters one more time. When their parents start to follow through again, the kids know they mean what they say. They are left with the feeling not that they are bad kids but that they are clever enough to figure out a solution to the problem and that cooperation is the most effective alternative.

Brad

I think the key to this tool is the "notify in advance" part. Kids thrive in an environment of structure where they know what to expect. I have admitted before in this book that I tend to be more reactionary than proactive. But I try to remedy that situation every day by using these Positive Discipline tools.

I often use this tool with regard to school. I have told my children in advance that school is their responsibility. I already spent eighteen years going to school and I don't plan on going through it again. So my children have learned that they need to have a plan for completing their homework and getting good grades.

My son was so good at signing himself up for the right classes and taking advantage of college credits in high school that he graduated from high school with more than thirty college credits. You'll be amazed what your children can accomplish when you turn over the responsibility to them!

Mary

The most important part of this tool is the follow-through. Children know when you mean it and when you don't. After all, isn't it their job to test you and your limits? Of course it is! This is why it is so important to only make promises (not threats) that you're willing to keep.

I've learned the hard way more than once, as while I'm in my flipped-lid state I've made some threats I would never follow through on when I'm calmer, and my kids know it. Listed are some of my personal favorites:

- Turn the TV off *now* or you won't watch it for an entire week.
- You and your brother better stop fighting, or I'm going to turn this car around and we'll go home.
- If you don't start sharing and being kind to your friends, then we're going to leave our playdate.
- If you don't brush your teeth right now, then you can forget about any sweets ever again.
- If you don't change your attitude, then you can forget about going to the _____!
- If you can't take better care of your bike [or baseball glove, or toy, or whatever], then I'll take it away from you and you won't be able to use it.
- If you don't stop asking me for everything in the store and start behaving, then we're leaving.

Of course, my oldest son tests me—and I feel just as sad as he does when I follow through on threats I wish I hadn't made. One day I explained to him that we were going to our friend's house for a playdate. I had taken time for training, and I went over the rules—sharing, taking turns, using nice words, no hitting, and so on. I then went on to explain that if we didn't follow these rules, we would need to leave. It was with one of my good friends, and so naturally I wanted to be at the playdate as much as my son did. Needless to say, they also lived forty-five minutes away.

Sure enough, less than an hour after we got there, he hit his friend and called him a name. I decided to follow through. I wasn't trying to make him pay for his behavior but was simply tired of having each playdate so consumed with making threats that I didn't keep. Deep down I knew it would be a painful lesson for both of us as well as a lot of gas and time wasted. (He cried himself to sleep on the way home.)

It wasn't a total waste, because he never forgot it. I felt like I earned his trust of knowing that when I said it, I meant it. I also learned to stop making threats, and instead decide in advance what I would do.

I'll always remember my mom saying, "The tongue in the shoe speaks louder than the tongue in the mouth." In other words, if you say it, mean it, and if you mean it, follow through.

If I had to do it over, I would let him know in advance that we would sit in the car until he's ready to use gentle hands and nice words. This would've accomplished the same goals for this tool and been easier on both of us.

SUCCESS STORY FROM RENO, NEVADA

My 9-year-old son played every sport in its season, and as his mom, I moved from gym bleachers for basketball to park bleachers for baseball to lawn chairs for soccer. He had good seasons and disappointing ones, but one constant in his athletic life was the laundry: he generated loads and loads of dirty socks.

Now, if you've never done the laundry of an active boy, you may never have encountered the "crusty wad," but it was a staple of my domestic life. Philip would peel his socks off his sweaty foot from the top down, creating a damp wad of sock with all the dirt and grass trapped inside, and toss the crusty wad of sock into his laundry basket.

When I went to do the laundry each week, I spent several unpleasant minutes straightening out the crusty wads and cleaning up the dirt and grass that inevitably dropped on the laundry room floor. And every week I became more irritated and cranky.

Like moms everywhere, I thought I had tried everything. I lectured. I asked for help. I checked to be sure that Philip knew how to remove his socks by sliding a finger down the back of his heel and easing the sock off right side out. (That move earned me some vigorous eye-rolling.) I'd get a temporary change, but sooner or later the crusty wads would return.

I finally remembered the Positive Discipline tool that calls for you to decide in advance what you'll do. One day I told Philip, calmly and respectfully, that I didn't enjoy unwadding the crusty wads, and that from now on I would wash, dry, and put his socks in his drawer just as he put them in the laundry basket. Now, this was not an easy thing for a clean-freak mom to do. But I threw the crusty wads into the washing machine. I threw the wet crusty wads into the dryer. And I threw the dried crusty wads into my son's sock drawer without saying a word to him. He never mentioned the change in his socks, but one morning I walked by his bedroom as he sat on his bed putting on his shoes. He was unwadding a clean crusty wad and muttering under his breath. And after that, believe it or not, the crusty wad problem was solved. Occasionally, though, one would slip through, and I'd wash it without fixing it.

Deciding what I would do and following through without lectures ended the crusty wad epidemic once and for all, and reminded me that the only person I truly can control is myself.

—Cheryl Erwin, coauthor of several Positive Discipline books

TOOL TIPS

1. There are several other parenting tools that are essential for this one to be effective: showing faith in your child (Chapter 4), letting go (the last section in this chapter), seeing mistakes as opportunities to learn (Chapter 3), being kind and firm (Chapter 1), natural consequences (Chapter 9), controlling your own behavior (Chapter 10), following through (the next section in this chapter), and acting without words (Chapter 8).

2. An important key is being kind and firm, informing your children in advance what you'll do, and then keeping your mouth shut.

3. In most cases, involving kids in solutions is the best motivator, but sometimes it is appropriate to allow your children to decide what they need to do in response to what you have decided you will do.

FOLLOW THROUGH

Man is no longer a servant; he is the master of himself.

—Alfred Adler

I f you say it, mean it, and if you mean it, follow through.

1. Kids know when you mean it and when you don't.
2. If you say "I will read a story at eight o'clock, after pajamas are on and teeth are brushed" and your kids aren't ready by eight o'clock, point out the time kindly and put the kids to bed without reading.
3. Be encouraging by saying, "You can try again tomorrow."

Jane

Julie complained that her 4-year-old son, Chad, is very responsive and cooperative with his father about going to bed, but when she puts him to bed and tries to leave, Chad yells for her to come back and wants her to lie down with him. Every time she tries to leave, he cries for her to come back. Julie feels exhausted and resentful that she can't have the evening to herself or enjoy time with her husband. She wonders why she can't get the same cooperation from Chad as Dad does.

Why is it that children behave one way with one parent and differently with another? Because they learn which parent they can manipulate and which one they can't. Children know when you mean what you say and will follow through, and when you don't. It is really that simple. If you mean it, say it; if you say it, follow through. The way you follow through (or fail to follow through) is an indication of your parenting style. A brief recap:

Permissive parents don't follow through because they are afraid their children will suffer trauma for the rest of their lives if every desire is not met. This parenting style emphasizes freedom without order. These parents do not understand the future impact of the beliefs that their children are forming. Children will suffer much more throughout their lives if they develop the belief that love means others should take care of them and give them whatever they want. They will suffer when they don't learn they can survive disappointments in life—and discover how capable they are in the process.

Strict parents want to make sure their children do not become spoiled, entitled adults. But parents who focus on order without freedom also do not understand the long-term results of the beliefs their children are forming. Their children often go to one extreme or the other, either rebelling ("I won't do what you want even if it is good for me. I refuse to be bossed around") or becoming approval junkies ("I will do whatever it takes to get your approval, even if it means giving up my sense of self").

Authoritative parents balance freedom with order. This is the Positive Discipline way. These parents understand the long-term consequences of the beliefs their children are forming and want to provide experiences where their children can learn responsibility and capability (along with the rest of the characteristics and life skills mentioned in Chapter 1) through problem solving. This is what Adler meant by the quote at the beginning of this chapter. An important goal of Positive Discipline is to help children be "masters of themselves." Research has shown that adolescents who perceive their parents as authoritative had higher levels of resourcefulness than adolescents who perceive their parents as more authoritarian.[17] Studies also show that authoritative parenting is consistently and significantly related to high academic performance.

We know that most parents choose their parenting style based on what they believe is best for their children. However, too often their choice is based on lack of knowledge about the long-term results of their actions. In this book we talk a lot about skills children need to learn, but it's up to parents to successfully teach them those skills. It's a two-way street.

Mary

The most difficult time for me to practice this tool was when my children were around the age of 2 and it seemed as though it was their job to test me daily. I knew it was important not to make threats I couldn't keep, and—more important—to follow through on whatever I said I would do. I referred to this stage as my "mean mommy stage." My mom simply reminded me that it was my "firm mommy stage."

Even though I know Positive Discipline tools are both kind and firm, I am the first one to admit that I am usually too kind until I get completely fed up. Then I become this really *firm* mommy and forget about the *kind* part.

The best part of this "firm mommy stage" was that it didn't take my kids very long to know that Mommy meant business. And 99 percent of the time I followed through with what I said I would do. Just like punishment, firmness without kindness can work, but none of us are left with good feelings, and we don't feel capable. I feel the most capable when I'm both kind and firm, and so do my children.

I am still working on following through with kindness and firmness. One night my oldest son had a major meltdown at bedtime. It was my fault because I let him stay up later than his bedtime (with no nap) to watch a movie that he had recorded the night before. When the movie was finally over, he went ballistic when it was time to brush his teeth and put on pajamas.

The more out of control he got, the more out of control I felt. I *told* him, which was my first mistake, "If you can't calm down and get control of your body, I will delete your movie and you won't watch any TV in the morning."

Sure enough, he acted more hysterical, and, in my flipped-lid state,

I marched downstairs and deleted his movie. Naturally this just made the situation worse, but I was so concerned about following through on my threat that I didn't focus on actually helping him calm down by making a connection before my correction.

After I walked away, went into my own positive time-out, and calmed down, we were able to reconnect, make apologies for our behavior, and finally go to bed.

The next morning he came downstairs and gave me another big hug and said how sorry he was for the night before. I too apologized and explained that I had been equally tired and was acting out of control. Unfortunately, his movie had already been deleted. Even though I didn't regret deleting the movie, I regretted how and when I did it—without kindness.

However, I made sure to follow through with no TV in the morning, and I reminded him why in a kind way. He wasn't happy with that decision, but we were able to turn it around with the fun and active morning we had together.

There is a moral to this story: control your own behavior before you expect your children to control theirs. It helps to remember the basic tool of connection before correction. When you use these two tools, kindness and firmness at the same time is a natural result, and you will be able to mean what you say without feeling guilty.

Brad

Making agreements with children is easy. Following through with those agreements is hard. My mom explains that children do not share the same priorities as parents. As a parent, my priority is managing the household. This includes such things as laundry, dishes, trash, recycling, vacuuming, grocery shopping, and preparing meals. It's no wonder children don't have the same priorities as adults. I don't even want those things to be my priorities! But the fact is that life involves managing the priorities of a household.

During family meetings I will make agreements with my children regarding chores. But my children usually don't follow through. So follow-through becomes another one of *my* priorities. The problem is, following through with children is more difficult than just doing everything myself.

For example, if I am upstairs preparing dinner and the trash can is overflowing because my son forgot to empty it, I can spend thirty seconds emptying the trash can myself or ten minutes tracking down my son and getting him to follow through with our agreement. I'm sure most parents can relate to this dilemma.

So does that mean we should give up and stop following through with our children? Absolutely not. But when do we get to reap the benefits from our efforts to follow through? Based on my experience and observation, the benefits of following through with our children usually take effect when our children move out of the house. That's not very comforting right now, but Positive Discipline is based on long-term results.

Occasionally we will catch a glimpse of success when our children surprise us by following through without any reminders. That happens in my home about once a week, and those little successes make it all worthwhile and remind me that my children might just make it in this world on their own someday.

SUCCESS STORY FROM OKLAHOMA

Not too long ago, my daughter knew she could get away with very little with her father. She went to bed for him like a saint. When it came to me, though, she knew she could push me to the ends of the earth and get whatever she wanted, even if the whole experience was negative. We spent hours at night with her making requests such as "Rub my back," "Put cream on my leg," "Fix my blankets"—all just part of a power trip she was taking me on. I felt guilty, and so I continued the long and drawn-out bedtime routine that left me exhausted and unable to finish my nightly duties.

Since reading the Positive Discipline books, I learned that much of her self-worth comes from doing things for herself and feeling accomplished. That opened my eyes. I cut out all the special services, knowing she can do things herself and that it is my job to encourage her to do so with kindness and firmness at the same time.

We follow the same bedtime routine every night. I read her a book and then I remind her that she is a big girl and she can put herself to sleep. If she gets out of the bed, without saying a word I walk her back to her bed. If it happens more than once, I remind her that I will no longer put her blankets back on, nor will I refill her water. She knows I mean what I say. After two nights of doing this, bedtime has changed all the way around. I am so thankful for what I learned in Positive Discipline. What was once a dreaded time is now a nice, quiet time to wind down from the day.

—Christine

SUCCESS STORY FROM CARLSBAD, CALIFORNIA

We had made an agreement in our family meeting for no electronics in bedrooms. One day, I came into our 13-year-old daughter's bedroom to speak with her. She quickly closed the closet door, but not before I caught a glimpse of what looked like a blue light. I asked her to open the door, and there was her iPad. I asked her what she was doing, and she said she was texting her friend. I asked her what our agreement was about electronics, and she responded, "Not in bedrooms."

Our daughter is not perfect, and like any child, she has misbehaved in the past. This time was different. I had never experienced the reaction of feeling angry and offended that not only had she not kept the agreement but she was being sneaky about it. I asked for the iPad and told her my husband and I would decide how to respond.

We decided there were two issues: responsibility about agreements, and being respectful to us and to herself because of trying to cover up her mistake. It was Friday, and we told her she would lose the privilege of using the iPad for the next three days, meaning she would not have it over the weekend, a time when she typically is in more contact with her friends. We told her she could still use her desktop computer for homework.

Her response was one I did not expect. She said, "That's fair," and my eyes welled up with tears. She has rarely been challenging to us by being sneaky (unless she was so good at it that we never found out), so we weren't used to having to take such a firm stand. The few times we have needed to be firm following misbehavior has been enough for her to learn we will act with firmness when needed.

I thanked her for understanding. I was grateful that she understood and accepted our decision. Because of the relationships we have created in our family using Positive Discipline tools, it made it easier for me to be firm, and for her to understand and be accepting.

This experience helped me see why it is sometimes difficult for parents to use the Positive Discipline tools, because our own beliefs can interfere. In any case, she was so involved in other activities during those three days without her iPad that I don't think she even missed having it!

—Lois Ingber, Certified Positive Discipline Trainer

TOOL TIPS

1. Remember your long-term goals as a parent—to help your children learn skills and capability.

2. Skills aren't learned in a day. That is why your children need you for at least eighteen years.

3. Model the skills you want them to learn. They will become responsible more quickly if they don't have to waste time rebelling against lectures and punishment or feeling a sense of low self-esteem because they can't live up to your expectations.

LETTING GO

Knowing what not to do is a great help in determining what should be done.

—Rudolf Dreikurs

Letting go does not mean abandoning your child. It means allowing your child to learn responsibility and to feel capable.

1. Take small steps in letting go.
2. Take time for training and then step back.
3. Have faith that your child can learn from his or her mistakes.
4. Get a life so that your identity doesn't depend on managing your child's life.

Jane

"Jimmy, time to get up! . . . C'mon, Jimmy, get up now! . . . This is the last time I'm going to call you!"

Sound familiar? Mornings in Jimmy's home are much like mornings in other homes around the world—hectic, argumentative, and full of hassles. Jimmy has not learned to be responsible because Mom is too busy being responsible for him. It gets worse as the morning continues.

"How should I know where your books are? Where did you leave them? How many times have I told you to put them where they belong? . . . If you don't hurry up and eat, you're just going to have to go to school hungry. . . . You're still not dressed, and the bus will be here in five minutes! I'm not going to take you to school if you're not ready—and I mean it!" And then on the way to school, "Jimmy, when will you ever learn? This is absolutely the last time I'll drive you to school when you miss the bus. You've got to learn to be more responsible!"

What do you think? Is this the last time Jimmy's mother will drive him to school when he misses the bus? No. Jimmy is very intelligent. He knows his mother's threats are meaningless. He has heard them many times and knows his mother will drive him to school when he's late. Jimmy's mother is right about one thing: Jimmy should learn to be more responsible. But through morning scenes like these, she is teaching him to be less responsible. She is the responsible party when she keeps reminding him of everything he needs to do.

It is possible to enjoy hassle-free mornings while teaching children self-discipline, responsibility, cooperation, and problem-solving skills. The key is letting go. Many parents are afraid that letting go means abandoning their children or giving in to permissiveness. In Positive Discipline terms, letting go means allowing children to develop their sense of cooperation and capability. Many of the following tips are covered in different chapters, but it's important to understand the many variations of all of them and how they often fit together.

SEVEN TIPS FOR LETTING GO, AVOIDING MORNING HASSLES, AND TEACHING RESPONSIBILITY

1. **Involve children in the problem-solving process.** When children are involved in solutions, they have ownership and motivation to follow the plans they have helped create.
2. **Involve children in the creation of a routine chart.** Part of Jimmy's bedtime routine could be to choose his clothes, put his backpack by the door, and put his lunch in the fridge the night before.
3. **Let go by allowing children to experience natural or logical consequences.** Jimmy will learn to be responsible when his mother stays out of the way and allows him to experience the consequences of being late.
4. **Decide what you will do.** Let your children know in advance what you plan to do. If you mean it, say it, and if you say it, follow through.

5. **Ignore the temptation to become involved in a power struggle or revenge cycle.** Children often show their need for independence by resisting when you won't let go.

6. **Things may get worse before they get better.** Children may try hard to keep you responsible, even if they resent your authority.

7. **Have faith in your children.** Children learn to be capable people when you teach skills, have faith, and let go.

If you want to turn morning hassles into morning bliss, and avoid many other power struggles (bedtime, chores, homework, picking up toys, listening, vacations, etc.), practice the steps for letting go outlined above. With practice, you and your children will feel more capable and will enjoy the benefits of responsibility, cooperation, and self-discipline.

Brad

I need to pay special attention to the first sentence in this section: "Letting go does not mean abandoning your child." I've never had a problem letting go. As a busy single dad, I am more than happy to let go and allow my children to take more responsibility. But occasionally (when my kids are being particularly annoying) my letting go looks more like abandoning.

Here's a perfect example. We were invited to go ice-skating and have dinner with friends. My daughter and I were excited by the invitation. Unfortunately, my teenage son was less than excited. He was grumbling and complaining, "Why do we have to go? Will we be gone a long time? I really don't want to go!"

We were in the car pulling out of the driveway and my son was still complaining and throwing his backpack down on the floor and just generally being belligerent and trying to make sure everyone would be as miserable as he was. We hadn't even left our street and I turned the car around, drove back to our house, and told my son to get out and have a nice day. I let go (abandoned) him for the afternoon so that my daughter and I could have an enjoyable time. And we did!

I don't think that is the spirit of this tool. It has more to do with letting our children have more responsibility so they can become capable, contributing members of society. It would have been much more effective if I had explored with my son the reasons he didn't want to go and then allowed him the dignity of skipping this activity without getting angry.

My daughter was able to put things into perspective as we drove away. She said, "Dad, that's just the way teenagers are. My teacher said that her daughter was disrespectful and grumpy until she turned 18 and now she is a joy to be around. So don't take it personally if I act the same way when I am a teenager. I might say that I hate you, but I won't really mean it. That's just what teenagers do."

Mary

A huge part of letting go is not only allowing my children to take more responsibility but also actually letting go of my ego and not caring what others may think or say. Positive Discipline taught me that giving up the need for others to think well of my parenting meant caring more about my children gaining a sense of self-confidence and capability.

Each one of my boys proved he was capable of getting dressed on his own around the age of 2. Letting go meant letting them choose what they wanted to wear, even if it meant wearing pajamas, last year's superhero cape, clothes on backward, and, of course, nothing that matched. I have taken several pictures over the years capturing their confident faces after they brushed their hair or dressed themselves.

When I was a young girl, my mom often silently applauded my strange and creative outfits. I now look at pictures of those days and am mortified. She teases me and reminds me not only of my fashion sense as an adult but also, and more important, my confidence.

I want to allow my children to learn capability by letting go. One day my 2-year-old was struggling to put on a T-shirt all by himself. I was so tempted to rush in and make it easier for him. Instead, I patiently observed him struggle inside the T-shirt trying to find where his head and arms go. What a tragedy it would have been if I had helped instead of waiting for his smile of satisfaction and capability as he emerged from the T-shirt and proclaimed that he had done it "all by himself." What I had interpreted as a struggle (since it seemed to take so long) was simply him enjoying the process of the challenge.

Mom's Story

Our oldest son is 12 years old and in middle school. He attends an academic magnet school and has daily homework and frequent big projects. We struggled a lot with him in fifth grade over keeping up with his work, and in sixth grade we *really* started with the power struggles. Sometimes we would have daily arguments about homework.

My husband decided it was time for us to cut the cord completely in this area just before Christmas. They wrote out a mutually agreed upon contract specifying that our son would come to us if he needed our help and that we would go to him if we got notification that his grades had dropped into the C range. We all read and signed the contract.

There have been a few times when I would start nagging about homework again and my husband would remind me about the contract terms. The first report card with our new approach came and he had straight A's. On the second one, he had all A's and one B. At breakfast one morning we were acknowledging his hard work, and it occurred to me in that moment that he had earned those grades by himself. I realized that by us "driving the boat," so to speak, it minimized his successes as well.

In the seventh grade, scores and grades ensure you a place in the academic high school. During that same breakfast he said, "Just wait until next year. I am going to knock it out of the park, because I am not going to let an 84 keep me out of Hume Fogg." It was great to see his attitude shift. A few months ago he didn't want to go to that high school—probably because of our insistence on it.

Dad's Story

During the conversation that Lisa referenced above, I told our son that I did not like the way I treated him when we had discussions around homework, and that I wanted us to be on the same page. I also was specific about my areas of concern: scheduling time for projects versus waiting until the last minute, him remembering to do his daily homework, him forgetting to turn in important papers, and what my role was when we got the grade notifications. I then simply asked him what he needed our help on in these areas.

Here's what he said with a little discussion:

1. If his grade drops below a B and we are notified, we remind him that we have a notification and he will access the website and find out what the issue is and take care of it within a week. If it's not taken care of within a week, we have his permission to talk with him about it and help him brainstorm a list of solutions to the problem.
2. On Tuesdays we sign off on his weekly agenda. If there are missing assignments, he gets a week to resolve it; then we follow step 1 above.
3. We agree that he will skip a sports practice if he has not resolved any issues within a week, and use that time to get caught up.
4. On projects, we will guide and schedule our time that we are available to help on Tuesdays during the weekly agenda review.

Contract signed by all three parties dated December 26, 2012. Not a power struggle since.

—Mr. and Mrs. Quinn

TOOL TIPS

1. It is difficult to watch your child suffer, even when you know the lessons learned will provide strength in the long term. Often it is harder on you than on your child. Hang in there.

2. Think about how much better it is for your child to make mistakes when you are around for support instead of when he's on his own.

3. Letting go allows your child to gain strength by building his or her "disappointment muscles" and problem-solving skills.

CHAPTER THREE

MAKING MISTAKES

UNDERSTAND THE BRAIN

*Man does not see reality as it is, but only as he perceives it,
and his perception may be mistaken or biased.*

—Rudolf Dreikurs

1. Do not try to solve a problem when you or your child is upset.
2. Wait until after a cooling-off period (a positive time-out), when you can both access your rational brains.
3. Putting the problem on the family meeting agenda (or asking your child to) is another way to allow for a cooling-off period.

Jane

When you've flipped your lid—meaning you've completely lost your cool—the "reptilian" part of your brain takes control and rational thinking is gone. With two flipped lids (yours and your child's), how much helpful problem solving do you think is happening? Who is listening?

Lectures are useless at best and damaging at worst because children, in a flipped-lid state, tune out lectures or process them through their mid-brains (the amygdala, where irrational beliefs and fears are stored), and they may be deciding to get even, planning to avoid getting caught in the future, or thinking, "I am a bad person."

When you understand the brain, you realize that children cannot learn anything positive when they feel threatened. They are capable only of fight, flight, or freeze—which may translate into rebellion or emotional withdrawal.

Learn self-regulation (positive time-out, in the next section) and then teach it to your children. This doesn't mean you will never again flip your lid, but at least you will know you can't teach anything productive in this state of mind; you'll catch yourself sooner, and you will reconnect through an apology and then focus on solutions after you have calmed down.

Brad

You may have noticed by now that I am often the example of how *not* to implement these Positive Discipline tools. Remember how we say that there are no perfect parents? If nothing else, at least after reading my stories a lot of you will feel a lot more perfect.

By a show of hands, how many people read the point above about not solving a problem when you or your child is upset, and said, "Yeah, right"? Most of us solve 90 percent of our problems with our children when we are upset. Or maybe I shouldn't say "solve" our problems, but we make the attempt when we are upset—and probably do more harm than good. The following story is a perfect example of how I tried to solve a problem while I was in my flipped-lid state.

I arrived home from shopping and began putting the groceries away. In the background I could hear the following discussion between Gibson and Emma.

GIBSON: Emma, why did you play with my Nerf gun?

EMMA: I didn't!

GIBSON: Yes, you did. It wasn't where I left it!

EMMA: I didn't play with your Nerf gun!

GIBSON: Since you played with my Nerf gun, I get to shoot you!

I had just begun to walk over to defuse the situation when Gibson pulled the trigger and shot Emma square in the face.

I grabbed the Nerf gun, furious. I yelled at Gibson and told him that if he ever shot Emma again I would break that Nerf gun into a hundred pieces! (I was totally flipped out.)

Then I went downstairs to watch basketball. For the next hour I didn't say a word to Gibson, who was lying upstairs on the couch. Then, mercifully, Gibson was invited for a sleepover at his friend's house. While I was driving him over to his friend's house, Gibson decided this would be the perfect time for us to bond.

"Now?" I thought. "When I am fuming and frustrated and can't wait to kick him out the door, he wants to bond?"

He started asking me why I hadn't come upstairs. I told him that I was very angry that he would shoot his sister in the face.

He said, "Come on, Dad, Emma forgave me. Why can't you?" Emma had gone over earlier and given Gibson a hug.

I told him that being mean to his sister was not a good way to earn brownie points with me. By that time we were sitting in the driveway of his friend's house. I guess he sensed that I was trying to get rid of him, so he sat there and continued talking to me. Finally after a couple of minutes he said, "Come on, Dad, how about a hug?" So I relented, gave him a hug, and he got out of the car.

The following day when my son got back from his sleepover, we were both feeling better. We were able to calmly discuss the events of the day before, talk about our mistakes, and vow again to do better.

Mary

I know summer is here when I have to stop myself from flipping my lid every day since school has been out. On one hand, I am truly grateful to have a career where I am able to spend every day with my boys, but on the other hand, I'm counting the days until school starts again.

I had fantasies of a fun-filled active summer full of swimming, play-dates, picnics at the park, lots of baseball, walks in our neighborhood, and so on. However, in between all those fun activities are trips to the grocery store, daily housework, and a few other boring errands. At the end of the day I'm exhausted, and it's much easier for me to flip my lid.

But all is not lost. There are many Positive Discipline tools that can help me and my children get back to rational thinking: connection before correction, positive time-outs, hugs, and this one, understanding the brain.

I watched a video of interpersonal neurobiologist Daniel J. Siegel, M.D., showing how to use the palm of the hand to explain the brain and what happens when we become upset, and taught it to my son, Greyson, using the following instructions:

1. Introduce the brain in the palm of your hand by asking everyone to hold up their hand in an open position. Ask them to follow along with what you do.
2. Point to the area from your palm to your wrist, and explain that this area represents the brain stem, which is responsible for the fight-flight-or-freeze response.
3. Fold your thumb over your palm. The thumb represents the midbrain (amygdala), where early memories that created fear and insignificance are stored. It works in conjunction with the brain stem.
4. Then fold your fingers over your thumb (so you now have a fist). This represents the cortex. The prefrontal cortex (point to the front of your fist where your fingertips touch the palm of your hand) is where rational thinking and emotional control takes place.
5. What happens when our buttons get pushed and we lose it? We flip our lids (let your hand open (fingers up) exposing your thumb (representing the exposure of your midbrain).
6. Now our prefrontal cortex is not functioning. In this state we cannot think or behave rationally.

Greyson now loves to remind me when I have flipped my lid by displaying his open hand with his thumb front and center.

I often need to remind myself that I can't expect to control my children's behavior when I don't control my own. The good news is that mistakes are wonderful opportunities to learn. Thank goodness my children are so willing to forgive me and then work on solutions.

We had planned a special trip to a fast-food restaurant all week—a very rare outing. When I let my 11-year-old son know we were ready to go, he abruptly told me he was not going and I should bring the food home to him.

I happily offered to bring the food home and suggested he cut up some apples to go with it before we got back (thinking this would respect his mood swing and need for time to calm down). He shot back at me that he would not and that it was stupid that I asked him. I was calmly telling him what I was willing to do when he stood up, stormed into his room, slammed the door, and yelled a not-very-nice word. At me!

I took a deep breath and thought about what I had learned about the brain. It was clear now that he had a flipped lid, even though I had not realized it before and had no idea why.

His sister looked at me and wisely said, "I am outta here."

I followed her insightful lead and we went to the restaurant. When I returned home I expected an apology, but noticed that he was still blaming me and it was not the time. He avoided me all night. I wanted to talk to him about it but remembered that it takes time to unflip your lid and that he was on his timeline, not mine.

The next morning he walked straight out of his room and gave me the sincerest apology I have ever heard. We agreed that if our relationship was as strong as we thought, he would not have called me that very nasty word. Together we decided that it was best to remove all distractions from building our relationship, including the television and video games. We decided we would play together for a few days, and then he would ask for them back.

It was a surprise when two weeks went by before he came to me and said he would like to watch TV again! It was not easy to avoid saying, "Don't ever talk to me like that again," immediately after it happened, but I made it through.

—Christine Salo-Sokolowski, Certified Positive Discipline Parent Educator

TOOL TIPS

1. Teach your kids about the brain and "flipping your lid."

2. When in a rational state of mind, make plans for calming down (taking a positive time-out) as soon as you realize you need it. Teach your kids to do the same.

3. Follow up by making amends, if needed, and/or finding solutions to the challenge that brought on your flipped lid, if needed.

POSITIVE TIME-OUT

The proper way of training children is identical with the proper way of treating fellow human beings.

—Rudolf Dreikurs

People do better when they feel better. Positive time-out helps us cool off and feel better.

1. Create a time-out space with your children. Let them decide what it would look like and what is in it.
2. Let them give it a special name.
3. When they are upset, ask, "Would it help to go to your _____ place?"
4. Model using positive time-out by going to your own special place when you are upset.

Jane

Most parents have good intentions when they use a *punitive* time-out. They really believe punishment and humiliation is the best way to motivate children to do better, or they simply don't know what else to do. Not doing anything feels like permissiveness to them.

Where did we ever get the crazy idea that we have to make children feel bad before they will do better? This crazy idea is the basis for all punishment, including punitive time-out. It doesn't work for children any more than it would work for adults.

If you are married, imagine your spouse coming to you and saying, "I don't like your behavior. Go to your room until you can act better."

In this scenario, what would you be thinking, feeling, and deciding? Would you say, "Oh, thank you so much. This is so helpful. I'm feeling encouraged and empowered and can hardly wait to do better"? Not likely. You are more likely to file for divorce—or get even in some other way.

When children are put in a "naughty chair," some are plotting how to get even or to avoid getting caught next time. Even worse, some are developing a sense of doubt and shame about themselves. Amazingly, adults would fold much more quickly if they were subjected to so much blame and shame. Children are very resilient and fight to keep their sense of self. This fight usually looks like rebellion or giving in. That is, until they become adults and all the discouragement catches up with them. They live the rest of their lives depressed or constantly trying to prove their worth.

There are several things that make a positive time-out different from a punitive time-out.

1. The purpose is to help children have a place that helps them feel better, not to make them suffer and "think about what they did."
2. It is essential to have your child help create a space that will help him or her feel better—to self-regulate.
3. To increase ownership, invite your child to give his or her space a special name.
4. During times when it might be helpful, allow your child the opportunity to "choose" her special place instead of sending her to it. You can say, "Would it help you to go to your special place right now?"

You might say to your child, "Let's create a place that feels special to you—a place where you can go when you feel mad or sad, or just need time to calm down. Would you like to find a place in your room or another room in the house?"

After your child chooses a place, ask, "What kind of things would you like to have in your space that will help you feel better? What about a pillow, a stuffed animal, some books, some music?"

Then ask your child what he or she would like to call his special place. Many parents have shared that their children have created special names for their cool-out space, such as Amazon Jungle, Spring Garden, Tree House, or Under the Sea.

Once this positive time-out space is created, don't *send* your child to her cool-out space. This defeats the purpose of self-regulation. Allow your child to choose to go to her special place. During a conflict you might say, "Would it help you to go to your feel-good place?" If your child says no, ask, "Would you like me to go with you?" Often this is encouraging to a child and helps increase the connection, as well as calm her down. If your child still says no or is having such a temper tantrum that she can't even hear you, say, "Okay, I'm going to my time-out place." She will notice you leaving and may run to keep up.

We now have a children's book called *Jared's Cool-Out Space*. Reading this book can help children feel excited about creating their own cool-out space for self-regulation. Many parents have read this book to their children and then sent us pictures of what their children have created.

Even positive time-out is rarely appropriate for children under the age of 3. If a child isn't old enough to design his own positive time-out area, he is not old enough to understand any kind of time-out.

Sometimes positive time-out is enough to change behavior. It is not necessary to engage in "I told you so" lectures (or any other kind of lecture). However, there may be times when follow-up is necessary, through curiosity questions, to invite problem solving. In many cases, another Positive Discipline tool might be more appropriate, such as inviting your child to see if it would be helpful to find something on the wheel of choice (see Chapter 5), or to put the problem on the family meeting agenda for discussion when everyone is calmer.

Mary

For many years I avoided creating positive time-out spaces with my boys. I found that too often *I* was the one who needed a time-out to calm down. I thought it was enough to model using positive time-out. I would say, "Mommy is really upset. I'm going to go take a time-out and cool off. I need to take at least five minutes so that I can take deep breaths and calm down. I don't want to say anything I'll regret."

I'd often have one or all of them say, "Can we come with you?" I would reply, "Of course, if you want to take deep breaths and calm down too." Almost immediately we would all calm down and want to reconcile.

Recently I realized how important it is not only to model taking time to cool down but also to give my boys the opportunity to create their own positive time-out spaces so they can practice this important self-regulation skill.

I was a little nervous that after reading *Jared's Cool-Out Space* they'd want to create an elaborate cool-out space and paint the walls black. I really didn't want to paint anything black, and I wasn't sure how to deal with our limited space, since they shared a room. What would happen if they created Positive Time-Out places in their room and needed to go at the same time? I remembered to show faith in my boys' ability to find a solution—and they did.

Greyson, who was 9, said, "Mom, if you or Dad just asked me to go to my room instead of told me, I'd go."

All I could say was, "Wow!" I continued by asking, "What would help calm you down when you're there?"

GREYSON: Well, you know how music always puts me in a good mood—in fact, it's instant.

ME: Of course. So will your CD player work?

GREYSON: Yes.

ME: What else helps you cool off?

GREYSON: Looking at the photo albums from when I was a baby.

ME: Those would help me calm down too. If you think of anything else, be sure to add it in your space.

GREYSON: Okay, Mom. Will you come with me sometimes? Because I always calm down when you rub my back and give me a hug.

ME: I'd be happy to so long as you don't mind waiting for a couple of minutes until I'm calm.

The next day Greyson got upset with his brother Reid because he wasn't playing fairly. I asked him, "Would it help you to go cool off in your room?"

Greyson said, "Yes. Will you come with me?"

I let him know that I needed to get his 4-year-old brother, Parker, distracted with something, or else I would have to bring him too. Greyson said it was fine if Parker came too.

Greyson became calm very quickly after a hug from Parker and me and some deep breaths. Then we talked about what made him so mad. Once he was calm, he came up with a logical solution to the issue. Calm and collected, he went back downstairs and let Reid know how he felt and how they had miscommunicated about the rules to the game. Reid said, "Okay," and they continued to play peacefully.

Reid, who was 7, decided to create Reid's Feel-Good Fort. There is a crawl space under Parker's bed. It has a door and is set up to be the perfect fort.

Reid said, "I can put blankets and a pillow there. I can have a flashlight, books, and some of my Legos."

He asked if he could have his tablet. I reminded him that although electronics are a great distraction, they're not helpful when trying to cope with feelings and problem solving. Screens numb your feelings and eliminate the process of dealing with them. I explained that having a time-out space without screens would create a great habit for dealing with his feelings and problems, a habit that will be very helpful when he's an adult. He was cooperative and understanding.

Within a few hours Reid got upset with one of his brothers. Before I could even ask, he said, "Mom, I'm going to my fort to calm down."

I was relieved that he remembered, and even more relieved that he didn't ask me to come with him. It would've been a tight squeeze through that little door, although it would've been a great laugh too.

Now the tables have been turned. My boys are modeling the use of positive time-out even more than I do.

Some parents complain about the terrible twos, but I found the age of 3 to be more challenging. My daughter, Claire, was developing greater independence and voicing her opinions with great enthusiasm. Most of the time I loved her spirit and her wonderful sense of humor. But sometimes she was stubborn and oppositional. That period could easily have been called the terrible threes.

One fall afternoon, my husband, John, and I had planned to take Claire to the park to enjoy the lovely weather. The day began on a rough note. Claire was in rare form, full of naughty energy. We had regular morning responsibilities to get through, but Claire dreamed up a thousand ways to avoid cooperating with John and me. We couldn't get her dressed. She wouldn't eat her breakfast. She threw her toys all over the living room . . . and she was laughing about it the whole time. We were never going to get out of the house!

She was so ornery, and it was difficult to get Claire to focus and listen to us. Finally I pulled her onto my lap and calmly said, "I can see you're having trouble doing the jobs we need to do before we go out. We need to wear clothes and have some breakfast before we can play at the park today. If you don't get dressed and have something to eat, we can't go out."

Claire burst into big, fake tears. Very dramatically she said, "I'm gonna go cry in my bed now, Mommy." She slowly walked into her room and climbed into the top bunk.

John and I had to run into our own bedroom before we exploded with laughter. Her dramatic exit was hilarious! Yet the tactic was very effective. She sat in her bed for a few minutes, and then emerged as if nothing had happened. She used a positive time-out to help herself calm down and refocus.

We even made it to the park!

—Amy Knobler, Certified Positive Discipline Parent Educator

TOOL TIPS

1. Learn the importance of taking a time-out for yourself to calm down before teaching positive time-out to your children.

2. Remember the importance of asking children if it will help them to go to their positive time-out, instead of sending them.

3. It helps to offer a choice: "Would it help you to go to your feel-good place or to put this problem on the family meeting agenda?"

MISTAKES ARE WONDERFUL OPPORTUNITIES TO LEARN

We cannot protect our children from life. Therefore, it is essential that we prepare them for it.

—Rudolf Dreikurs

See mistakes as opportunities for learning.

1. Respond to mistakes with compassion and kindness instead of shame, blame, or lectures.
2. When appropriate, use curiosity questions to help your child explore the consequences of her mistakes.
3. During dinnertime, invite everyone to share a mistake they made during the day and what they learned from it.

Jane

Many children are taught to be ashamed of mistakes. Adults who teach blame for mistakes mean well. Again, they believe that shame will motivate children to do better. It might—but at a heavy cost to their healthy sense of self-worth. If you were raised this way, it may be time to "re-parent" yourself, so that you can create new beliefs about mistakes.

1. Close your eyes and remember the messages you received from parents and teachers about mistakes when you were a child. Did you receive the message that you were stupid, inadequate, bad, a disappointment, a klutz?

2. When hearing these messages, what did you decide about yourself and how to react in the future? Remember, you were not aware that you were making a decision at the time. But if you examine your reaction when you make a mistake in the present day, the long-term effects of those messages are usually obvious.

3. Some people decided they were bad or inadequate. Others decided they should not take risks for fear of humiliation if their efforts fell short of perfection. Many decided to become approval junkies and try to please adults at great cost to their self-esteem. Some are obsessed with the need to prove their worth. And some decided they would be sneaky about their mistakes and do everything they could to avoid getting caught. What did you decide?

4. While teaching your children that mistakes are opportunities to learn, you will be able to make some new decisions for yourself.

When parents and teachers give children negative messages about mistakes, they are trying to motivate children to do better, for their own good. They haven't taken time to think about the long-term results of their methods and how the decisions children make are crucial to their development.

So much parenting and teaching is based on fear. Adults fear they aren't doing a good job if they don't make children do better. Too many are more concerned about what the neighbors will think than about what their children are learning. Others are afraid that children will never learn to do better if they don't instill fear and humiliation in them. Most are afraid because they don't know what else to do—and fear that if they don't inflict blame, shame, and pain, they will be acting permissively.

There is another way: teaching children to view mistakes as learning opportunities. It is not permissive, and it truly motivates children to do better without paying the price of a lowered sense of self-worth.

It can be helpful to turn the idea of learning from mistakes into a family tradition. At least once a week, during dinnertime, ask everyone to share a mistake they made and what they learned from it. It would be wonderful to hear an adult say to a child, "You made a mistake—that's fantastic! What can we learn from it?" And I do mean "we." Many mistakes are made because we haven't taken time for training and encouragement. We often provoke rebellion instead of inspiring improvement.

Children need daily exposure to the value of mistakes—and they need to be able to learn from them in a safe environment. Children can truly learn the courage to be imperfect when they can laugh about and learn from mistakes.

Mary

Once again I get to share how fortunate I was to be raised learning that mistakes are wonderful opportunities to learn. Throughout my childhood we always celebrated our mistakes. (At the time, I thought that's what everyone did.) My parents taught me that life is about learning lessons, and when we make mistakes, we can either learn from them or continue to make the same mistakes until we do finally learn.

I think we can all relate to a painful mistake we've made in our life that's ended up being a valuable opportunity to learn. It wasn't until I went off to college that I experienced how often people don't like to admit that they're wrong or imperfect or that they made a mistake.

As a mother of three young boys, I have the opportunity to make mistakes daily. Even though I am a practicing Positive Discipline mother, I am still a human being. Luckily, I have kids who are truly forgiving and have no problem accepting me while I continue to learn and grow with every mistake.

Every night when I tuck my boys into bed, we end our day with our happiest and saddest moments of the day, and at least one mistake.

Then we discuss what we learned from them. It's a great advantage to learn from each other and continue the ongoing message of unconditional love and support.

Instead of feeling sorry, rescuing, shaming, or expecting perfection, think of the courage and self-confidence your children will develop when they are invited to see their mistakes as learning opportunities.

My oldest son, Greyson, recently made a mistake, although he was so ashamed that he didn't even want to talk about it. I found out from the school principal that he said something completely inappropriate to another student on the playground. When I tried to bring it up with him, he said, "I don't want to talk about it."

I attempted to talk about it a few times that day, and realized the importance of timing and connection. I wasn't going to be able to do it either in the car or at the dining room table, so I waited until it was just the two of us at bedtime. We talked about other things until I felt we were connecting. I then said, "Greyson, do you think Mommy has said things she didn't mean, especially when I was mad?"

Greyson replied, "Well, probably not as bad as what I said."

"I doubt it," I said. "When I am mad I can say things that I would never even think of, let alone say, when I'm not mad. I know for certain that when I feel hurt, I will say things to hurt back. How about you start with what happened that hurt you?"

Greyson explained how some boys on the playground hadn't been playing wall ball fairly and were being mean to him by excluding him and saying mean things to him. He still didn't want to tell me what he'd said. I knew he felt embarrassed and ashamed.

I told him, "Greyson, you're 8 years old. You're supposed to make mistakes every day. I'm 39 years old and still make mistakes almost every day. I try to learn from them so I don't make the same mistakes, and sometimes I make the same mistake over and over. The reason I make mistakes daily is because I'm human and, as you know, I'm not perfect."

Greyson, who loves math and word problems, said, "Mom, that would mean you've made over ten thousand mistakes."

I said, "Exactly. And I'm still not perfect, and I'm still continuing to make mistakes and learning from each one."

After Greyson realized he wasn't alone and how accepting I was of his mistakes, he gave me a huge hug and told me what he'd said.

We continued to talk about the situation and focused on positive and productive ways he could handle a similar situation next time. I was reminded of what I have learned over and over in Positive Discipline—what a wonderful gift I'm giving to my kids by acknowledging how imperfect I am.

Brad

I make a *lot* of mistakes. I make mistakes as a parent. I make mistakes at work. God knows I make mistakes with women. If mistakes are wonderful opportunities to learn, I should be the smartest person in town by now.

My children also make a lot of mistakes. Sometimes in the heat of the moment, it is difficult to "respond to mistakes with compassion and kindness instead of shame, blame, or lectures."

When my son was younger, we made a trip to the grocery store so he could buy some snacks for his school lunches. We had finished picking out our groceries and approached the self-checkout station. As I began to scan the items, I noticed that the computerized voice kept scolding me on every item. "Please place the item in the bagging area! Press skip bagging if you would like to skip bagging! An attendant has been notified to assist you!"

I was standing there frantically pushing buttons trying to appease the voice. Finally one of the employees walked over and said, "Sir, your son is leaning on the scale." I looked over and explained to Gibson that he couldn't lean on the scale because it messed up the weight of our groceries.

I was scanning the rest of our items when the computer voice started yelling at me again. I looked over at Gibson, who was gently touching the scale. I said, "Gibson . . . you *can't* touch the scale!" I guess he was trying to see how much pressure it would take to set the thing off, but I was not in the mood to experiment with the computer voice.

I managed to get a few more items scanned before the computer voice started in on me again. You can imagine my frustration at this point. I looked over at Gibson and saw that he was touching the top part of the scale. I was speechless for a moment. At last I said, "Gibson!" and looked meaningfully at his hand.

He said, "Oh . . . I didn't know that was part of the scale too."

Finally we got all of the items checked out and left the store.

As you can tell, I didn't do a very good job with the first part of this tool, so I moved on to the next suggestion: "When appropriate, use curiosity questions to help your child explore the consequences of her mistakes."

I asked Gibson, "Do you understand why I got upset in the store?"

"Yes," he said.

Then I asked, "What do you think we could do next time so we don't have that problem?"

He said, "You could let me scan the groceries."

I replied, "That's a great idea! Let's do that next time."

In the next section we discuss the 3 R's for recovery from mistakes. One of the steps is to reconcile by apologizing. I recognized my part in the grocery store checkout fiasco and apologized to Gibson for getting so upset. The next time we went shopping together, Gibson scanned all the groceries and the computer voice stayed out of it.

SUCCESS STORY FROM COSTA RICA

One morning my middle son, Daniel (he is 8 years old), came to my room and told me: "Mom, stay in the bed. I'm going to make you breakfast!"

I did as he said, and I could hear him in the kitchen by himself. Suddenly I heard the very loud sound of something breaking. I didn't get up or say anything to him.

After a while he called, "Mom, breakfast is ready."

When I got to the table I saw that he had put out the plates, forks, napkins, juice, everything. He had made fried eggs for himself, me, and a friend, and scrambled eggs for his brother. It was so sweet that he thought of what each of us liked and how to put it all on the table.

"Daniel, thanks for this food," I said. "It is really good."

I started eating, and after a while I asked him, "Daniel, what was that sound I heard in the kitchen?"

He said, "Nothing."

I said, "Are you sure?"

"Well, Mom, I broke the butter cover. But don't worry, Mom. I cleaned everything up."

I said, "Oh. Okay. Thanks. So what did you learn about that?"

He answered, "I have to be more careful, and I can clean up when I make a mistake."

I said, "Great," and continued eating.

—Georgina Gurdian, Certified Positive Discipline Parent Educator

SUCCESS STORY FROM VISTA, CALIFORNIA

As a parent, I feel grateful to be able to celebrate being imperfect and role-modeling for my children that it's okay to be who they are, mistakes and all.

When my oldest son was in the fourth grade, he brought home a test with a failing grade. This took me by surprise because it was way out of character for him, and I gasped.

His response was, "What's wrong, Mom? It just means I have more to learn."

I was so grateful that he had been raised with Positive Discipline and completely understood that mistakes are wonderful opportunities to learn. We immediately sat down at the table and began reviewing each mistake.

—Joy Sacco, teacher and Certified Positive Discipline Trainer

TOOL TIPS

1. Model being excited about your own mistakes by sharing them without blame or shame.

2. Introduce the idea of learning from mistakes as a family tradition. At least once a week, during dinnertime, ask everyone to share a mistake they made and what they learned from it.

3. Use the 3 R's of recovery from mistakes (next section), and teach them to your children.

3 R'S OF RECOVERY FROM MISTAKES

Perfection never exists in reality, but only in our dreams.

—*Rudolf Dreikurs*

Making mistakes isn't as important as what we do about them. Use these steps after you have had a chance to cool off.

1. Recognize your mistake with a feeling of responsibility instead of blame.
2. Reconcile by apologizing.
3. Resolve the problem by working together on a respectful solution.

Jane

Seeing mistakes as opportunities to learn is easier said than done. Is it instinctual to feel we aren't good enough when we make a mistake, or is it learned? In any case, the 3 R's of recovery from mistakes can help because they provide skills to make amends that you can learn and teach your children.

Modeling isn't one of the steps, but children do learn best from watching your behavior. Catch yourself making mistakes. Practice saying, "Whoops—I wonder what I will learn from this one." Then follow the steps.

Since you are a human being, I can almost guarantee that you won't always catch yourself soon enough to prevent all mistakes. Sometimes you will say and do things you regret—especially to your children. Even though you love them, you may let it slip that you feel upset or disappointed about something they have done.

The good news is that it is never too late to follow the 3 R's of recovery from mistakes. Once you have calmed down, acknowledge the mistake you made, first to yourself. Then go to your child, take responsibility for your mistake, and apologize. This is when you learn about the true nature of children. They are immediately forgiving: "That's okay, Mommy."

When others have been involved in your mistake, you might need to make amends that extend beyond an apology. You will need to figure out how to fix the problem. It may require brainstorming for solutions (see Chapter 5) or putting the problem on the family meeting agenda so everyone can be involved in brainstorming for solutions.

Teaching children that it's okay to make mistakes, and teaching them the skills needed to recover from those mistakes, can save them from the challenges of perfectionism.

Mary

Fortunately, I have never had a problem admitting when I'm wrong or owning my mistakes and apologizing.

Recently a parent asked me, "Is there a way to not react when your buttons get pushed?"

I replied, "I wish! If I knew that answer, I could save myself a lot of heartache and guilt." Since I'm Jane Nelsen's daughter, a Positive Discipline parent educator, and a marriage and family therapist, I often put pressure on myself to enact Positive Discipline techniques perfectly.

My mom keeps reminding me that it is very encouraging to the parents I work with to know that I mean it when I say, "There is no such thing as a perfect parent. Fortunately, the 3 R's of recovery from mistakes provide a tool for making amends. We can also teach this skill to our children so they can learn skills and techniques for recovery when they make mistakes."

My biggest button pusher is when my boys fight. I can stay out of fights and practice what I teach about 50 percent of the time. When I do, I feel good about having faith that they can work it out. But when I do get sucked in, I get to practice the 3 R's of recovery from mistakes.

First I own it (recognize): I acknowledge my behavior and reiterate that Mommy has lost it again. I have raised my voice or threatened to take away something that, of course, was totally unrelated to what they were fighting about.

Then I apologize (reconcile): "Mommy's buttons were pushed again, and instead of counting to ten or walking away, I let my emotions take over and I reacted instead of respectfully responding. I apologize."

I'm really great at apologizing, and my boys are so forgiving, like most kids. My apology is always more than saying, "I'm sorry." I am specific in saying what I'm sorry for. Then we focus on solutions (resolve). When we've connected and calmed down, we focus on what I and/or they will do differently next time they fight. A few of our latest examples include:

1. A code word ("leprechaun")
2. A silent signal (four fingers up, which is the sign for a flipped lid)
3. Putting the issue on the family meeting agenda
4. Sense of humor (tickling them or doing something crazy that totally distracts them)
5. Pulling over in the car and reading my book until they both tell me they're ready to stop fighting
6. Putting music on and starting to dance (it's difficult to be mad when your favorite song is on, or when your crazy mom starts dancing)
7. Leaving the room and letting them work the issue out (as long as there's no danger of physical violence)

If they try to get you involved, don't bite the bait. Let them know you have faith in their ability to work things out, or that you will be happy to get involved later if they want to put the problem on the family meeting agenda for discussion when everyone has calmed down.

When there has been some physical violence and I don't intervene, it has been amazing to experience their genuine remorse and compassion. The one who hurt his brother will quickly respond with an ice pack, hug, or apology. When I intervene, they take on the roles of victim or bully and become defensive or blaming.

Brad

Finally . . . a chance for me to recover from my many parenting mistakes! Whew! I'm sure I am not alone in being relieved. We are all human, so mistakes are a part of the process. Don't beat yourself up. Instead, use the 3 R's of recovery from mistakes.

As you might imagine, I've needed to apologize to my son quite often. When we have both calmed down, I usually go into his bedroom, sit down beside him. and go through the steps.

> DAD: Son, I'm sorry I got so upset today.
>
> GIBSON: That's okay.
>
> DAD: What do you think we can do in the future so it doesn't get to that point?
>
> GIBSON: I don't know.
>
> DAD: Would you like to hear my ideas?
>
> GIBSON: Sure.
>
> DAD: Maybe when your sister is getting on your nerves, you can walk away?
>
> GIBSON: That won't work—she'll just follow me.
>
> DAD: Do you have any ideas?
>
> GIBSON: Yeah—she could stop being so annoying!
>
> DAD: Ha! I'm not sure that will happen. Younger sisters are usually annoying to older brothers. Maybe I could just take you next time we need to go somewhere and I'll have Jessica come over and babysit Emma?
>
> GIBSON: That would be good.
>
> DAD: Okay, let's try that.

SUCCESS STORY FROM SHENZHEN, CHINA

I asked my 4-year-old daughter, Serenity, to clean up the Lego garden house she'd built on the floor. I told her the cat, Peace, would step on it and make all those small pieces scatter everywhere.

She said with full confidence, "Peace won't! I told her, she understood!"

"Serenity, clean up all the Legos, please! And put all of them into the box so you won't lose any, please."

"No! I'm leaving my garden house on the floor. I want it to be there!"

"Serenity, would you like to clean it up by yourself? Or do you want Mummy to help you?"

"I want nothing! It's my choice! Not your choice!" She is just as strong-willed as I am.

I raised my voice: "Serenity! Clean it up, right now!"

Serenity looked at me, angry and (I guessed) a bit scared, and started walking to her room, saying, "I am upset. I am going to my tent to calm myself down!" (Her tent is one of her positive time-out spots.)

The words from this 4-year-old little girl filled my heart! How many adults could say and do this?

I softened my voice right away: "Sweetheart, please come back. Mummy has something to say to you."

I squatted and held her shoulders gently. Serenity said: "Mummy, you raised your voice, you were loud, and it hurt my feelings."

I gave her a big hug and whispered sincerely, "Serenity, I am very sorry. Please forgive me for hurting your feelings."

She hugged me back. "It's okay, Mummy. I feel much better now!"

She figured out the solution to the Lego problem after I asked, "What can you do if you don't want Peace to destroy your work?"

We put it on the top of a shelf!

—Elly Zhen, Certified Positive Discipline Trainer

TOOL TIPS

1. It is never too late to use this tool, but it can be too soon. Wait for a cooling-off and calming-down period.

2. Remember that most mistakes made by parents and children are made from a flipped-lid state of mind. Take time to access your rational brain and then use encouragement—which is the essence of the 3 R's of recovery from mistakes.

3. Deal with your own issues about mistakes. This may require re-parenting yourself while parenting your children.

4. Find stories to read to your kids about the mistakes of great men and women. Edison is famous for telling a reporter that he didn't make ten thousand mistakes while trying to discover electricity—he just learned ten thousand things that didn't work.

5. Give up all guilt about past mistakes. Guilt that lasts longer than a few minutes is useless and debilitating to you and others. Use the 3 R's of recovery from mistakes and move on.

CHAPTER FOUR

HOW TO CONNECT

SPECIAL TIME

If we are to have better children, parents must become better educators.

—Rudolf Dreikurs

S chedule special time that is different from regular time.

1. Take the phone off the hook or put your cell phone on silent.
2. Take turns choosing an activity you both enjoy from a list you have brainstormed together.

Jane

You may already spend lots of time with your children. However, there is a difference between have-to time, casual time, and scheduled special time. For special time, it's important for children to know exactly when they can count on time that has been set aside especially for them on a regular basis.

We suggest that parents take the phone off the hook to emphasize that this is special, uninterrupted time. However, one mother would leave the phone on the hook during her special time with her 3-year-old daughter. If the phone rang, she would answer and say, "I'm sorry, I can't talk with you now. This is my special time with Lori." Lori would grin as she heard her mother tell other people how important it was to spend time with her.

How often do you say, "I can't. I'm too busy right now"? Adding a few words can make all the difference to your child: "I can't right now, but I'm looking forward to our special time."

Children feel a sense of connection when they can count on special time with you. They feel that they are important to you. This decreases their need to misbehave as a mistaken way to find belonging and significance.

Mary

Special times with both of my parents are some of my fondest memories of my childhood. We called them "date nights," and would take turns each week in different combinations. For example, it'd be my mom and me one week, while my brother and Dad went out on a "date." The next week we would switch, so I would be with my dad and my brother would be with Mom. The third week we would have a family date night, and the final week would be just my parents for their date night.

Many of our date nights didn't involve going out or spending money. I love the memories of building a fort with my brother and dad, or baking cookies with my mom. They were special because my brother and I brainstormed what we wanted to do and put our ideas on a list, and our parents enthusiastically agreed.

I have continued this tradition with my family and my boys. My oldest son and I would have our special time at least once a week when my youngest son was still in his crib. We would put him to bed and then have our date night—usually playing a game of his choice, followed by a movie and popcorn in bed.

I learned that while a movie and popcorn in bed may not seem that special to me, calling it our date night, planning for it, and anticipating it have made it more special for my son. He would ask me all week if it was Saturday, our date night, yet.

A key factor in having special time is making sure your child knows in advance that it's his special time with you and getting him involved in the planning.

Brad

I already spend plenty of time with my children. In fact, I probably spend too much time with them. But this is "special time," which is different. If I am spending time with both children, there is still that element of competition for my affection. So I wondered if spending special time with each child individually would have an effect on the sibling rivalry in our home.

We had planned our special time for Friday. The kids had the day off from school, so I was going to play tennis with Gibson and practice softball with Emma. Then we woke up Friday and opened the front door to see snow on the ground! Not exactly tennis and softball weather.

This actually turned out to be a good thing, because I was having computer problems and I was able to spend the day getting those issues resolved. We had to be flexible and decided to reschedule for Saturday, when the snow had melted enough for Gibson and me to play tennis.

There was just one problem. You see, when you involve your children in this process of using the Positive Discipline Tools, they actually understand the process better than you. When Gibson and I arrived at the tennis courts, we rallied for ten or fifteen minutes. Then I said, "Okay, let's play. You can serve."

Little did I know that my perception of tennis and Gibson's perception of tennis were completely different. It took me about thirty minutes to figure out Gibson's version of tennis, during which he reminded me several times, "Dad, this is my special time. I want to play fun tennis."

For those of you unfamiliar with "fun tennis," let me enlighten you. First of all, you are not allowed to call out the score: "love-fifteen," "love-thirty," and so on. I learned this early on when Gibson said, "Dad, be quiet!"

"What?"

Gibson said, "Stop talking!"

"I'm just calling out the score," I said.

Gibson said, "Yeah . . . stop doing that. I want to play fun tennis."

Okay, lesson learned.

Then after Gibson served twice and missed, I said, "Double fault—move to the other side."

To which Gibson responded "Dad . . . stop doing that!"

I said, "Stop doing what?"

Gibson said, "Stop telling me what to do. This is my special time!"

Okay, lesson number two learned. In fun tennis you always serve from the right side.

Then it was my turn to serve. Gibson was standing in the middle of the court, so I said, "Gibson, you had better move over a little."

Gibson didn't move. So I served to the right service court, and the ball landed in and then bounced to the fence.

Gibson said, "Dad, you did that just to prove a point."

I said, "No, I didn't. That's how you play tennis."

Gibson said, "I just want to play fun tennis."

Lesson number three learned: in fun tennis none of the rules of normal tennis apply.

Finally after several missteps, I learned all the rules to fun tennis and Gibson and I started having fun. After tennis, I took him to get some food, and our special time ended up being a success.

Since the snow hadn't quite melted off the grass, Emma and I decided to go to dinner together at Olive Garden. It was a Saturday night, and by the time we got there it was an hour wait for a table.

Emma said, "That's okay—this is our special time. I don't mind waiting." That made my heart smile, and so we waited for a table and had a wonderful time together.

Just a few final points about special time. As a busy single dad, I found myself looking at my scheduled special time with my kids as just another item to check off my already overwhelming schedule. I realized that I needed to change my attitude about my special time with the kids. Nobody wants to be an item that is just there to be checked off a schedule. It even helps to show our kids that we are excited about our special time together. Then they'll realize that they are much more important than all the other events we have scheduled that week.

SUCCESS STORY FROM SAN DIEGO, CALIFORNIA

My husband and I took our Positive Discipline parenting classes very seriously when our girls were 4 and 6 years old. We decided to schedule regular family meetings.

One of the first things we did was create a list of all the tasks in the house. Our girls loved helping us think of all the things we needed to do to help our home run smoothly.

Then we divided up the tasks, such as cooking, shopping, laundry, and cleaning. Later we added the names of who would work on specific tasks in teams with a parent. We switched the tasks and which parent and child would work together until we all agreed. We had outlined four weeks with various tasks, which included going out with Mom and going out with Dad for special times. We enjoyed shopping, playing, and doing many things together over many years until the girls went away to college. Each girl got to share her interests with us and we got to show them some of the things we loved doing.

Family meetings helped us schedule special time, in addition to getting family chores done. These were the most special days, when we all had fewer breakdowns and more fun times as a family.

—Yogi Patel, Certified Positive Discipline Trainer

TOOL TIPS

1. Scheduled special time is a reminder of why you had children in the first place—to enjoy them.

2. When you are busy and your children want your attention, it is easier for them to accept that you don't have time when you say, "Honey, I can't right now, but I sure am looking forward to our special time at four-thirty."

3. Plan the special time with your children. Brainstorm a list of things you would like to do together during your special time. When first brainstorming your ideas, don't evaluate or eliminate. Later you can look at your list together and categorize. If some options cost too much money, put them on a list of things to save money for.

SHOW FAITH

We must realize that we cannot build on deficiencies, only strength. We cannot help our children—or anyone else—to have faith in themselves if we have no faith in them.

—*Rudolf Dreikurs*

We underestimate grossly what our children can do.

1. When we show faith in our children, they develop courage and faith in themselves. Instead of rescuing, lecturing, or fixing, say, "I have faith in you. I know you can handle this."
2. Children develop their problem-solving skills and "disappointment muscles" through experiences.
3. Validate feelings: "I know you are upset. I would be too."

Jane

One of the biggest mistakes some parents make when they decide to try Positive Discipline is becoming too permissive because they don't want to be punitive. This is a mistake because it is not respectful to pamper children. However, it is respectful to validate their feelings: "I can see that you are disappointed" (or angry, or upset). It is also respectful to have faith that your children can survive disappointment and develop a sense of capability in the process.

Have faith in your children's ability to handle their own problems. You can offer support by validating feelings or giving a hug, but not by rescuing or fixing.

Patience is probably the most difficult part of showing faith in our children. It is almost always more expedient to solve problems for our children. This is particularly true when we are under time pressure. In these cases we can take time later to explore solutions for the future. Ask your children exploratory questions: "What happened?" "What caused it to happen?" "What did you learn?" "What can you do in the future?"

Practice having faith in your children on a daily basis. Allow them to solve problems on their own. Allow them to feel a little disappointment. Allow them to work through their feelings. They will need these skills in the future.

It may help to remember that who your children are today is not who they will be forever. Someday they will be nagging their own children to put their dishes in the sink and to clean their rooms. Remember that example is the best teacher. Model what you want for your children, take time for training so they learn skills, have regular family meetings, and then have lots of faith in them to become the best they can be.

Mary

With my two older boys, I wasn't aware that I could skip Pull-Ups or nighttime training diapers altogether. With them, I accepted that there would be a few accidents, but that they would take place in the training diapers, so I wouldn't have to wash sheets. I didn't know that keeping them in nighttime diapers would extend the nighttime training time. Instead, they developed the habit of wearing diapers instead of discarding them when they were developmentally ready and experiencing the feeling of capability that comes from self-control.

When it came time to potty-train my third son, Parker, I decided to skip Pull-Ups and nighttime diapers. I thought it would help him if I didn't allow him to have any water starting at least one hour before bedtime. I'm not sure if it was because he was really thirsty or if it was that he sensed my energy and fear, but he insisted on having water. The more I tried to redirect him or tell him that if he drank the water he would wet his bed, the more he insisted he had to have it. The more I persisted, the more he resisted.

I realized that this was my opportunity to show faith. I knew it would be more effective if he learned through his own experience (the wet way) and knowledge rather than mine. That said, I needed to let go, show faith, and allow him to experience the natural consequences of his actions.

Sure enough, he guzzled down about eight ounces of water and—wouldn't you know it—wet his bed. He learned his lesson without any lectures or "I told you so's" from me. The next night he went to take a sip of water and said, "I'll only have a little bit, so I won't wet the bed."

Showing faith that he would learn about water before bed through his own experience sped up the process once again. He wet his bed only one more time before he was able to stay dry at night.

I know it's tempting to explain to our children that we know what will happen, but simply allowing them to experience it on their own is much more valuable.

I also allowed him to help me clean up his mess—no shame, just the task of changing his sheets and washing the old ones. He loves any opportunity to help. This also allowed for some curiosity questions. Even though I knew the answers, I asked him so that I could invite him to really think about and answer the questions.

ME: Why do you think you wet the bed last night?
PARKER: I drank too much water.
ME: Do you think you should drink water before bed tonight?
PARKER: Just a little bit.

Because I showed faith in him, Parker learned about water before bed and I learned that it's age-appropriate for him to test and explore. He was definitely testing his power the first few times. I know this because I was immediately drawn into a power struggle with him. Trying to insist on him not having water only made him want it more. I'm still convinced that he wasn't even thirsty but was just seeking a reaction from me.

I had to ask myself, "What's more important, for him to fight me and have a nightly power struggle or go through one morning of messy sheets?" The latter created a respectful relationship with Mom and an overall sense of self-reliance.

Brad

I find that being brutally honest to everyone about your shortcomings as a parent is hard. This tool talks about showing faith in our children so they can develop courage and faith in themselves, but I think it is the parents who need the courage and faith. Let's face it—having faith in our children takes a lot of courage. And sometimes showing faith means allowing our children to make mistakes.

One day I picked my son up from school and he excitedly announced that he was going to make cheesecake. I too was excited, because cheesecake is my favorite dessert. So I said, "Great!"

Then Gibson explained that he had watched his friend make cheesecake. He started describing the recipe to me. It went something like this: You take some graham crackers and grind them up and mix them with butter for the crust. (So far, so good.) Then you take some whipped cream and mix it with some sugar and melt down some chocolate chips and mix that in and then add some more whipped cream. (This is what I heard . . . sugar, sugar, sugar.) Then you put it in the freezer.

I looked at Gibson. I tried my best to show faith and resist the temptation to speak, but the words just came out. "That's not cheesecake."

Gibson said, "Dad, why do you always do that?"

I said, "The reason they call it cheesecake is because one of the ingredients is cream cheese."

Gibson said, "Dad, it *is* cheesecake!"

It went on like that until we got home and I tried to show Gibson a cheesecake recipe online. But he refused to look, so I finally gave up.

Gibson wanted to make his cheesecake right away, but I explained that we didn't have any whipped cream. He wanted me to go to the store, but I told him that I had work to do and that I would add it to the shopping list.

Fast-forward to Friday. I had bought the ingredients and Gibson started making his cheesecake while I was out running errands and picking up dinner. When I returned home he was up to his elbows in whipped cream and chocolate chips. Even though I was convinced that this whole experience was going to give me heartburn, I was very supportive of his efforts. He wanted me to taste his chocolate cream concoction, but I told him I would wait for the final product. Gibson finished making his cheesecake and put it in the freezer.

After dinner, we finally were ready to sample the cheesecake. Gibson cut everybody a piece. Emma took one small bite and said, "Hmmm, not bad. I give it two and a half stars out of five." But she didn't eat any more.

Not wanting another teenage meltdown, I ate my entire piece of cheesecake. I tried to be encouraging and supportive. Then I started cleaning up from dinner and the mess that was made from the infamous cheesecake experiment.

Now comes the priceless part of the evening. Gibson's friend came over—you know, the one who started this whole cheesecake controversy. I was in the kitchen cleaning up as Gibson proudly displayed his cheesecake.

Gibson's friend related the story of his first attempt at making cheesecake: he'd made some cheesecake for a party he was attending, and the cheesecake came out all lumpy. But his mom let him take it to the party anyway, and he was the only one who ate it. They both laughed.

Gibson's friend tried a bite, and they began discussing the ingredients and the steps for making a good cheesecake. Suddenly I heard "cream cheese." I perked right up and looked over at Gibson, who looked back at me rather sheepishly. So I walked over to Gibson's friend, put my arm around him, and said, "Do you mean to tell me that when you make cheesecake you use cream cheese?"

Gibson's friend said, "Yeah."

I started laughing uncontrollably.

Gibson said, "Uh . . . I didn't know it was cream cheese. It just all looked like white stuff to me."

I was still laughing, and Gibson said, "Dad . . . you don't have to make a scene."

I said "Gibson, you raked me over the coals for having the audacity to bring up the fact that cheesecake has cream cheese. Isn't it possible that your dad isn't quite as stupid as you think he is?"

Gibson said, "Dad, I don't think you're stupid."

It really helps to write these experiences down. I can see now that I failed miserably at all three principles of the showing faith tool:

1. Instead of rescuing, lecturing, or fixing, say, "I have faith in you. I know you can handle this."
2. Children develop their problem-solving skills and "disappoint-ment muscles" through experiences.
3. Validate feelings: "I know you are upset. I would be too."

I'll know better for next time. Who cares if he butchered his first attempt at making cheesecake? I'll just need to keep a stock of Rolaids in the medicine cabinet.

SUCCESS STORY FROM CAIRO, EGYPT

My 14-year-old daughter often gets upset and barely ever says what's wrong or why she's upset. I was feeling frustrated and guilty because I didn't know what to do or how to help her.

I would ask, "What's wrong?" Then, when she wouldn't tell me, I would try to guess. I would ask her if I'd done something to upset her. I made a fuss trying to figure out what was wrong so that I would be able to help her feel better, but her response was to retreat further and not share anything with me. I decided to try the following:

- To have faith in her ability to deal with her feelings without me fussing and trying to rescue her.
- To offer to talk with her about what's bugging her when she's ready, and to wait so that she has time to take the first step.

Having faith in her ability to handle her own ups and downs has allowed me to see how much she actually *can*. And I believe it's beginning to work, because she seems to trust that she can too.

She still gets upset, and hurt, and sometimes cries. I give her a hug and offer to talk when she's ready. I find that she is able to deal with her worries eventually and to move on after a while with most issues.

Because I now wait rather than fuss, and make sure to let her know that I'm there for her when she needs, she now initiates when she is ready. She has started coming to me so she can share her worries sometimes. We have great discussions when she does. We often share problem-solving ideas, and enjoy the lovely connection with one another that I have always been hoping for.

—Shaza A. S. Salaheldin, Certified Positive Discipline Parent Educator

SUCCESS STORY FROM SAN DIEGO, CALIFORNIA

My family and I started camping together as soon as the children were old enough to walk (I was never brave enough to go with a non-walker). But this camping weekend turned out to be extra special.

My husband was on a trip, and my firstborn was in college on the East Coast, so my 15-year-old son, Adrien, and I decided we should go camping on our own. He used our checklist to prepare all our supplies and packed the car on his own, and he even got annoyed with me because I wasn't ready on time for our trip! It truly does pay off to give our children the time and space to discover what they are capable of.

When my children were younger I would give them time to figure things out while I observed their efforts. Like any other parent, at times I was impatient and would try to help them or do things for them. But I learned that if we take the time to guide them and show them how to fend for themselves, the payoff is immense. During our camping trip, we socialized with a couple who was constantly telling their children what to do and not do. I had a proud parenting moment when my son noticed this and thanked me for not being like them.

It's easy to fall into the trap of thinking we need to direct our children's every move. But letting them figure things out on their own is much more empowering for them! As Dr. Montessori said, "Follow the child." Step back and observe your child; you'll be amazed at what they can accomplish.

—Jeanne-Marie Paynel, Certified Positive Discipline Parent Educator

TOOL TIPS

1. Note how much resistance you may invite from children because you try to control them instead of having faith in them.

2. Tame your ego.

3. Take Rudolf Dreikurs's advice and stop underestimating your children.

4. Have more faith in yourself and your children—you can learn from mistakes and have more fun making them.

COMPLIMENTS

The beneficial effects of building morale, providing a feeling of togetherness, and considering difficulties as projects for understanding and improvement, rather than as objects of scorn, outweigh any possible harm.

—Rudolf Dreikurs

Compliments and appreciations bring us closer together. Focus on accomplishments and helpfulness to others:

1. "I appreciate how quickly you get dressed and ready for school."
2. "I notice how kindly you cared for Anna when she felt sad. I bet it helped her feel better."
3. "Thank you for setting the table."

Jane

Siblings don't have any trouble bickering and putting each other down, but strangely enough they struggle with the idea of appreciating each other. Giving and receiving compliments is a skill that needs to be taught and practiced. Family meetings provide that opportunity.

Hearing my kids be mean to each other was very difficult for me, so I was thrilled that the hurtful comments were reduced significantly when we held regular family meetings starting with compliments.

So often we are focused on what our children have done wrong. It is much better to focus on what they have done right and give them appropriate compliments. This simple act will change the atmosphere in your home.

Brad

We start all of our family meetings with compliments, which help set the tone for a more positive experience. During one meeting I complimented Gibson on learning two new songs on the piano. Throughout the week I gave him positive feedback on his creative thinking and told him that I was impressed with his initiative. You can always find something to compliment if that is your focus. There is something about taking the time at a family meeting to make a specific compliment that makes it more meaningful.

I complimented Emma for helping me with one of my daily chores when I was running late for a very important meeting. (By "important meeting," I mean I had a tee time at the golf course at 8:00 a.m.) Emma doesn't like doing the dishes, but she willingly helped me because the kitchen needed to be cleaned before some guests arrived. I thanked her at the time, but I also made a specific compliment at the family meeting.

You should see my children light up when they receive a specific compliment. Never underestimate the power of a compliment, especially when you take time to give it in front of the rest of the family.

Mary

One of the things that instantly causes me to lose my cool is when my boys fight. This morning they were playing really well together. But I knew it was only a matter of time before they'd start arguing. So before they did, I complimented them by saying, "Look at how nice you boys are playing together! I really appreciate it."

I went on to say, "Greyson, I love how nicely you are speaking to your brother, and how patient and calm you are being with him."

And to Reid, "I notice how well you're working with your brother—what great teamwork."

I could almost see them glow, and they played together cooperatively for a noticeably longer time before they started bickering. Sigh! My mom keeps telling me to think of them as bear cubs—fighting is what they do. Family meetings will teach them to focus on what they appreciate about each other, so they'll at least know how.

Another situation that makes me lose my cool is trying to get out the door without having to nag them several times. This morning they were having so much fun playing together and having their morning dance party. I set the timer for twenty minutes and asked them what they would need to do to be ready to go when the timer went off. Surprisingly, they named a few more things than I was thinking—what a bonus! Naturally, they waited until the last five minutes before they made a mad dash to beat the buzzer.

I was sure to use compliments by stating how "quickly they were cleaning up" and "how fast they were getting dressed." I then asked if they'd be able to brush their teeth and comb their hair within three minutes. When they did, I told them how much I appreciated it and how excited I was about the day we had planned together.

These tools work when I work the tools. Yes, it takes a lot of thought, especially at first. But it's the kind of work that is much preferable to nagging and anger.

It is my hope that someday the "bear cub" fighting phase will end, and they will be left with the skill of appreciation and compliments. And I'm sure their wives will thank me.

SUCCESS STORY FROM PASADENA, CALIFORNIA

You know that warm, fuzzy feeling you get when you receive a genuine compliment? We all need more of that feeling in our daily lives!

It's just as gratifying to express heartfelt appreciation. When I let my daughter, Claire, know how much I appreciate her efforts, it forges an instant connection in the moment.

Claire loves helping me prepare meals for our family—it's one of our favorite ways to spend time together. She recently asked if I could make quesadillas for dinner so she could prepare her famous guacamole to serve on the side. It's a simple avocado mash that even toddlers can prepare with little assistance. We both got to work.

When the quesadillas and guacamole were done, Claire excitedly told me she had a surprise planned, and she asked me to go wait in the bathroom! I laughed and did as I was asked. I could hear her working on something involving dishes and trays. After several minutes, she said, "Okay, come out for your surprise!"

Claire led me from the kitchen to my bedroom, where she had plated and displayed our meals, on trays, on the bed! (She even made my bed first—something I never do!) She said, "I want you to pretend this is our hotel room and we're having room service!"

I was so touched by Claire's thoughtfulness (and by how nicely she'd made the bed) that I got a little teary-eyed. I thanked her wholeheartedly for the surprise and complimented her on her bed-making skills, which she clearly didn't learn from me! She just beamed.

Claire's sweet, simple gesture made me feel warm and fuzzy inside, and in turn, I returned that good feeling with heartfelt appreciation. Presto: instant connection! And this was just one of many times that cooking side by side has brought us closer together.

—Amy Knobler, Certified Positive Discipline Trainer

TOOL TIPS

1. Compliments and appreciations create connection.

2. Children do better when they feel better. One way to help them feel better is to compliment them on their strengths.

3. Keep an appreciation journal where you write down the things you appreciate about each child. Make a check mark every time you verbalize a specific appreciation.

4. Provide lots of practice for giving and receiving compliments during regular family meetings.

CLOSET LISTENING

Seeing with the eyes of another, listening with the ears of another, and feeling with the heart of another.

—Alfred Adler

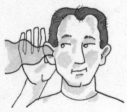

Hang out with your kids and don't force conversation by asking questions. They might start talking.

1. During the week take time to sit quietly near your kids.
2. If they ask what you want, say, "I just wanted to hang out with you for a few minutes."
3. If they talk, just listen without judging, defending, or explaining.
4. If they don't talk, just enjoy their company.

Jane

Have you ever tried talking with your children only to be frustrated by one-word, unenthusiastic, totally bored-sounding responses?

"How was your day?"

"Fine."

"What did you do today?"

"Nothing."

Try closet listening. Closet listening means you find times to be near your children, hoping they will talk with you, but not being obvious about it. Your chances of hearing them talk increase when you avoid the "third degree," which seems to annoy kids so much.

I tried closet listening with my daughter, Mary, when she was a teenager. While Mary was getting ready for school, fixing her hair and makeup at the bathroom mirror, I would go in and sit on the edge of the tub. The first time I did this, Mary asked, "What do you want, Mama?" I said, "Nothing, except that I just want to spend a few minutes with you." Mary waited to see what would come next. Nothing did. She finished fixing her hair and makeup and said, "Bye, Mama."

I continued to do this every morning. It wasn't long before Mary got used to having me there. I didn't ask any questions, but before long, Mary would chat away about all the things that were going on in her life.

Children often feel interrogated when you are ready to talk and they aren't. Just sit there. Perhaps children who resist questions will respond when you make yourself available and just listen.

Mary

Closet listening should be one of the easiest tools, and yet I find it one of the most difficult. All you really need to do is sit with your child and not say anything. I found this difficult, because it's not my personality to just sit and not initiate the conversation. In fact, even with my own children, I feel uncomfortable with silence. When I sat with them quietly, it felt almost like I was ignoring them. Greyson at 6 years old even asked me, "What's wrong?" I responded by saying, "I just want to sit by you and be with you." That was strange for him compared to my usual behavior.

We ended up putting a puzzle together. I made a conscious effort to not initiate any conversation and just waited to see what would come up. This is when I discovered how difficult it is to listen without judging, defending, or explaining.

He asked me if we could go to the store to buy some more toys. He went on and on about how he didn't have enough toys and we definitely needed to buy at least a new puzzle. I just nodded and made a few loving gestures, like rubbing his hair and giving him a wink.

Rather than feeling annoyed and irritated that our conversation yet again was about what he wanted or wanted to buy, I just listened and avoided a lecture that would lead to disconnection. Soon I quit feeling anxious about wanting to talk him out of wanting what he wanted, and the need to give excuses for why he couldn't have what he wanted. Then I really did relax and just enjoy his company.

Brad

With my daughter I don't even really have to make an effort at closet listening, because she is *always* talking. I find it very entertaining to just sit and listen to all of her random thoughts.

With my son I have to make a conscious effort to "listen without judging, defending, or explaining."

I tried to practice a version of closet listening one night with Gibson. The conversation went something like this:

GIBSON: I don't know what to do about math.

DAD: Oh?

GIBSON: Yeah . . . I've never had an incomplete in math before.

DAD: What is an incomplete?

GIBSON: If you don't pass a quiz, you get an incomplete.

DAD: Oh.

GIBSON: Yeah, if you get more than two answers wrong on the quiz you get an incomplete.

DAD: Oh.

GIBSON: I just don't really understand what we are doing right now. [This is where Gibson went into great detail about the mathematical equations he didn't understand. I will spare you the details.]

DAD: Wow! That sounds hard.

GIBSON: I guess I'll go talk to my math teacher tomorrow and ask him for help.

DAD: That sounds like a good idea. Hey, do you want to play Ping-Pong before you go to bed?

GIBSON: Sure!

Now I'm not sure if "Oh" is the best response when talking to your kids. That's just usually what happens when my son starts talking about math. I get a deer-in-the-headlights look on my face and say, "Oh." The point is that I took the time for closet listening with Gibson and allowed him to process his thoughts and feelings out loud.

Gibson is a straight-A student, so having an incomplete was a big deal for him. Instead of trying to fix the problem, I just listened and he was able to come up with his own solution.

SUCCESS STORY FROM NORTH CAROLINA

Every night I spend time in each of my kids' rooms for some one-on-one time. When they were little, this may have included reading storybooks, but now there's lots of closet listening. This is the time I hear about all the things they might not share in the car with their siblings or at the dinner table.

As middle and high school students, my kids are usually studying or catching up on reading every evening. But even when they are super busy we end up talking for a while. I have found that my kids are more likely to do schoolwork in the kitchen if I'm there, sometimes doing my own work. Soon they are chatting away without me asking a single question.

Closet listening is a tool that has helped keep us close even during the busiest of times, when we have club soccer, cross-country, Irish dance, and everything else. Now that they are older, I notice they listen really well to each other. It's great to see them use Positive Discipline tools to connect with each other.

—Paige O'Kelley

TOOL TIPS

1. Find times to hang out with your kids with no agenda in mind except enjoying their company—not even the agenda of hoping they will talk with you.

2. Make a conscious effort to avoid starting a conversation. Just be available.

3. Practice until you can be comfortable with silence if that is all that happens.

4. If your child does start talking, "Oh" is a response that may invite your child to provide more information. "Anything else?" is another invitation for more sharing.

CHAPTER FIVE

CHAPTER FIVE

SOLVING PROBLEMS

PROBLEM SOLVING

Our children have become immune to adults' domination in the process of a democratic evolution which provided them with a sense of equality.

—*Rudolf Dreikurs*

U se daily challenges as opportunities to practice problem solving *with* your children.

1. Brainstorm for solutions during family meetings, or with one child.
2. Ask curiosity questions to invite your child to explore solutions.
3. When your kids start fighting, tell them to figure it out themselves and come back with a plan.
4. Brainstorm what chores need to be done and invite your kids to create a plan. Be willing to try their plan for a week.

Jane

Children are great problem solvers when we give them the opportunity to brainstorm and come up with solutions. We can use daily challenges (and it is the nature of parents and children to have many) as opportunities to practice problem solving with our children.

One summer we went backpacking with several friends. Our 10-year-old son, Mark, was a very good sport and carried his pack the long six miles into the canyon. When we were getting ready for the long, steep trek back out, Mark complained about how uncomfortable his pack was. His dad jokingly remarked, "You can take it. You're the son of a Marine." Mark was in too much pain to think this was very funny, but he started the climb anyway. He hadn't gone very far ahead of us when we heard his pack come crashing down the hill toward us. I thought he had fallen and asked, with concern, what had happened.

Mark angrily cried, "Nothing! It hurts!" He continued climbing without his pack.

Everyone else observed this with interest. One adult offered to carry the pack for him. I was feeling very embarrassed—and had the additional social pressure of having written a book on Positive Discipline!

I quickly overcame my ego and remembered that the most important thing was to solve the problem in a way that would help Mark feel encouraged and responsible. I first asked the rest of the party to please hike on ahead so that we could handle the problem in private.

I said to Mark, "I'll bet you feel really angry that we wouldn't pay serious attention when you tried to tell us your pack hurt before we even started."

Mark said, "Yeah, and I'm not carrying it."

I told him I didn't blame him and would feel exactly the same way under the circumstances.

His dad said he was sorry and asked for another chance to solve the problem.

Mark visibly dropped his anger. He was now ready to cooperate. He and his dad figured out a way to stuff his coat over the sore part to cushion the pack. Mark carried the pack the rest of the way with very few, minor complaints.

Mary

If there's anything I've learned, it's that I cannot solve problems when I'm in a flipped-lid state. My family and I have been reminded that when we are in our "reptilian brain" there's no rational thinking taking place.

I've been role-modeling this for my children by demonstrating that I need to cool off and take a positive time-out. I need to calm down, which gives them time too. It's after this cooling-down time that we are able to shift into problem-solving mode, find solutions, brainstorm ideas, and role-play.

One day when my oldest son was 5 and his younger brother was 3 I received a last-minute invitation from a brave super-dad of a neighbor to take both my boys for an evening playdate. My first instinct, of course, was to say, "Absolutely yes!" But then I started feeling hesitant about how they might behave. Reid's favorite word at the time was "stupid" (that's a whole other story). Coincidentally, he seemed to be saying it more than usual that day. Also, they seemed to be fighting more than usual and not listening.

Anyway, instead of denying them (and me) their playdate, I decided to have a mini family meeting and a few role-plays about their behavior and my expectations for them. It was so cute to have my 5-year-old son take the lead on the role-plays and the several different problem-solving ideas they had for the evening.

For instance, I asked them, "What will you do if your friend doesn't want to share the toy that he's playing with?"

Greyson replied, "If he doesn't want to share, I'll ask him which toys I can play with, or I'll ask him when it will be my turn."

I then proceeded to ask, "What will happen if Reid says 'stupid'?"

Greyson said, "I'll whisper in his ear and remind him we use the word 'silly' instead."

We then role-played the dinner scenario and practiced our manners. I was beginning to wonder if I had gone a little overboard with all the talking and role-playing.

After everything was said and done, my neighbor said they had a great night and my boys were very well behaved. I was proud, relieved, and impressed by the effectiveness of our problem-solving role-plays.

Brad

We do most of our problem solving during our weekly family meeting. In the family meeting album (available at www.positivediscipline.com) there is a problem-solving worksheet. The format of the worksheet is:

1. Write down the problem or challenge.
2. Brainstorm ideas. (It is important to write all the ideas down, even the silly ones.)
3. Choose a solution.
4. Follow up the next week to see how it worked.

I pulled out our family meeting album and looked at some of the past problem-solving worksheets. It was quite entertaining. Here are two examples:

Problem #1: Toilet

When you have girls and boys in a household, inevitably there will be issues with how the boys use the toilet. Emma brought up the problem of boys who either miss the toilet or don't flush the toilet.

Among the ideas we brainstormed were:

1. Aim better.
2. Don't drink so much water.
3. Gibson can go pee in the backyard.
4. Use bathroom downstairs.
5. New toilet for bathroom.

The solution chosen was to use the bathroom downstairs. At our one-week follow-up, Emma reported that the solution was working great!

Problem #2: Gibson Hitting Emma

For this one, we brainstormed the following ideas:

1. Use a get-along shirt (this was a popular social media photo of two squabbling kids made to wear the same T-shirt).
2. Ground Gibson.

3. Live on separate floors of the house.
4. Sign up Emma for karate.
5. Emma stops calling Gibson names.
6. Gibson stops being so sensitive.
7. Gibson leaves the room to cool down.

The solution chosen was for Gibson to leave the room to cool down. At the one-week follow-up, the consensus was that this had worked okay—one time—but that the problem should be put back on the agenda. As you can see, this agreement required further follow-up.

We revisited the problem-solving sheet, looked at the ideas we'd previously brainstormed, and decided to use a version of the same solution. Instead of relying on Gibson to leave the room until he could cool down, we thought it might help if Emma left the room.

When we followed up the next week, Emma reported that leaving the room when Gibson was bugging her worked very well. Simple, but effective.

SUCCESS STORY FROM OAKLAND, CALIFORNIA

Thursdays are piano days for two of my kids. Their babysitter picks them up from school and goes straight to piano lessons, so they need to pack their piano books in the morning and take them to school.

This particular morning, it was time to head to the car and the piano books were not yet packed. I reminded my kids to pack them. Jessie complied without complaint. Serena, however, thought her backpack was already too full and so asked Jessie to pack her piano books for her.

Jessie said no. "Today is art day and I want to leave room in my backpack for my art projects."

Serena protested, "Your backpack is empty. My backpack is super-heavy. See?"

Serena tried to put her backpack onto her sister. Jessie stepped away and said, "Stop it, Serena. I want to leave room in my backpack today."

"Come on, Jessie, don't be so mean," replied Serena. "You have lots of room in there. Also, I always forget my piano books. If I put them into my locker at school, I'll forget them."

Jessie didn't respond and began walking down the stairs from the kitchen to the garage. From the top of the stairs, Serena threw her piano book bag down at her sister, hitting her in the head. Jessie began to cry and rub her head.

You may be asking, "Where was Mom?" I was at the bottom of the stairs, watching all of this in wide-eyed horror. I decided to intervene.

"Whoa, there! What was that about? I'm pretty sure I heard Jessie say no! Okay . . . now I just need to be quiet for a minute because I am so angry right now!"

After a few seconds of breathing deeply, I said, "I'm sorry that happened. Jessie, do you need an ice pack?"

Jessie shook her head through the tears and made her way to the car. Everyone was silent (or crying quietly) as we got into the car. But as soon as we were in, Serena said, "Jessie, why can't you just take my piano books?"

I'd been doing pretty well calming down until that point, but then I lost it. "Are you kidding me, Serena? You just hit Jessie in the head with your books and now you're back to badgering her? How can this still be about you?"

"But Mom—" Serena tried to interrupt.

"You just hit her in the head! Maybe the better thing to say right now would be 'I'm sorry I hit you. Are you okay?' How about that?" I offered with frustration.

In a robotic, monotone voice, Serena said, "I'm sorry I hit you. Are you okay? Now, will you take my books?"

Exasperated, I intervened again. "Serena! I heard 'no' several times now. It looks like you're going to have to come up with another solution. Can you do it? Or do you need some help?" We pulled out of the garage and started driving to school.

Jessie offered one: "How about you write yourself a note?"

Serena quickly shot it down.

Then I offered one: "How about you put your piano books into your backpack after you unload your binder?"

Again Serena refused. "I carry my whole backpack around to my classes. That won't work."

Then, after taking a deep breath, I said, "Serena, I know you are creative and resourceful. What could you do to make sure you remember your piano books?"

And Serena replied, "Jessie could take them."

"Okay, that's it," I said. "I'm pulling the car over and will wait until you can let that idea go, Serena."

I pulled the car over to the side of the road and waited, fuming but silent. After about two minutes Serena said, "Fine! I'll smush my piano books into my backpack! Let's just go." By this time her eyes were welling with tears.

"Thank you, Serena," I said, and pulled back onto the road.

After a few moments, though I tried, I could no longer resist The Lecture. "You know, Serena, sometimes you just need to take no for an answer. I'm not sure why this is so hard for you. You don't always get your way in life, and you've got to move on anyway . . ." blah blah blah.

We finally got to school and I pulled over to let my kids out. I turned around to say goodbye but Serena was already halfway out the door, looking hurt and angry. She turned her back and walked into the school.

I pulled away from the curb feeling pretty crappy and proceeded to rethink the whole episode while driving to work. What could I have done differently? Why hadn't Jessie wanted to help? What had made it so hard for Serena to cooperate? Why couldn't I have thought of something more helpful?

I called my friend and Positive Discipline colleague Lisa Fuller to get her perspective. After hearing my story, she told me I'd done a really good job under tough circumstances and could think of little to do differently. We took a moment to point out all the things I'd done well, like biting my tongue and taking a breath when angry, encouraging Serena by showing faith in her ability to find a constructive solution, inviting problem solving with "what" and "how" questions, and being kind and firm while pulling over the car.

Then we identified a few things I could have done better, such as empathizing with Serena and skipping the lecture—or at least saving it for later when we were both calm.

And then Lisa said, "You know, you can lead a horse to water, but you can't make it drink."

Whoa. Excellent point.

Here I was, examining everything I'd done right or wrong, thinking that I'd had control over the outcome, but my kids had owned the way that morning turned out too. I'd tried to help them find a constructive solution to the problem, but in the end, I could not make them "do the right thing." The morning didn't work out very well, but as with everything, the experience was a life lesson for all of us.

And here was my lesson: I can't make my kids be understanding, kind, or respectful. I can lay the groundwork, teach them, and model the best I can. Also, I have to be okay with them failing, and have faith that they are learning something in the process, just as I did.

—Marcilie Smith Boyle, Certified Positive Discipline Trainer

TOOL TIPS

1. Take time to teach brainstorming—and to have fun with wild and crazy ideas as well as practical and respectful ideas.

2. After brainstorming, involve children in eliminating the suggestions that are not practical, respectful, and helpful.

3. Kids are more likely to follow solutions they have helped create.

FOLLOW THROUGH AFTER AGREEMENTS

People before long must agree on something—even if it is to disagree.

—*Rudolf Dreikurs*

1. Have a discussion where each person can voice his or her feelings and thoughts on an issue.
2. Brainstorm solutions and choose one everyone can agree to.
3. Agree on a specific deadline.
4. If the agreement is not followed, avoid judgment and criticism. Use nonverbal signals or ask, "What was our agreement?"
5. If the agreement still is not followed, start again at step 1.

Jane

In my classes, I love asking for a volunteer to role-play a child while I demonstrate the following steps regarding the challenge of getting kids to keep their agreements—in this case about unloading the dishwasher.

FOUR STEPS FOR RESPECTFUL AGREEMENTS
1. Have a friendly discussion where everyone gets to voice his or her feelings and thoughts around the issue.
2. Brainstorm for possible solutions and choose one that both you and your child agree to.
3. Agree on a specific deadline (to the minute).
4. Understand children well enough to know that the deadline probably won't be met, then simply follow through with your part of

the agreement by holding them accountable. (We don't role-play this last step, but its importance is discussed later.)

Then I set up scene 2 by asking the person who is playing the child to now pretend he or she is deeply engaged in playing a video game, while I play the parent.

FOUR HINTS FOR EFFECTIVE FOLLOW-THROUGH
1. Keep comments simple and concise: "I notice you didn't unload the dishwasher. Please do that now."
2. In response to objections, ask, "What was our agreement?"
3. In response to further objections, shut your mouth and use non-verbal communication. Point to your watch. Smile knowingly with the "nice try" look. Give your child a hug and point to your watch again.
4. When your child concedes to keep the agreement (which he or she will do if you repeat step 3 long enough), say, "Thank you for keeping our agreement."

Usually, a couple of parents interject and tell me that this wouldn't work with their child. That is when I go through the next four steps, checking in with the child to see how well I followed each one.

FOUR TRAPS THAT DEFEAT EFFECTIVE FOLLOW-THROUGH
1. Wanting children to have the same priorities as adults. Unloading the dishwasher is usually nowhere near a child's priority list. (I ask the child how high on his priority list is unloading the dishwasher. Usually not very high if on the list at all.)
2. Getting into judgments and criticism instead of sticking to the issue. (I ask the child if at any point he felt I was judging or criticizing him, to which he responds no.)
3. Not getting agreements in advance that include a specific time deadline. Including the specific time makes it less likely for children to feel that they can wiggle out of it. (I ask the child how

important it was that he had agreed to a specific time. The answer is "Very.")

4. Not maintaining dignity and respect for the child and yourself. (I ask the child if there was any time I failed to show respect for him and myself. The answer is "No.")

At this point, the complaint from observers is that they don't want to have to remind their kids. They want them to be responsible.

I jokingly ask, "How's that working out for you?"

Of course it isn't working out, but most parents prefer to keep doing what doesn't work (nagging, punishing, lecturing) over and over instead of taking the time and effort to kindly and firmly follow through with agreements.

If kids were responsible, why would they need you? Haven't you noticed how magically they become responsible when they grow up and have kids of their own to nag?

We will keep referring back to a basic premise of Positive Discipline: helping children develop valuable social and life skills and a strong belief in their personal capability. Supporting your children by involving them in agreements, following through, and allowing them to learn from mistakes does not mean you are a bad parent. It means you are a courageous parent who is allowing your child to develop courage—and eventually responsibility.

Brad

Agreements and problem solving go hand in hand. The goal of problem solving is to find a solution. Often that solution is an agreement. After the agreement is made it is time to follow through.

This came up regarding chores. Originally when we tried to figure out how to divide up the jobs, I had the kids create a job wheel. Eventually they got tired of that, and I got tired of constantly reminding them. So we put the problem on the family meeting agenda.

We started brainstorming solutions for getting the family chores done without reminders. While the idea chosen from our first brainstorming session wasn't successful and required too much follow-up from me (no technology until chores are finished), the idea we picked from our second brainstorming session was a hit.

We play a lot of board games in our home, so somebody came up with the idea of using dice for the daily family chores. We created a list of the chores that needed to be done and numbered them 1 through 5. The number 6 represented a day off. Each day the kids would come home from school and roll a die. Whatever number came up, they would do that chore from the list—or, if they were lucky enough to roll a 6, they got the day off.

My children couldn't wait to come home and roll the die. It didn't require any reminders from me, and the chores got done.

Mary

This tool helped me realize how often my husband and I decide what the agreements should be and then have our boys say they "agree"—willingly or unwillingly. I then follow up by saying, "What was our agreement?" even though they were never really involved in making the agreement. It would have been more accurate to say, "That isn't what I told you to do. Why don't you listen?"

It's embarrassing how often I can forget that one of the most important concepts of Positive Discipline is to have your children involved in problem solving. The more involved they are, the more likely they will follow through—especially when it comes to agreements.

Recently I found that I was resenting the TV, and my boys for wanting to watch it. Every time it was supposed to be turned off, I was getting attitude or grief from one or all three of my boys. I was about to eliminate TV altogether, but then I realized we'd never really come up with an agreement. Time to start over:

ME: Boys, I realize how much you enjoy watching TV and how easy it is
to get comfortable and not want to do anything else once it's on. It's

important to me that we have a peaceful and timely bedtime routine. Rather than me getting upset with you for not turning it off when I say it's time to do so, I'd love to hear your thoughts.

GREYSON: We just don't like it when you turn it off when we're in the middle of watching a show.

ME: That makes sense. I would be upset too if I was in the middle of a show and had to go get ready for bed.

REID: What about, instead of giving us a five-minute warning, you give us a thirty-minute warning, or let us know that we need to turn it off at the next commercial?

ME: What happens if you don't turn it off at our agreed time?

BOYS: Then you can turn it off, and we won't give you a hard time . . . we promise.

ME: That seems extremely fair. I'll even offer to record it on the DVR so that you can finish it the next day.

Our agreement has been extremely successful. I know that it has a lot to do with coming up with an agreement together, and that the boys felt heard and respected. It's amazing how much cooperation can happen when mutual respect is involved.

SUCCESS STORY FROM MONROE, WASHINGTON

Agreements are a major tool in our house. I love the way the process unfolds, allowing for shared control within the context of a certain expectation.

One agreement that has shown up in my home (and needs to be revisited ASAP) is around texting. My daughter, now nearly 13, wanted to get a texting app on her iPad. I said no, but she pressed the issue continually. It became clear that I was holding on to control for the sake of holding on to control, and not really listening to her. So we made an agreement.

I shared with her what my fears were: that she would become obsessed with texting, that it would open the door to all that could go wrong. Then she had the chance to share with me why she wanted to be able to text—basically it was a fun way to stay connected with her friends.

We started the brainstorming process. It was here that I shared the counteroffer idea with her. I said, "Let's start by sharing how we each would like it to be, then make tweaks to get to a place we can both agree to."

So she started with, "I can text with my friends whenever I want."

I counteroffered with, "You don't need to text."

Ha! She looked at me, mortified, and then I said, "Counter my offer."

She then said, "I can text with my friends between getting home from school and dinner."

I countered with, "You can text with friends after your afternoon routine is finished, and only for half an hour."

This continued back and forth until finally we found a place of agreement.

It helped me to realize, too, that texting for her was like getting on the phone for me. And when I was her age, I was on the phone a lot with my friends. She didn't want to send a text just to send a text; she actually wanted to have conversations with her friends. Duh, Mom.

So we agreed that she could spend the first twenty minutes that she was home texting with friends. After that she would get her routine done, and then she could use the rest of her screen time (another, previously made agreement) for texting.

What I love about this process is that it isn't something that is set in stone. We revisit, tweak, and revise the agreements we make all the time. And that, ultimately, is what it's all about! Through this process, the kids are using their voice, feeling heard, practicing negotiation skills, and really exploring the space of designing their experience. My willingness to be open, available, and nonjudgmental allows for a stronger, authentic relationship.

—Casey O'Roarty, Positive Discipline Trainer

TOOL TIPS

1. You will make yourself miserable if you expect your kids to remember to do things that are on your priority list but not theirs.

2. If kids were responsible, they might not need parents; and they need parents for at least eighteen years.

3. Following through with a kind and firm reminder is easier and more effective than nagging.

ASK FOR HELP

The desire to be "good" mothers makes them the worst mothers. These "good" mothers are America's tragedy.

—*Rudolf Dreikurs*

Telling children they are capable is not effective. They must have experiences where they feel capable.

1. Children feel capable, belonging, and significance when they contribute.
2. Look for every opportunity to say, "I need your help."
3. Be sure to let your children know how much you appreciate their help.

Jane

Mothers (and fathers) don't realize how much they can damage their children's character when they do too much for them in the name of being a good parent, and in the name of love.

When parents do everything for the child, it is likely that the child will decide, "I'm not capable," or "Love means getting others to do things for me." Then parents wonder, "Why does my child act so demanding after all I have done for her?"

Alfred Adler taught that the measure of good mental health was the level of *gemeinschaftsgefüel,* a German word he coined. The word has so much meaning that it is difficult to translate into English, but "social consciousness" and "social interest" come close. Adler believed that mentally healthy people had a desire to contribute to their social community, beginning with the family. Research keeps proving what Adler taught: allowing children to make meaningful contributions in their homes is a key to the development of a healthy sense of self-worth and capability.

Brad

This tool card comes up most often around dinnertime. I am admittedly not the best chef in the world. My cooking gives people heartburn. So when I ask my kids to help prepare dinner, they are more than happy to take over.

Recently my daughter was assigned a project of planning and preparing dinners at home for two weeks. Those were the best two weeks of meals we have ever had in our home. And you should have seen how my daughter was beaming with pride every night at dinner!

Mary

I believe the desire to help starts at an early age—as soon as they start walking and talking. I have vivid memories of all three of my boys saying, "Me do it."

Yes, it requires a lot of patience and some training, but the more my boys did, the more confident they became. Below is a list of examples you might try that worked in our home.

HELP FROM 1-YEAR-OLDS
- Putting the diapers away and in the trash
- Picking up toys (lots of modeling and mirroring)
- Cleaning up messes with wipes
- Kissing boo-boos better and offering a hug when someone is hurt or feeling bad

HELP FROM 2-YEAR-OLDS
- Buckling their car seat (or at least trying to)
- Stirring the mix for muffins (even cracking the eggs)

- Getting themselves dressed, starting with pajamas (they likely need help with zippers, buttons and snaps)
- Clearing their dishes from the table
- Putting toys away
- Pushing buttons on washer and dryer
- Folding laundry (starting with washcloths and socks)
- Pushing the stroller (or at least attempting)
- Carrying groceries (make sure to pack a couple of light bags)
- Looking for groceries in the store (for example, asking for help finding the milk, bananas, or bread)
- Sweeping and cleaning (having supplies made for little hands, such as a kid-sized broom or little spray bottle filled with water, helps them feel like they're contributing to the chores)
- Throwing out trash (toddlers love to throw stuff away)
- Washing their bodies and hair in the bathtub

HELP FROM 7- AND 9-YEAR-OLDS
- Help creating grocery lists
- Help with preparation of meals
- Folding and putting laundry away
- Bringing up trash cans from the bottom of the driveway
- Cleaning their rooms (this one requires the use of many Positive Discipline tools)
- Clearing dishes at mealtimes
- Unloading dishwasher
- Vacuuming
- Sweeping leaves
- Wrapping gifts for birthday parties
- Creating paper bags of goodies for the homeless
- Decorating for every season

Some of these chores are done with more enthusiasm than others. It would be easier to do many of them myself, but I keep the long-term results in mind. I want my boys to be contributing members of society, not spoiled brats. Someday the wives of my boys will thank me.

An important tip to remember: I'm doing the lists above *with* my children. The tool involves asking for help—not doing it yourself.

My boys love baseball, and I love being a baseball mom. We have created a motto: There is no "I" in team. The TEAM acronym stands for "together everyone achieves more." When we work together we all feel a sense of teamwork.

SUCCESS STORY FROM UNION CITY, PENNSYLVANIA

My daughter was overtired, and after her bath she was just crying and would not hold still. I tried putting on her diaper, I tried distracting her with a balloon, I tried giving her a book to read, but she ran off and climbed up on the couch.

So, figuring I had nothing to lose, I took a deep breath and said, "Leni, Mommy needs your help!" She looked at me skeptically. "You need to wear your jammies, but I can't put them on unless you help me. Can you show me where your arm goes?"

She looked curious, but I wasn't sure if she was going to go for it.

"Does your arm go in here?" I held up the sleeve and she reached her arm out and smiled. Then I asked her to show me how to put a diaper on. I slid the diaper under her, and she lay still and said "snap" to tell me when to snap it on her. Then I put one leg in her jammies, and she put the other leg in herself and said "zip," and I zipped them up. By that time she had a big grin on her face!

I was so amazed it actually worked! I have been noticing a lot less conflict overall since I have been trying to have her "help" with things like carrying things to or from the car, putting away groceries, and even sitting on the counter helping me mix bread dough or something. So instead of expecting her to just stay out of the way, I try to involve her in whatever I am doing. It seems so obvious, but I didn't think of it that way before I started reading parenting books. It was just constant frustration and wondering, "Why won't she let me get anything done?" I just wish I had figured this out sooner!

—Lilly Himrod

TOOL TIPS

1. Let your highest goal be to provide opportunities for your children to feel capable and learn the inner joy of contribution.

2. Be aware of the beliefs children form when they are given opportunities to feel capable—and the beliefs they form when too much is done for them.

3. Children usually respond to sincere requests for help.

4. Even when children resist contributing at first, they are left with a feeling of capability and accomplishment when they do.

FOCUS ON SOLUTIONS

Sometimes the problem can even be solved by discussing it with the children and seeing what they have to offer.

—Rudolf Dreikurs

Instead of focusing on blame, focus on solutions.

1. Identify a problem.
2. Brainstorm as many solutions as possible.
3. Pick one that works for everyone.
4. Try the solution for a week.
5. In a week, evaluate. If it didn't work, start over.

Jane

It is very common to ask, "What punishment should be applied for this behavior?" This is the wrong question. Punishment is designed to make kids pay for what they have done in the *past*.

"What is the solution that will solve this problem?" is a better question. Focusing on solutions helps children learn for the *future*.

Teaching children to focus on solutions is a great life skill. Another question to keep in mind is, "What is the problem and what is the solution?"

Be ready for initial resistance. Children don't know how capable they are when they haven't been provided with opportunities to discover and practice their problem-solving skills. If your child says, "I don't know," respond by saying, "Take time to think about it. You can tell me what you come up with in a few minutes."

Of course it helps if you are having regular family meetings where they are practicing their problem-solving skills on a weekly basis, and if you are regularly asking curiosity questions that invite your child to think and to search for solutions.

Mary

There were two Positive Discipline sayings that were drilled into my head growing up: (1) mistakes are wonderful opportunities to learn, and (2) are we looking for blame or are we looking for solutions?

One of my favorite memories from my childhood was my mom complaining about the dishes that were left in the sink. My brother quickly responded, "Are you looking for blame or are you looking for solutions?"

I think all my mom could say was, "Touché."

This week I went out of my way to repeat that very same question— "Are we looking for blame or are we looking for solutions?" I interrupted my boys several times when they were arguing and kindly reminded them that I had faith that they could find a solution to their problem. If they weren't able to solve the problem, we would stop whatever activity they were doing until they could both agree on one or several solutions. My youngest son willingly joined the problem-solving "game" and came up with the idea of using a timer. It's so great to see the seeds that I've been planting for so long finally grow.

Focusing on solutions is the foundation for successful family meetings. It helps parents avoid the temptation to lecture about items on the agenda. It also helps children stop complaining.

Brad

One of the most important things to remember when focusing on solutions is to involve your children in the process. I learned that the hard way when trying to find a solution to the clothes on my son's bathroom floor.

Focus on Solutions: Part 1

Gibson was trying to set a Guinness Book of World Records for clothes on his bathroom floor. Every morning I observed the pile of clothes in his bathroom getting bigger and bigger, while the hamper in his bedroom remained empty. I decided to continue to observe him in his natural habitat for a while and see if he would pick up the clothes without a reminder from me.

Focus on Solutions: Part 2

My son might make it in the world after all. Without any prompting from me, he finally picked up the clothes in his bathroom and moved them to the hamper in his bedroom. Of course, he then started a new pile on the bathroom floor. But even though he is not following the system we agreed on, he apparently does have a system. Sometimes I guess we need to allow our teenagers to figure these things out on their own, even if it doesn't exactly match our schedule or preferred method.

Focus on Solutions: Part 3

On my blog, some people recommended putting a hamper in Gibson's bathroom to solve the problem of clothes on the floor. After all, how hard could it be to drop his clothes in a hamper that is two feet away? I finally had time to go to buy a hamper, and you'd think the problem would have been solved. But the next day there were more clothes on the floor in the bathroom right next to the brand-new (but empty) hamper!

Focus on Solutions: Happy Conclusion

Did you notice in all the scenarios above who was *not* involved in the solutions? I never once asked Gibson if he had any ideas for solving the problem. Finally I put the issue on the family meeting agenda.

During the family meeting I asked Gibson if he had any ideas for a solution to the problem of clothes on the bathroom floor. He said, "Sure—you could buy a bath mat. I only put the clothes on the floor so I don't have to step on the wet floor when I get out of the shower."

What? Can you believe how easy that was? It was such a simple solution to the problem. I had been battling the problem of clothes on the bathroom floor for weeks on my own and all I needed to do was involve my son in finding the solution. After purchasing the bath mat, I was able to remove the hamper from the bathroom and we haven't had clothes on the floor since.

SUCCESS STORY FROM MISSION VIEJO, CALIFORNIA

Dinnertime in our home used to be something we all dreaded. My youngest son has always been a very picky eater.

My husband's philosophy is that you eat what is served to you. Mine is that you don't eat what you don't want. For a while, I tried making a separate meal for our youngest son—which often went untouched.

Finally we stopped looking for blame and focused on finding a solution that was respectful, reasonable, related, and helpful. The results were amazing.

We decided that while I made dinner, our son would be there with me and cook his own meal using the same ingredients. He was 6 years old at the time.

He is now 15 and is an incredible chef. And some of my most precious memories are from spending time in the kitchen with my son.

—Joy Sacco, teacher and Certified Positive Discipline Trainer

TOOL TIP

1. Let yourself be amazed by the capability of children to find solutions when they are invited to do so.

2. Understand that you're helping your children develop a stronger sense of capability every time they are respectfully involved in solutions.

3. Don't expect solutions to be magic and solve the problem forever. As soon as a solution no longer works, start again to find another solution.

WHEEL OF CHOICE

Kids are our greatest untapped resource. They have a wealth
of wisdom and talent for solving problems when we invite them
to do so.

—Rudolf Dreikurs

Using the wheel of choice is one way to teach problem solving.

1. Brainstorm (with your children) a list of possible solutions
   to everyday conflicts or problems.
2. On a pie-shaped chart write one solution in each section
   and let children draw illustrations or symbols.
3. When there is a conflict, suggest the children use the
   wheel of choice to find a solution that will solve the
   problem.

Jane

Focusing on solutions is a primary theme of Positive Discipline, and
kids are great at focusing on solutions when they are taught the skills
and are allowed to practice them.

The wheel of choice provides a fun and exciting way to involve kids
in learning and practicing problem-solving skills, especially when they
are involved in creating it.

Make sure your child takes the primary lead in creating his or her
wheel of choice. The less you do, the better. Your child can be creative
and decide if he or she would like to draw pictures or symbols to represent solutions, or to find pictures on the Internet. Then let your child
choose (within reason) where to hang his or her wheel of choice.

Older kids may not want to create a wheel, but could benefit from brainstorming ideas for focusing on solutions and writing them down on an easily accessible list. It is helpful when you have other options for finding solutions, such as family meetings. Then you can offer a choice: "What would help you the most right now—your wheel of choice or putting this problem on the family meeting agenda?"

Helping your child create a wheel of choice increases his or her sense of capability and self-regulation. From Mary's story you will gain a sense of why it is best to have your kids make their own wheel of choice from scratch instead of using a template.

Mary

It was such fun creating a wheel of choice with my son Reid when he was 7 years old. We purchased a few supplies in advance: poster board, stickers, scented markers, scissors, and colored paper. None of these materials are required, but I knew it would make it more fun.

It turned out to be even more of an advantage than I thought because his 3-year-old brother, Parker, wanted to be involved too. He had fun making his own wheel of choice (even though he didn't really understand it). This was a great distraction for Reid's little brother, who felt like he was involved in the process.

I started by asking Reid, "What are some of the things you do or can do when you are having a challenge?"

I was really impressed with how easy it was for Reid to come up with so many solutions. He had already been using many of these skills, so he created his list very quickly.

1. Walk away or go to a different room.
2. Take deep breaths.
3. Put it on the family meeting agenda.
4. Use a different tone.
5. Ask Mom or Dad for help.
6. Count to ten to cool off.
7. Hit the "reset button" and try again.

He had fun writing them all on his pie graph. The scented pens added to his enthusiasm. He wanted to "practice" writing them on a piece of scratch paper before he officially drew them on his poster board.

I loved how he handled it when he misspelled a word or when his circle wasn't even. He just crossed out the word and rewrote it. I was tempted to give my two cents and step in to fix it for him, but I remembered how important it was for him to do it by himself. I could see the pride in his grin and his little happy dance movement in his chair. I was relieved when Reid patiently allowed his little brother to be involved by adding stickers to his finished project.

Reid was so proud when he held up his wheel of choice. Even Parker was proud. They were both posing for a photo, and Reid even wanted me to take a video as he described it.

About two hours later he had his first challenge: his older brother, Greyson, was saying, "Reid smells like a fart." Then he started mimicking everything Reid said.

Reid came to me and said, "Greyson keeps bugging me."

I said, "You're having a challenging moment. Would it help you to go to your wheel of choice to choose something you could do?"

He went to his wheel of choice, looked at it, and did his own little process of elimination. He said, "I've already walked away and he keeps following me. I'm asking you for help."

I asked, "What else could you try?"

Reid started taking deep breaths. Then he said, "I'm going to try asking him in a calm voice to please stop, and lie on the bed while you read us a book."

It worked!

Before I could even fully process this magical moment, all three boys were lying next to me while we read a book.

One of the most valuable lessons I learned was that he had the tools and skills to solve his problems on his own. Knowing that he had his wheel of choice reminded me to not get involved in solving the problem. After all, getting me involved wasn't one of his "solutions." (Yes, asking me for help was one of his solutions, and I used my judgment to know he could find something that didn't involve me. If he had been in physical danger I would have helped.)

My 3-year-old, Jake, created a wheel of choice with my help. Jake chose the clip art he wanted to represent his solutions. He called it Jake's wheel of choice.

It wasn't long before he had a chance to use it. Jake and his sister (17 months old) were sitting on the sofa sharing a book. His sister took the book and Jake immediately flipped his lid. He yelled at her, grabbed the book, and made her cry. She grabbed it back.

I walked in slowly and asked Jake if he'd like to use his wheel of choice to help—and he actually said yes! He chose to "share his toys." He got his sister a book that was more appropriate for her, and she gladly gave him his book back. They sat there for a while and then traded.

It is so rewarding to have tools that help my children learn problem solving at such a young age.

—Laura Beth

Each year we create a wheel of choice in my classroom. At a certain point in the school year, I noticed that the wheel of choice was not being used as much as I had hoped. Therefore, I offered the class a variation on this project in order to ignite an interest in the tool. I was particularly thinking of a 4-year-old boy who always refused my invitations to use it when I knew he really needed it and could benefit from its use.

The children made their own portable mini wheels out of small paper plates, selecting, writing, and drawing four of their preferred things to do when they needed to solve a problem. Then they punched holes and used a piece of yarn to help them wear their wheels around their necks.

Everyone had so much fun making their own wheel and they were very happy with it. The act of creating and wearing their personal wheel made it more relatable, and it surprisingly worked very well for the boy I had in mind.

When the boy took his portable wheel of choice home, his mom told me that he was very excited about it and shared its use with her and his grandmother. She said that she couldn't believe her eyes that evening when she saw him get in a conflict over something with his father. The boy was about to flip his lid. His usual reaction was to throw a tantrum. Instead, he ran straight to his wheel of choice and said: "I choose to walk away." And he did walk away!

—Saleha Hafiz, Certified Positive Discipline Parent Educator

TOOL TIPS

1. During a family meeting you might want to practice with "pretend" challenges and role-play how a solution from the wheel of choice might look.

2. Invite your child to create another wheel called the anger wheel of choice.

   - Invite him or her to share some disrespectful or hurtful ways people express their anger. Write them down on a flip chart.
   - Brainstorm together appropriate ways to express anger. Let your child choose his or her favorites to put on their anger wheel of choice.
   - When your child is angry, you might ask, "Would it help you to use the wheel of choice to find a way to express your anger?"

CURIOSITY QUESTIONS
(MOTIVATIONAL)

Stimulate children to find solutions. Don't tell them.

—Rudolf Dreikurs

Asking instead of telling invites children to think and to feel capable.

1. "What do you need to do to be ready for school on time?"
2. "Oops! What do you need to do about the spilled milk?"
3. "How can you and your brother solve this problem?"
4. "What do you need to take if you don't want to be cold outside?"
5. "What is your plan for getting your homework done?"

Jane

"Won't listen" is on every list of challenges described in the Introduction. When questioned what this means, most parents will admit, "My child doesn't obey." This provides an opportunity to introduce an experiential activity to help them understand why their children don't listen or obey. You can now participate in this activity vicariously.

Pretend you are a child listening to the following "telling" statements from a parent. Notice what you are thinking, feeling, and learning.

"Go brush your teeth."
"Don't forget your coat."
"Do your homework."

"Stop fighting with your brother."

"Put your dishes in the dishwasher."

"Hurry up and get dressed or you'll miss the bus."

"Stop whining."

"Pick up your toys."

As a child, are you feeling respected and capable? Not likely.

What are you learning? Go to the list of characteristics and life skills in the Introduction. Are you learning anything on that list? Not likely.

Then look at the list of challenges, also in the Introduction. As a child, are you feeling inspired to engage in any of these behaviors? Probably.

Participating in this activity helps parents get into a child's world to understand how they help create some of the challenges they complain about.

Now pretend you are a child listening to the following "asking" statements from a parent. Again, notice what you are thinking, feeling, and learning.

"What do you need to do so your teeth will feel squeaky clean?"

"What are you taking so you won't feel cold outside?"

"What is your plan for doing your homework?"

"How can you and your brother solve this problem?"

"What did we decide about what to do with our dishes when we are finished eating?"

"What can you do so you will catch the bus on time?"

"What is your responsibility when you are finished playing with your toys?"

In your role as a child, what were you thinking, feeling, and learning? If you go back to the list of characteristics and life skills, are you learning anything on the list? When we do this activity in our workshops and classes, the volunteer who role-plays a child always tells us she does not learn any characteristics and life skills from the "telling" statements, but learns many of them from the "asking" statements.

This activity illustrates brain science and physiology. Telling creates physiological tension in the body, and the message that is sent to the brain is "resist." No wonder children don't listen or obey.

On the other hand, hearing a respectful and sincere question (an "asking" statement) creates physiological relaxation, and the message that is sent to the brain is "search for an answer." When children are searching for an answer, they feel respected and capable and are more likely to feel motivated to cooperate.

Parents seem to have an ingrained habit of telling instead of asking. They tell kids what happened, what caused it to happen, how they should feel about it, and what they should do about it. So kids learn to tune out. Then adults wonder why their lectures seem to go in one ear and out the other. I jokingly challenge parents to notice over a period of two weeks how often they "tell," and to put a quarter in a jar every time they do. At the end of two weeks they will have more money than they thought possible. Once they notice themselves telling, they can start to think about how they could ask instead.

Motivational questions are very short and don't necessarily require a verbal response from the child. They invite a child to think and to decide. If the question doesn't motivate the child to cooperate, try a different tool. Conversational curiosity questions (see Chapter 6) are designed to invite conversation, and problem solving. Remember, there isn't any one tool that works for every situation.

Mary

My husband, Mark, and I both found ourselves feeling discouraged that the motivational curiosity questions weren't working as well as we thought they should. After checking in with my mom, we quickly learned that we had false expectations of how these questions were supposed to work. We thought that if we *asked* instead of *told,* we would invite our boys to comply with what we wanted them to do.

Mom pointed out that these are *curiosity* questions, not *compliance* questions. Instead of hearing us asking in a way that might inspire them to think and feel motivated from within, they caught on to our agenda to get them to comply.

Of course we hope they will choose what we want them to do, but there is a fine line between asking in a way that invites resistance and asking in a way that promotes cooperation. When our children feel we are truly curious, they search for an answer. However, if they sense "compliance questions" instead of true curiosity, they are more likely to resist.

As usual, one of my greatest teachers, my 9-year-old son, Greyson, verified what I had just learned from my mom.

I told Greyson, "I wish I didn't care about your teeth."

He laughed and gave me a hug.

Then I said, "Our relationship is more important to me than your teeth. What can I say or do to motivate you to brush so that I don't need to play tooth-brushing cop?"

GREYSON: You could try not saying anything.

ME: How will I know if your teeth are brushed?

GREYSON: Before you tuck me in, I'll either breathe on you so you can smell my breath, or I'll just tell you after I did.

ME: You mean, I don't even need to ask?

GREYSON: You've been asking me every night since I was born. I think I know by now that you want me to brush.

ME: Touché.

What a concept! I think we were both sick of me asking or nagging him about his teeth. I was also quickly running out of creative ways to kindly and respectfully ask, and I was definitely running out of patience. I found that too often we were getting into power struggles and feeling disconnected, all because of teeth.

When all else fails, try asking your children what will motivate them. The next night I didn't ask, and he brushed his teeth without any reminders (first time ever). We did our bedtime routine totally connected, and I know we both felt better.

Brad

I am the king of telling instead of asking. So my kids were thrilled when I decided to try the experiment of putting a quarter in a jar every time I would tell them something instead of asking a curiosity question. They were mostly thrilled because I agreed to give them all the money in the jar after two weeks. You would be surprised how observant your kids can be when there is money involved.

Those two weeks did not go well for me. "Don't forget your lunch" and "Hurry up, you're going to be late" were just two of the statements that cost me a quarter.

When it was all said and done, both my kids were able to buy a new video game of their choice. And I learned that it's very helpful to have those on-the-spot reminders from your children.

SUCCESS STORY FROM SAN DIEGO, CALIFORNIA

We had our weekly family meeting tonight and one of the items on the agenda was sweets. Like me, my kids love sweets and eat too many of them! I had placed this item on the agenda to hear the kids' ideas on what we can do to eat more healthfully. My 5-year-old, Lilly, shared that we do eat healthfully; we just eat too many sweets. Then she got up and role-played, with her 3-year-old sister, Rose, what it looks like to eat too many sweets. In the role-play, they tempted each other with pretend sweets and then ate them all up.

Then they wanted to role-play eating fewer sweets, so when Lilly offered the pretend sweets, Rose said no, she wouldn't eat it because of Mom.

I asked, "Are you not eating the sweet because of me or because it is not healthy for your own body?"

Lilly quickly answered that it was because it was not good for her own body.

Then they sat down and came up with how they wanted to keep track of their own intake of sweets. They decided to do a "sweets monitor" with everyone in the family's name on it. Then, whenever anyone eats a sweet, that person puts a tally mark beside his/her name. That way we can see how we are doing and try to do better each week.

The kids decided that we would begin keeping track of our sweets intake from yesterday, so we all thought back on how many sweets we had eaten. We had just gone to the zoo and eaten cotton candy, and also had fortune cookies at a Chinese restaurant for lunch, so we all made marks by our name.

We had decided earlier on in the family meeting that we would end today's family meeting with dessert. Rose was saying that she wanted cherries for dessert, and I also opted for cherries. Lilly said that she wanted cake, and my husband went to get that for her from the top of the refrigerator. Then she stopped him and said that she was choosing to have cherries too—nature's candy. I love family meetings and how they empower the children to choose from within.

—Julie Iraninejad, Certified Positive Discipline Trainer

SUCCESS STORY FROM PASADENA, CALIFORNIA

My daughter, Claire, has always enjoyed cooking as a tactile experience. She loves squishing bread dough in her hands, crushing flaky sea salt with her fingertips, and chopping vegetables into different shapes.

This began when Claire, as a toddler, found my spice containers in the pantry. She was filled with curiosity. I taught her the names of the ingredients and put a pinch of each into her hand so she could sniff some nutmeg or crush dried dill between her palms.

When she was 3, Claire figured out how to open the spice jars on her own . . . and discovered her greatest joy. She loved "cooking"—combining dried herbs and spices with water to create bizarre, fragrant concoctions. She was enthralled! She adored mucking around with the dry ingredients, mixing them with water, and exploring the results. Claire was obsessed with "cooking"—she wanted to do it every day. At first I cleaned out my spice rack and gave her the old jars I hadn't used in years. But those were gone in one afternoon! I realized I'd soon be completely out of spices if I didn't intervene.

I explained, "We can't use up all the spices because our family needs them to cook our meals." Claire was devastated. She sadly told me, "Mommy, I cook for us!" Her disappointment was real—in her mind, she was cooking for our family! I loved that Claire felt she was making an important contribution, and I wanted to encourage her. I thought about how I could share power with her without going broke buying new spices or wasting good ingredients. I realized that I needed to use another one of the tools, taking time for training.

I offered Claire a pantry shelf for her very own ingredients. I took her shopping at the local dollar store, explaining we could spend $10 for her to choose her own spices. She took her task very seriously, carefully examining each bottle at the store and filling her basket with assorted bottles.

Arriving home, we faced our next challenge: Claire wanted to dump the entire contents of the spice bottles all at once! This presented a great opportunity to use the tool of limited choices combined with some curiosity questions, and then allow her to experience the natural consequences of her choices. We discussed what would happen if we emptied all the bottles that day. Claire understood that we'd have no spices left, and we wouldn't be buying any more for a while.

I asked Claire to choose four bottles of spices to use that day and decide which ones to put on her pantry shelf for the future. Then it was up to her to decide how to use her four bottles. I asked, "Would you like to use up the four bottles all at once today? Or use a smaller amount so you'll have some left to use tomorrow? You decide."

You can probably guess what she chose. With great enthusiasm, she dumped the contents of all four bottles into a big bowl of water and sloshed away. She loved smelling the spices, naming them, and running her hands through them to see how they felt. She was in the zone!

Claire started out in the kitchen as a pint-sized mad scientist, mixing crazy herbal sludge and calling it dinner! Now 8 years old, she is a competent young chef who is quite skilled at combining ingredients to invent delicious recipes.

Asking curiosity questions and offering Claire limited choices empowered her to "cook" the way she envisioned. While she was disappointed when her ingredients ran out, over time she learned the value of thinking ahead and managing her resources. These are invaluable skills, in the kitchen and in life!

—Amy Knobler, Certified Positive Discipline Parent Educator

TOOL TIPS

1. Instead of lectures that attempt to stuff in, try curiosity questions to draw forth.

2. Don't ask questions if either of you is upset. Wait until you are both feeling calm.

3. Make sure your questions are not "compliance" or "manipulation" questions.

4. When children hear a respectful question, they are likely to feel capable and to cooperate.

AVOID PAMPERING

Any child who is over-dependent is over-demanding. A dependent child is one who tyrannizes others, who puts everyone in his service.

—Rudolf Dreikurs

Parents make a mistake when they pamper in the name of love.

1. Pampering creates weakness because children develop the belief that others should do everything for them.
2. One of the greatest gifts you can give your children is to allow them to develop the belief "I am capable."

Jane

Be willing to take a look at how you might be encouraging your children to believe you will always rescue them or fix their challenges, instead of having faith in them to work things out with empathic support. When we avoid pampering, we are in essence showing faith in our children.

Have you taught your children that it is your job to "make" them happy? If so, they will want to make sure you don't quit that job. On the other hand, the skills and competencies you are helping them develop are the best platform they can build for happiness.

Let's define what we mean by "avoid pampering." We are *not* talking about love, affection, and connection. Giving hugs is not pampering. Giving compliments is not pampering. Validating feelings is not pampering.

Pampering is doing things for our children that they are perfectly capable of doing for themselves. Children are born with an innate desire to do things for themselves (and to help others). They begin to express that desire around the age of 18 months. We are all familiar with the toddler who says "Me do it!" Too many parents say, "No, you are too little. Go play." Then when they are older and we ask them to help, we are surprised when they say, "No. I'm playing."

Parents often do things for their children for expediency. They may be in a hurry or they are afraid their children will not do it "right" or perfectly. That is why it is important to take time for training. This means showing them how to do things such as dressing themselves (including picking out their own clothes), letting them be in charge of their schoolwork (including allowing them to experience the consequences of not doing it and then helping them figure out solutions for next time), and letting them cook some meals (even if they turn out like Gibson's cheesecake). Letting them practice, make mistakes, and learn.

Do things with young children until they are old enough and practiced enough to graduate to doing things by themselves. Everything will take longer, and it won't be perfect, but remember that we are striving for long-term results. Give your children opportunities to become responsible, capable young people, which cannot happen when you pamper. Remember, research has shown that the authoritative parenting style is associated with social maturity, responsibility, and academic success.

Mary

I haven't met a parent who doesn't pamper their kids, at least sometimes. I say that without judgment since I know I'm not alone when it comes to doing too much for my kids and trying to rescue them to save them from disappointment. I also know we all do this in the name of love.

How many of you have driven back home (even been late to work) to bring your child's homework to school? Maybe you have written a note or made a call with whatever excuse you could come up with to rescue your child from experiencing the consequences of his or her actions. What about running back inside the house to grab coats, lunch pails, backpacks, sports gear, or whatever else they may not survive without? I'm guessing that this "favor" also came with at least a tiny lecture about what would've happened or how they would've felt had Mom not rescued them.

How about this one: have you made separate meals for each child because it was easier than hearing them complain about what you cooked—or you couldn't stand the thought of sending them to bed starving?

While working on this tool, I have to wonder why I'm still washing their hair, re-brushing their teeth, tying their shoes, and picking up the stuff they've left on the floor or counter. Mainly it's quicker, more efficient, less hassle, I don't have to listen to their excuses, and I'm sick of constantly repeating myself.

Please tell me I'm not alone. Tell me you need this tool as much as I do. Do you feel as guilty as I do to realize I'm robbing my children of so many opportunities to feel capable?

Okay, so it's not all about guilt. It is about awareness and understanding. We can learn from our mistakes and work on improvement. A few thoughts that can help:

1. I can learn to stop taking my kids' forgetful, picky, age-appropriate, and sometimes annoying behaviors personally.
2. I can remind myself that it's not about me and what others will think. It is about my children's abilities and capabilities for the future.
3. I can remember that my job is not to make my boys suffer, but to *allow* them to suffer so they can build strong "disappointment muscles," resilience, and the feeling of capability to solve problems.
4. I'm more effective as a mom when I take time for training and allow my extremely capable boys to do more for themselves.

What a gift to them. And what a gift to myself.

I was provided with one opportunity to avoid pampering when I received a call from my son Greyson's school. When I saw the school's number on my caller ID, I immediately panicked. When I heard his sweet voice, I panicked even more. (Since when do they let you call home for forgotten homework?)

Greyson said, "Hi, Mom. I left my homework in your car. Is there any way you could bring it to me? If I don't have it by recess, I'm going to have detention."

I immediately visualized my poor boy trapped inside instead of doing what's natural and downright necessary—playing outside. Ugh! His precious voice was pulling on my heartstrings, and I was struggling big-time not to say, "I'll be there in fifteen minutes."

Instead, I thought about this as an opportunity to build his resilience and learn from his mistake, even if it meant he would be mad at me for not rescuing him. I can guarantee it was harder on me than him when I said no.

Of course he survived. He was able to sit in the classroom and redo his homework and then help the teacher, which he admitted to loving. Because I avoided rescuing him, he had the special time with his teacher, and he hasn't forgotten his homework since then.

I was reminded of the time I was in the second grade and I forgot my lunch. My teacher had me go to the office to call my mom so she could bring it. The conversation went like this:

"Hi, Mom. I left my lunch on the table. Will you please bring it to me?"

My mom replied, "I'm so sorry, honey, that doesn't work for me."

She didn't lecture. Instead, in a kind way, she validated my feelings and said, "I know you're disappointed, and probably mad that I won't bring it to you. I'm happy to brainstorm solutions when you get home."

Some parents gasp in horror at the idea of letting their child go hungry for one meal. First of all, I know this won't hurt them nearly as much as me depriving them of the deeper, internal hunger to feel capable. Secondly, I know they won't go hungry. They will have plenty of opportunities to eat the healthful sandwich their friend was going to throw in the garbage.

I remember how surprised the office staff was when I told them my mom wasn't bringing my lunch. I wasn't surprised. By now I had enough experience to know that basically I needed to learn the natural consequences of my actions.

Many years later I can attest that I never forgot my lunch again, and am now pretty responsible about remembering to bring whatever I need for the day. Had my mom rescued me, I can almost guarantee I would've forgotten my lunch again.

Brad

I pamper my children. I'm not proud of this. I am by my own admission a super-dad, always ready to leap tall buildings to rescue my kids from disappointment. If my daughter forgets her lunch, I will drop everything and bring her lunch to school. If my son doesn't like doing a chore, I will do that chore and let him do something easier.

My kids are still very capable and independent. However, they are not very good at handling disappointment. As my mom says, "Kids need to develop their 'disappointment muscles.'" Now that my kids are getting older, I notice that when the going gets tough, they tend to quit.

Now I am trying to play catch-up and teach them to be more resilient. Trust me, it is a lot more difficult when your children are older. So this is a cautionary tale. If you want your kids to develop resiliency and the ability to achieve difficult goals, you must allow them to develop their "disappointment muscles" at an early age.

SUCCESS STORY FROM ATLANTA, GEORGIA

My daughter is 4 years old. Overall, she is very well behaved. However, we are now in a place where she sometimes does not want to do what she is asked to do. For example, she has long hair, but does not want to brush it; yet she complains when I brush it. She never wants to straighten up her room after she's been playing and has dragged most of her toys out onto her bedroom floor.

It makes me irritated, annoyed, and impatient. I tend to respond by doing many of the behaviors in the third column of the Mistaken Goal Chart. For example, I almost always end up brushing her hair myself. I have a little more success with getting her to clean her room, because she likes receiving compliments after showing us how nice her room looks after she puts her toys away.

But there are other times when she initially refuses to pick up toys and clothes and gets involved in another activity, hoping I'll just do it for her. And sometimes I do it for her to avoid deeper feelings of being outwardly irritated and annoyed as those feelings begin to bubble up. I often have to remind her to do the same things repeatedly.

Just as described in the fourth column of the Mistaken Goal Chart, she brushes her hair begrudgingly and poorly, leaving numerous tangles for me to fix before we can leave home.

Per the fifth column of the Mistaken Goal Chart, it seems that her belief is "You can't make me!" This resonates with me the most. She wants to be her own boss.

I came up with the following ideas:

- My daughter enjoys being helpful. "Let me help" might be what she needs during these instances. Perhaps I can find a more effective way for her to feel as though she's helping me, and herself, when she cleans her room, instead of me simply repeatedly asking her to do it, then giving in when she does not.
- "Give me choices" also comes to mind. For example, I have suggested that we cut a couple of inches off of her hair to make it easier to brush, and she has agreed to this, but I have not followed through. If she felt more involved with how her hair looks, maybe she would become more inclined to take care of it.
- I'm going to set aside a specific time each day for cleaning up her room, probably at the end of the day. I will set a timer for ten

minutes or so, which I think she will enjoy. I can say, "Let's see how pretty you can make your room in ten minutes, before the timer goes off!"

- I usually read her a story right before bed, and I can offer to do so after she cleans her room by letting her pick a book of her choice, to be read following her timed cleanup session. Perhaps this can be established as a routine.

Results: For the last couple of evenings, I have created a "game" for her. I set the timer on my phone for five minutes to see how quickly she can straighten up her room before the alarm sounds. She enjoys trying to get it looking nice before the timer goes off. This is going well so far. Hopefully I can make it part of our evening routine by offering to read her bedtime story (which she loves) only after her room is tidy.

—Joel Devyn Carter, Certified Positive Discipline Parent Educator

TOOL TIPS

1. Pampering is not an act of love. Yes, kids love it. However, it is a disservice to them for healthy skill development.

2. Keep in mind the beliefs your children are forming, and create experiences to help them believe in their resiliency and capability.

Sometimes it is the experiences that are the hardest for you and your children that will be of greatest service to them for the rest of their lives.

CHAPTER SIX

WORKING THROUGH IT

HUGS

Security comes from a feeling of being able to deal effectively with anything life may have to offer.

—*Rudolf Dreikurs*

Children do better when they feel better—and so do you. Hugs help us feel better.

1. When your child is having a tantrum, try asking for a hug.
2. If your child says no, say "I need a hug" a second time.
3. If your child says no again, say, "I need a hug. Come find me when you are ready," and then walk away. You might be surprised at what happens.

Jane

Connection before correction is one of the first tools we present because it is foundational to every other tool. No one, parent or child, can be at his or her best until the feeling of connection is established. Asking for a hug is just one of many ways to establish a connection with your child.

I learned the value of asking for a hug while watching a video of Dr. Bob Bradbury, an Adlerian who facilitated the "Family in Focus" demonstrations in Seattle, Washington, for many years. Dr. Bradbury would interview a parent or teacher in front of a large audience. During the interview he would determine the mistaken goal of the child being discussed and would then suggest an intervention that might help the discouraged child feel encouraged and empowered. Bob shared the following example.

A father wondered what to do about his 4-year-old, Steven, who often engaged in temper tantrums. After talking with the father for a while and determining that the mistaken goal was misguided power, Dr. Bradbury suggested, "Why don't you ask your son for a hug?"

The father was bewildered by this suggestion. He replied, "Wouldn't that be reinforcing the misbehavior?"

Dr. Bradbury said, "No. Are you willing to try it and let us know next week what happens?"

The father agreed, with misgivings. However, the next week he reported that the next time Steven had a temper tantrum, Dad got down to his son's eye level and said, "I need a hug."

Between loud sobs, Steven asked, "What?"

Dad repeated, "I need a hug."

Steven was still sobbing but managed to ask incredulously, "Now?"

Dad said, "Yes, now."

Steven stopped sobbing and said reluctantly, "Oh, all right," as he stiffly gave his father a hug. But after just a few seconds he melted into his father's arms.

After they hugged for a few more seconds, Dad said, "Thanks. I really needed that."

Steven sniffled a bit and said, "So did I."

You may wonder why the father said "I need a hug" instead of "You need a hug." This story makes several points:

1. Since the mistaken goal in this case was "misguided power," to suggest that his son needed a hug would likely invite the boy to say, "No, I don't," in order to intensify the power struggle. But how could Steven argue with the fact that his father needed a hug?
2. Children have an innate desire to contribute. Contribution provides feelings of belonging, significance, and capability. Steven gave his father a hug, even though it was begrudging at first.
3. Children do better when they feel better. Once Steven felt better

by giving his father a hug, he let go of his tantrum and the power struggle and enjoyed the hug with his father.

Brad

We absolutely love this tool in our home. When I introduced this tool to my kids, Emma said, "Well, I'm not hugging Gibson." But pretty soon Emma was hugging Gibson, Gibson was hugging Emma, we were having group hugs . . . it was an all-out hugfest in our home.

Last night my son and I were having a disagreement about something. Suddenly he stopped, put his arms out, and said, "Dad, hugs!" We stopped arguing and gave each other a hug.

What a great tool! Everybody could use more hugs, and this is a perfect chance to focus on giving our children more hugs. The tool mentions giving a hug when your child is having a tantrum, but we certainly don't need to wait for a tantrum to give a hug.

Some of us may not be very good huggers (myself included), so we can use this opportunity to get a lot of practice.

Mary

One evening Greyson, who was then 3 years old, Reid, 1 year old, and I took a stroll around the block. We came upon a neighbor's house where kids were playing. Greyson was fascinated by all the different activities going on. There were kids from all different age groups playing basketball, playing catch, and riding scooters. So we stopped for about five minutes to watch them.

It grew darker and colder. Reid started getting fussy. I began feeling a little awkward just standing in front of this neighbor's house while Greyson watched with fascination. When I told Greyson that it was time to go, he was not ready. He wanted to stay and watch "the people."

I explained to him all the logical reasons why we needed to go. After asking him for a second time, and him still refusing, I told him that he had a choice: either he could walk with me and hold my hand or I would pick him up and carry him away. Either way we were leaving.

Of course he did not want to hold my hand, but his brother was in the baby carrier I was wearing, so I firmly grabbed Greyson's hand and said it was time to go. He started crying at the top of his lungs. Greyson has always had the loudest, most ear-piercing cry of any child I or anyone else has ever encountered. Of course one of my neighbors was walking her dog and looking at me as if I had just beaten him. From the sound of his cry, it sounded like I had.

I was desperately trying to be calm, ignore his crying, and let him have his feelings, but we were both just getting more upset. I knew what to do, but I did *not* want to do it. However, at the risk of embarrassing myself with the rest of the neighbors, I got down to his level and told him I needed a hug.

He immediately fell into my arms, lovingly willing to give me a hug. Instantly we both felt better, the crying stopped, and we walked home feeling calm and connected.

The moral of this story is that as much as I knew it would work to give him a hug when we were both feeling upset, I didn't feel like asking him for a hug. Hugging in the middle of a temper tantrum is easier said than done. However, after hugging, we both felt better—and behaved better.

SUCCESS STORY FROM PLEASANTON, CALIFORNIA

Last week on my way home from work, my wife, Stephanie, sent me a text that our daughter Grace, age 5, was being a handful, was in a horrible mood, and that Stephanie had had it with her.

When I got home, I walked into the house and went straight to Grace and asked her for a hug. At first she turned her back, crossed her arms, and said no. I decided to ask her one more time, and after a five-second pause, she turned and gave me a big hug. Stephanie said it was like someone flipped a switch on Grace. She went from being in the worst mood to acting as if she was having the best day ever.

It's amazing to see the kind of impact and dynamics that something as simple as asking for a hug can have on a 5-year-old. Honestly, before taking the Positive Discipline class, I probably would have come home and punished Grace for misbehaving, and the entire afternoon would have been ruined for the entire family.

—Eric Santos, participant in Lisa Fuller's Positive Discipline class

SUCCESS STORY FROM SHENZHEN, CHINA

I asked my husband to take care of our 3-year-old son for thirty minutes so I could take a nap. Seven or eight minutes after I lay down, I heard a big noise from the living room, and then I heard my husband yelling at our son. Then my father-in-law was yelling at my husband and my husband was yelling back at his father.

This has happened in our family many times. I used to suffer from this. However, this time I felt different. After I took the Positive Discipline parenting classes, I understood myself, my husband, and my father-in-law much better.

I got up from my nap. My father-in-law had taken our son out to the playground. My husband was playing something on the Internet. I could tell that he was very angry, even though he was silent.

I walked to him and said, "Stand up."

He was very confused. "Why?"

"Nothing, just stand up."

He stood up slowly.

I opened my arms and hugged him. After a few seconds I could feel his whole body soften in my arms. We hugged for a little while, and then he left his computer and went downstairs to look for my father-in-law and our son. His anger was gone and we enjoyed a peaceful evening.

—Participant in Elly Zhen's Positive Discipline class

TOOL TIPS

1. Do not take it personally if your child does not want to give you a hug. Allow your child to have feelings, and have faith that she will learn how to manage them in her own time.

2. During a calm time, have a conversation about how giving and receiving hugs can help people feel better.

3. Assure your children that it is okay to feel what they feel, and that they can decide if and when they are ready for a hug.

4. Have your child think of a signal to give you if and when he is ready to give or receive a hug.

EYE TO EYE

We can change our whole life and the attitude of people around us simply by changing ourselves.

—Rudolf Dreikurs

It isn't respectful (and doesn't work) to sit on the couch and yell at your child from across the room.

1. Stop whatever you are doing. Get up and get close enough to your child to see his or her eyes.
2. You'll notice that you speak more softly when you make the respectful effort to see your child's eyes.
3. Model eye to eye in your adult relationships.

Jane

Some moments are so profound that they stick in your memory. For me, one of those moments was reading a women's magazine sometime during the sixties. I don't remember the title of the article, but it must have been on listening to your children, because the message conveyed in the photo is indelible in my mind. It showed a mother at the sink who had obviously stopped doing what she was doing to turn and listen—"eye to eye," as it were—to her child, who had just come through the back door.

I remember thinking, "Wouldn't it be something if I could remember to stop whatever I'm doing and really listen to my children? What better way to let them know how much I care?" One reason this photo had such an impact on me is that I know how bad I can be at paying more attention to whatever "important" thing I am doing than to listening "eye to eye."

Did the photo change my behavior and make me a perfect eye-to-eye listener? No. I still get distracted. I hope it helped me remember to listen a little more often, and I also hope that just writing about it will inspire me again to stop what I'm doing and really listen.

Mary

I'll share one recent story that drove home to me why it is so important to get eye to eye with my child when trying to communicate.

The boys and I (6½-year-old Greyson and 4½-year-old Reid) were enjoying our Friday evening movie. We were having our typical movie treats, popcorn and ice cream. While we were all lying on the couch, Reid decided to help himself to some orange juice. On one hand, I was happy to have my 4-year-old son helping himself to a drink when he was thirsty. On the other hand, I was annoyed that he had poured himself a full cup of juice right before bed.

I turned my head to acknowledge him and what he had poured and gave him a little lecture about how he should have chosen water since it was right before bed and how I didn't want him to pee in his bed and have all that sugar.

Naturally, I expected him to say, "You're absolutely right, Mom!" Yeah, right. He just continued to drink it until it was almost gone, at which point I firmly said, "Reid, stop drinking that juice!"

He obviously did not like how I was speaking to him. To my surprise, he got right in my face and shouted at me, "Okay, Mom!"

I was so upset, and felt so disrespected. I told him he was done watching the movie and that he needed to go upstairs and go to bed.

It didn't take us long to feel bad about our behavior. We both apologized and said we wanted to try again. Reid melted and crushed my heart at the same time when he told me, "I just don't like it when you yell at me."

What I learned from this moment was that if I had actually gotten up off the couch and looked at Reid eye to eye while explaining all my concerns about his drink of choice, he would have heard me. If I had used a respectful and calm tone, he would have felt respected and responded respectfully.

Brad

I'll admit, as a busy single parent I have become a bit of a yeller. I'll be upstairs doing the dishes and yell at my kids, who are downstairs. I didn't realize how annoying this was until my kids started doing the same thing to me. I was very annoyed the first time I was relaxing downstairs in my La-Z-Boy and my daughter yelled something at me from upstairs. My first response was to yell back at her, "Come down here if you want to talk to me!"

Lesson learned. Sometimes if you take the time to put yourself in your children's shoes, you gain a new perspective. I now try my best to not yell; instead, I go find them and communicate eye to eye. Or if I'm feeling really lazy, sometimes I'll send them a text message. Teenagers love text messaging.

SUCCESS STORY FROM PASADENA, CALIFORNIA

Like many toddlers, my daughter, Claire, was a hands-on learner. That meant everything in her environment was something thrilling to be explored with her hands—even things adults find gross. Things like garbage.

One afternoon when Claire was about 14 months old, I left her sitting on the kitchen floor while I went into the living room. I came back a few moments later—I swear it was just a few moments. But a curious toddler can create quite a bit of havoc in just a few moments.

Claire still wasn't walking, preferring to scoot around on her bottom faster than I'd ever seen a baby crawl. It hadn't occurred to me that Claire could pull herself up on the trash can. Well, she proved me wrong. Not only had she pulled herself up, she had lifted the trash can lid and removed something from the top of the pile.

I returned to the kitchen to find Claire clutching a used coffee filter overflowing with wet grounds. The coffee grounds were *everywhere*. There were wide smears on the floor she'd made while scooting back and forth through the mess on her bum. Bum tracks! There were also coffee handprints on the white cabinets, the white trash can, the white shelves.

She was squealing with glee, and while I stood there in shock, she yanked the filter into two pieces, sending grounds flying everywhere.

Regrettably, my first reaction was yelling, "Claire! No!" But that didn't stop her. She was in her own world, having so much fun.

Sitting down on the floor, I took a deep breath. I got down at eye level and gently held her flailing arms. I calmly said her name several times. She finally looked at my face, and as soon as our eyes connected, she got the biggest smile on her face. That connection helped to refocus her attention, and she stopped tossing the coffee grounds around.

But here is what I found so surprising: that eye-to-eye connection was all I needed myself. Seeing her joyful grin, I felt more centered and ready to tackle the mess. In fact, I realized how funny it was. The very next thing I did was grab my camera so that I could document this hilarious story for my family.

Claire was pretty young, so there wasn't much she could do to help me clean up. I showed her how I cleaned up the black smears with paper towels, so she took her own paper towel and proceeded to smear the coffee grounds even further across the floor. It was truly ridiculous. And honestly, it's one of my favorite memories of a time I felt really in sync with my kid.

—Amy Knobler, Certified Positive Discipline Parent Educator

TOOL TIPS

1. Remember that Babe Ruth made it into the Hall of Fame with a .342 batting average (per baseballreference.com). You don't have to be perfect to get into the Eye-to-Eye Listening Hall of Fame.

2. We live in a sped-up world, which has increased its speed tenfold because of screens. Be aware of how often you avoid eye-to-eye listening because you are paying more attention to your cell phone than to your child.

3. Know that ten or twenty years from now, you won't remember what the "important" distraction was; but you will experience the results of the connections you made with your children.

SMALL STEPS

We cannot protect our children from life. Therefore, it is essential to prepare them for it.

—*Rudolf Dreikurs*

Break tasks down to allow children to experience success. Example: A preschooler struggles to write his or her name.

1. Model correct pencil grip.
2. Work on one letter at a time. You do one and then let your child do one.
3. Teach a skill but don't do the work for him or her.
4. Children give up the belief that they can't when they achieve small steps.

Jane

As parents, we can of course do everything better and quicker than our children. But how does this help your child? You have to decide if perfection and expediency are more important than encouraging your child to develop a deep belief in his or her capability.

Parents may not realize that doing too much for children (usually in the name of love) is discouraging. A child may adopt the belief "I'm not capable" when adults insist on doing things for him that he could do himself. Another possible belief is "Being loved means people do things for me."

It may be helpful to remember that healthy self-esteem comes from having skills, and that pampering a child actually discourages the development of skills. Stop doing things for your child that he can do for himself and make room for him to practice—even when he does things imperfectly. When he says, "I can't," have patience and say, "I have faith that you can handle this task. I'll show you the first step and then you show me the next step."

Encouraging a child who believes that he is inadequate requires a great deal of patience, faith in the child's abilities, and gentle perseverance in showing small steps instead of taking over.

Mary

When my almost 5-year-old son started kindergarten, he was given homework. I really struggled with this for the first few days, for several reasons. First, isn't seven hours each day enough time to teach them? Second, he'd been napping for almost two hours a day in preschool less than a month earlier. Thank goodness we lived twenty minutes from school, so he could fall asleep on the way home.

My biggest frustration was that I missed him all day while he was at school, and then I found us battling about homework instead of enjoying family time. Even though I knew better, I was bribing, threatening, praising, and then wanting to reward him just to get him to trace and color his letters. Then I remembered this very simple and powerful Positive Discipline tool: small steps.

I sat next to him and shared that my writing was really sloppy and that I wanted to relearn my letters to look like his. My son's face lit up. I asked him if I could have my own homework that could be just like his. He loved this idea and was quick to say, "Sure, Mom!"

I started practicing my A's while he practiced his. I believe that he felt connected and encouraged to do his. When he started getting sidetracked I asked if he could go over my work. He enthusiastically said yes and then started demonstrating and comparing my work to his. It melted my heart when he would support me with words of encouragement I used with him in the past, such as "Way to go, Mom," and "You must be so proud of yourself."

Another way we practiced "small steps" was when brushing his teeth. Sometimes I would use a small step by saying, "You brush the top, then I'll brush the bottom." This worked every time. Another small step was having him help me pack his lunch. I had him choose which part of his lunch he wanted to pack. He had the choice to put his fruit and crackers in the bags or to make his sandwich. I loved how we worked side by side as a team, helping each other rather than fighting and going through daily power struggles.

You may have noticed how so many of the tools are used in combination with other tools. For example, connection and encouragement are essential parts of small steps. But small steps turned out to be big steps when I realized how they eliminated all the extra baggage involved in power struggles, temper tantrums, and disconnect. Taking small steps is so much more rewarding!

Brad

One summer we went on a trip to California so the kids could have a vacation before school started. I put suitcases in their rooms so I could start packing when the laundry was finished. Emma decided to take matters into her own hands and pack her own suitcase.

The following is a sampling of what she packed:

1. An old lunch box full of seashells from our last trip to California
2. A tape measure (don't ask me why)
3. Her entire Pokémon collection
4. Her unicorn figurine
5. A spiral-bound notebook of lined paper and a pencil

The following is a list of what she didn't pack:

1. Shoes
2. Socks
3. Underwear
4. Swimsuit
5. Toothbrush

This is where I had to step in and use the small steps tool to help Emma pack for our trip, and provided her with a small backpack for her "treasures." First I asked her what clothes she might need for a trip to the beach. She immediately ran to get her bathing suit. Then I asked her if she would need anything for her feet if there are rocks on the beach. She excitedly exclaimed, "Flip-flops!" and packed her flip-flops in the suitcase. Next I said, "What about when we are not at the beach? What else will you need?"

This process continued until Emma had completely packed her suitcase. I could tell she felt very capable and proud.

SUCCESS STORY FROM ARIZONA

We have not consistently been trying to get our son to put his own shoes on when getting ready to leave the house. Today it was time to get going and I asked him to get his shoes and try to put them on while I was upstairs, and that if he needed help I would be down in a little bit.

When I came downstairs he was still struggling with the first shoe. Usually this is when I would just step in and do it for him. In fact, he kept asking me, "Mommy, you do it, please."

But instead of swooping in, I thought about small steps. I offered to show him step by step with the first shoe and then he would try on his own with the second. When it was his turn, I kept encouraging him and reminding him of the steps. He eventually got it himself.

There were a few things I could have corrected (such as straps that were too loose) but—and this was a huge success for me—instead of fixing it, I just let it be. I figured if they were actually too loose, he would have the natural consequence and we would just stop so he could fix it. This was really a major success for me and my son. I am always just swooping in and doing things for him or fixing things, and he definitely has some issues with assumed inadequacy as a result. I've really been trying this week to not do that to him. I felt really proud of myself and of him.

—Sarah G.

TOOL TIPS

1. Give up all expectations of perfection, which can be extremely discouraging to children.

2. Encourage improvement, not perfection.

3. Practice patience. Of course you can do it better and quicker, but this doesn't help your child develop a sense of capability.

ENCOURAGEMENT VERSUS PRAISE

The child should be commended for what he has done, and not for what he is, be it good, nice, handsome, pretty, or cute.

—Rudolf Dreikurs

Teach self-reliance instead of dependence on others. Encouragement invites self-evaluation. Praise invites children to become "approval junkies."

Examples:

Praise: "I am so proud of you. Here is your reward."
Encouragement: "You worked hard. You must be so proud of yourself."

Praise: "You are such a good girl."
Encouragement: "Thanks for helping."

Jane

Carol Dweck's extensive research has shown how rewarding children with praise can undermine intrinsic motivation. Dweck's research provides support for Positive Discipline tools and validates what Adler and Dreikurs taught about encouragement versus praise as far back as the early 1900s. Unfortunately, rewarding children with praise is a common response across many cultures. Research, however, supports the use of process-oriented feedback that provides encouragement. Dweck found that when children were praised, their motivation decreased. When children were given feedback about their effort and encouraged, they were more engaged and showed increased self-motivation. Dweck also found that praise can hamper risk taking.[18]

Children who were praised for being smart when they accomplished a task chose easier tasks in the future. They didn't want to risk making mistakes. On the other hand, children who were encouraged for their efforts were willing to choose more challenging tasks when given a choice.

As Dreikurs said, "Encourage the deed [or effort], not the doer." In other words, instead of "You got an A, I'm so proud of you," try "Congratulations! You worked hard. You deserve it." A subtle difference, but it will change your child's perception.

The differences between encouragement and praise can be difficult to grasp for those who believe in praise and have seen immediate results. They have seen children respond to praise with beaming faces. However, they don't think about the long-term effects. Praise is not encouraging because it teaches children to become "approval junkies." They learn to depend on others to evaluate their worth. Encouragement leads to self-reflection and self-evaluation. Praise doesn't help children foster good skills for coping with failure—if they are praised for the good result instead of the effort, it can be much more detrimental to their self-worth when they do make big mistakes as an adult.

Praise is like candy: a little can be very satisfying, but too much can cause problems. Awareness is the key. Notice if your kids are becoming addicted to praise and need it all the time to complete tasks. Those who want to change from praise to encouragement may find it awkward to stop and think before making statements that have become habitual.

Mary

There's a fine line between encouragement and praise, and it's very tempting to want to praise your kids, especially when you feel so proud. This fine line took place for me when my son hit a home run. It took everything in me not to tell him how proud of him I was (but dang it, I was). I didn't tell him I was proud, because what would that mean the next time he's at bat and he doesn't hit a home run?

I knew how proud he was of himself, and I could tell he knew how proud we all were—it was undeniable. Instead of praise, I offered encouragement: "You must be so proud of yourself!" Then I got even more specific with my encouragement: "All that hard work at the batting cages paid off! You've been swinging for the fences every pitch—I'm sure you knew it would eventually make it over."

His smile was so gratifying. I was a proud mama for sure!

Are there times when it is okay to say "I'm so proud"? Of course! I just try to be careful about when and how often I say it. If I used it in the instance of his home run, then I could have been setting him up to feel disappointed in himself in the future; even worse, he might think I'm disappointed in him.

The next game he struck out. He handled it with true sportsmanship. I have reminded my boys so many times, "It's not what happens in life but how you handle it."

After I saw Greyson strike out, I immediately noticed that he did not pound home plate with his bat, mope back to the dugout, pout, or give the umpire the stink eye. He kept his composure. I was proud, but I knew in that moment he wasn't proud of himself. I knew that he needed to hear lots of encouragement for his good attitude.

After the game, I reminded him about Babe Ruth's statistics and how he struck out 1,330 times but was remembered for his 714 home runs. Babe Ruth was also known for positive self-talk when he struck out. He respected competition and had a love for his boss and teammates.

I think we can all agree that most of the time, praise sounds and feels good. When we hear it too much, either we can become dependent on it, which may turn into the "disease to please," or the total opposite could happen and we could become so accustomed to hearing how proud our parents are for every little thing we do that it means absolutely nothing.

I will continue to praise my kids—I simply can't help it—but it's important to always keep in mind how much more powerful encouragement is for them. Before I give them praise, I ask myself, "Is this about them or me?"

Brad

My kids and I discussed this tool together one afternoon, and my daughter had a very profound insight: "Yeah, Dad, if you give people a reward or praise for doing something, they might not want to do it if they don't get the reward or praise."

I think that pretty much sums up this tool. It is all about learning the intrinsic value of accomplishment. It's also about teaching our children that sometimes it just feels good to help others, even if they get nothing in return. I do believe, however, that it is fine to be enthusiastic in our encouragement. Some people (including my mom) might think of this as a form of praise, but I like to be enthusiastic.

My first thought is a quote from Toni Morrison: "Do your eyes light up when they walk into the room?" I decided to focus on lighting up when my kids walk into the room. What could be more encouraging than that?

As I thought about how I could accomplish this goal, I noticed how easy it is to light up when my dog, Gracie, walks into the room. Those of you who are dog lovers know what I mean. When Gracie comes walking into the room with her tail wagging, I get a big smile on my face and I have to give her some love and attention.

What if I treated my kids like a dog? I wondered. What would their reaction be if I greeted them with the same gusto?

"Emmmmmmmmmaaaaaaa! How's my girl today? You look so cute! Come give me a hug!" So I tried it . . . and guess what? My kids loved it!

Think about it. No matter how bad your day has been, if somebody greets you with that much enthusiasm, you can't help but smile. And that's what happened. My kids smiled and basked in the attention. Not only that, but I felt better too.

Treat your kids with the same enthusiasm and you might be surprised how much more joy there is in your home.

Several years ago a client, whom I'll call Isaac, taught me the difference between praise and encouragement. He was about 13 years old at the time.

I had already attended my first Positive Discipline workshop but didn't completely understand (or buy into) the idea of the praise-versus-encouragement stuff.

I was doing a home visit with a family and asked how things were going. Mom mentioned that Isaac had been taking out the trash every day and she was really happy about that. Isaac rolled his eyes, and I asked what was wrong. He seemed really frustrated and got a little teary-eyed when he responded in a tone mocking his mom's, "All she keeps saying is, 'Good job Isaac, good job, Isaac.'"

Mom looked hurt, and I was a little confused about why this was a problem, since I was pretty sure it was my suggestion that she tell him "Good job" when he did well.

I said, "She's just trying to show you that she notices and appreciates that you're helping around the house. If you don't want her to say 'Good job,' what do you want her to say?"

That's when he started to cry and said, "She could just say 'Thank you.'"

At that point his mom and I both got, for the first time, the major difference between praise and encouragement. In the conversation that followed, Isaac explained that when she said "Good job" it felt condescending—and he didn't really believe her. He said taking out the trash wasn't even hard, so having her say "Good job" was stupid. He saw it as something she was just saying because I'd told her to praise him and not because it really mattered to her. What he wanted from her was to really see and acknowledge that he was trying hard to do better and contributing to the household in ways that were useful. The praise wasn't accomplishing that.

This was a major aha moment for me, and it was the first time I really got what it felt like to be on the receiving end of empty praise. For the mom, who teared up herself after hearing his perspective, it was a major aha moment as well. She got better quickly at encouraging—first through noticing and showing gratitude for the ways he contributed, and then in more complex ways, such as being able to recognize progress versus just the final products, asking curiosity questions to get his perspective versus sharing her judgments, and giving him more challenging work so that he had a chance to experience more successes and feel capable.

When he started feeling like his mom really saw and appreciated his efforts, their relationship improved and a lot of the behaviors we were working on started to get better.

—Aisha Pope, Certified Positive Discipline Trainer

TOOL TIPS

Ask yourself:

1. Am I inspiring self-evaluation or dependence on the evaluation of others?

2. Am I being respectful or patronizing?

3. Am I seeing the child's point of view or only my own?

4. Would I make this comment to a friend? The comments we make to friends usually fit the criteria for encouragement.

CURIOSITY QUESTIONS (CONVERSATIONAL)

Parents can't get along with their children if they assume that their children can be subdued.

—*Rudolf Dreikurs*

Don't ask trick questions in order to get a certain answer. It is a trick question if you already know the answer.

1. Ask open-ended questions, and then listen:
   • What happened?
   • What do you think caused it to happen?
   • How do you and others feel about it?
   • How could you solve this problem?
2. Don't use a script. Ask questions appropriate for the situation.

Jane

Conversational curiosity questions differ from motivational curiosity questions (see page 184) in that they are designed to invite your children to share their perceptions of what happened, what caused it to happen, how they feel about it, how others may feel, what they learned from it, and what ideas they have to solve the problem. This happens only when children know they can share what they are thinking and feeling without having to listen to lectures about what they should be thinking and feeling.

Too often adults *tell* children what happened, what caused it to happen, how they should feel about it, what they should learn from it, and what they should do about it. It is much more respectful and encouraging to ask, "What happened? What do you think caused it to happen? What were you trying to accomplish? If you were to take responsibility, without blame, what would be your part? How can you use what you learned?" And then listen without judgment. This is the true meaning of education, which comes from the Latin word *educare,* meaning "to draw forth." Too often adults try to stuff in instead of draw forth, and then wonder why children don't listen.

You'll notice that "Why?" isn't one of the suggested questions. "Why?" usually sounds accusatory and invites defensiveness. However, this isn't always the case. Even "what" and "how" questions can be asked in an accusatory tone of voice. "Why?" can work when children feel that you are truly interested in their point of view.

Conversational questions will not be effective if you are expecting to get the answer you want. **Then they would be called "compliance questions," not "curiosity questions."**

When your children do something annoying, you may be tempted to use criticism or lectures. When you are angry, you may feel the need to defend yourself, lecture about your point of view, or tell your children that they should feel differently. When your children are upset, you may feel the need to solve their problems or tell (lecture) them about what to do. This is a subtle form of criticism that says, "You are not capable enough to handle problems or to deal with being upset."

Instead of telling, try asking, "Can you tell me more about that? Could you give me an example? Is there anything else you want to say about that? . . . Anything else? . . . Anything else? . . . Anything else?" You may ask "anything else" several times before your child digs so deep that he or she can't think of anything else.

Sometimes children discover their own solutions through the process of responding to curiosity questions. If they haven't thought of a solution through the process of thinking it through, you could ask, "Would you like my help to brainstorm possibilities?" Avoid the temptation to assist if your child doesn't ask for your help. When you have permission, you can help your child explore possibilities by asking curiosity questions.

The operative word is "explore." Helping children explore the consequences of their choices is much different from imposing consequences on them. Think of a situation where you engaged in a lecture by telling your child what happened, what caused it to happen, how he or she should feel about it, and what he or she should do about it. Write it down. Then write a new script about how you could use that situation to ask curiosity questions that would help your child feel capable.

If possible, find someone who will role-play with you. First you can ask your partner to role-play you in the first description of what you did during your lecture while you play your child. Then you can ask your partner to role-play your child while you practice asking curiosity questions. After each role-play, ask your partner to share what he or she was thinking, feeling, and deciding during the role-play. Then share what you were thinking, feeling, and deciding in the role you were playing. This will give you great insight into what may be going on with your children.

Practice using curiosity questions, and keep a journal about the results. Reading your journal will provide you with inspiration for the future.

Mary

One day my son, who was 8 at the time, told me that he had a friend who was using profanity during recess and he wanted to be honest with me and share his experience. I avoided the temptation to overreact and jump into "mom mode." (Or should I say protective "mama bear mode"?) In the past I might have started asking questions such as, "Who is this kid? What's his name? Where does he get off? What's his mother's number?" I would have ended with my ultimatum: "You need to stop hanging out with him!"

Why is it that lectures and lots of "telling" seem so much easier in the moment? Believe me when I say that I've been there and done that, and it's not effective at all. Just ask my children.

But in this case I actually practiced the tool of conversational curiosity questions:

GREYSON: Mom, you know that boy at school I told you about that likes to cuss and say inappropriate stuff?

MOM: Yeah. What did he say?

GREYSON: When we were at recess he used inappropriate words like "racist," "retard," and "lesbo."

I sighed. Then I remembered my face needed to match my intention. When I was ready with my calm face and tone, I said, "Tell me what happened."

Greyson repeated the many inappropriate words his friend had used.

MOM: Why do you think your friend uses these words?

GREYSON: I think it's because he hears his older brother talking that way and he thinks it's cool.

MOM: Do you think it's cool?

GREYSON: Not at all.

MOM: What do these words mean to you?

GREYSON: I don't even know what some of them mean, but I'm guessing they're inappropriate.

MOM: How did you respond when you heard these words?

GREYSON: I sometimes laugh and other times I don't say anything.

MOM: What do you think others think of him when he says things like this?

GREYSON: Well, he actually has a reputation for being mean and a bully, but he's also popular.

MOM: What will your friends think of you if you laugh or say the same things?

GREYSON: Probably surprised or confused, because I don't talk that way.

MOM: What are some different responses you could say when he talks like this?

GREYSON: Maybe if I don't laugh, or I could even just say, "Bro, that's not appropriate."

MOM: How do you want to be perceived by your friends?

GREYSON: I don't want people to think that I'm like him.

The more I asked these questions, the more I saw the wheels spinning in his head as he searched for his answers. I noticed that instead of lecturing him and inviting him to be defensive, I invited him to think and to come up with the answers on his own.

I was really grateful that he was willing to share this situation. My goal is to never invite him to feel defensive with topics that will come up in the future. I also want him to feel supported and unconditionally loved and not judged. More important, I want him to be able to come up with the answers on his own.

Brad

I was driving Emma to her chorus practice one day and had the following conversation, full of curiosity questions.

> EMMA: Dad . . . I don't want to watch movies with swear words anymore.
>
> DAD: Sweetie, what movies did you watch that have swear words?
>
> EMMA: Remember that movie with the guy who is supposed to be a superhero, but he's not really a superhero? [It was *Hancock*, with Will Smith.]
>
> DAD: Ohhh yeah . . . That wasn't a very good movie.
>
> EMMA: Yeah. And now those words are stuck in my head.
>
> DAD: Well, I just think of different words to replace them. Like "Fahrvergnügen" and "shitake mushrooms." [Emma laughed.]
>
> EMMA: What about the *A*-word?
>
> DAD: How about "asteroids"?
>
> EMMA: What about the *B*-word?
>
> DAD: The *B*-word?
>
> EMMA: Yeah, you know, B-I-T—
>
> DAD: Ohhh . . . uhhhh . . . I don't know. Let me think about that one.

After chorus practice Emma jumped in the car.

> EMMA: Did you come up with a word?
>
> DAD: Yes—"biscuit." Like "son of a biscuit"! [Emma laughed.]

EMMA: Dad . . . you know how when it's Friday we like to say TGIF?

DAD: Yes?

EMMA: Well, I have a new one.

DAD: What's that, sweetie?

EMMA: TBIT.

DAD: TBIT?

EMMA: Too bad it's Thursday.

SUCCESS STORY FROM SAN DIEGO, CALIFORNIA

My 4½-year-old daughter drew a rudimentary picture of a bunk bed and wrote her name and the name of her sister on the family meeting agenda sheet that was posted on the fridge in our kitchen.

We started our family meeting with compliments and then addressed this item on the agenda, asking her to share what was bothering her. She said that she didn't like being on the bottom bunk of the bunk bed.

We passed around the talking stick and wrote down all the solutions suggested, including creating a schedule so that they could share the top and bottom bunks equally, which was suggested by her older sister. After we all went around the circle and shared our ideas, we asked my youngest daughter which one she thought would be helpful.

To my surprise, she didn't like any of them. So I asked her some curiosity questions, including "What is it about being on the bottom bunk that you don't like?"

She said she didn't like looking up at the wooden slats.

This gave us a whole new line of problem-solving solutions. We went around the table again and shared more suggestions.

My daughter happily chose the solution of making a collage poster to cover the wooden slats. She made the poster that day and we never heard another complaint about it!

—Julie Iraninejad, Certified Positive Discipline Trainer

TOOL TIPS

1. Wait until you and your child are calm before asking curiosity questions.

2. Make sure a loving connection with your child is your primary goal.

3. Be truly curious about what your child is thinking and feeling.

4. Kids know when you are truly curious and when you have an agenda for how they should answer. The former invites them to think. The latter invites them to shut down.

5. Ask curiosity questions from your heart and inner wisdom that fit the situation.

6. Have faith in your children to figure things out with your subtle guidance.

LIMITED CHOICES

Kindness implies a genuine respect for another individual. It does not require submission.

—Rudolf Dreikurs

Limited choices provide small steps in shared power.

1. Say, "It is time to leave. Would you like to hop like a bunny or clomp like an elephant to the car?"
2. If your child doesn't want to leave, kindly and firmly say, "Staying is not a choice," and repeat the two choices.
3. It can be empowering to add "You decide" after giving two choices.

Jane

Children often respond to choices when they will not respond to demands, especially if you follow the choice with "You decide." Limited choices should be respectful and should focus attention on the needs of the situation. For example, the needs of the situation may be tooth brushing. Children may not have a choice about whether or not to brush their teeth, but may have a choice about which toothbrush to use. They may not have a choice about doing homework, but they can be offered a choice as to when they would like to do it—right after school, just before dinner, or after dinner.

Choices are directly related to responsibility. Younger children are less capable of wide responsibility, so their choices are more limited. Older children are capable of broader choices, because they can assume responsibility for the consequences of their choice. For instance, younger children might be given the choice of going to bed now or in five minutes. Older children might be given full responsibility for choosing their bedtime, because they also take full responsibility for getting themselves up in the morning and off to school without any hassles.

Choices are also directly related to respect for, and the convenience of, others. When getting ready for school, younger children might be given the choice of putting on their shoes before we leave in five minutes or putting them on in the car. Older children might be given the choice of being ready in five minutes or riding their bike. Either way, Mom has to leave in five minutes.

Whenever a choice is given, both alternatives should be acceptable to the adult. My first try at choices was to ask my 3-year-old, "Do you want to get ready for bed?" She didn't. Obviously, the choice I offered didn't incorporate the necessity for her to go to bed, and the choice I offered did not include an alternative.

I waited five minutes and started again by asking, "Would you like to wear your pink pajamas or your blue pajamas? You decide." She chose her blue pajamas and started putting them on. Adding "You decide" after a choice is very empowering for the child, adding emphasis to the fact that she does have a choice.

What if the child doesn't want either choice and wants to do something else? If the something else is acceptable to you, fine. If it is not, say, "That isn't one of the choices," and then repeat the choices and "You decide."

Limited choices provide an excellent example of kind and firm parenting behavior. There is firmness in making sure that certain things get done and kindness in providing some choices, even if they're limited.

Mary

I use the limited choices tool daily, especially with my youngest son, Parker. I have found that unlimited choices can be overwhelming for my children, as it is with most adults. Less is more when using this tool. When I offer unlimited choices—for example, "What would you like to wear today?"—I'm setting my son up to change his mind several times. Other times he is having such fun being in the spotlight that he milks it for all it's worth, so a decision is not made—at least not in a timely matter.

I offer limited choices such as "Would you like to wear your Crocs or your Vans?" Or "This pair of shorts or these pants?" This speeds up the process of getting dressed, which happens quickly and without a power struggle. It also helps us to get out the door on time.

I have also noticed that there are three things you can't make your toddler do: eating, sleeping, and toileting. Offering limited choices during these times will usually lessen, if not eliminate, any potential power struggles.

For eating: apple or grapes, ham or peanut butter sandwich, fried eggs or scrambled eggs. At bedtime: one book or two. For toileting: walk like a duck or like an elephant to the potty.

The next time you find yourself feeling overwhelmed or irritated with your child, try offering him a limited choice. If he does not choose one of the two, you can follow up by saying, "That wasn't one of the choices." If and/or when my son continues to resist, I kindly and firmly say, "You can decide or I can decide for you."

One last key point to remember is the energy you offer when using the limited choices tool. I know for certain that when I'm frustrated and irritated and offering limited choices, I do not get the same enthusiasm and cooperation I get when my tone and energy are calm and inviting. When I'm calm and inviting, limited choices invite not only cooperation but also more connection in our relationship.

SUCCESS STORY FROM CHINO, CALIFORNIA

As a mom of three children under the age of 6, one of whom has ADHD, I need all the techniques I can get my hands on for encouraging cooperation. As soon as my first (and most challenging) child turned 2, I was at my wits' end. Moving from one activity to another had become tantrum-filled. The worst experience always occurred when it was time to leave the park. That is when I stumbled upon Dr. Jane Nelsen's *Positive Discipline for the First Three Years*. I suddenly had an array of strategies to use, and over the last few years, I have used pretty much all of them.

The most used technique, and the one that gets me a lot of accolades from other moms at the park, is limited choices. As the time to leave approaches, I ask my children if they would like to leave in five or ten minutes. Of course the longer time is selected, and rarely do I lack a consensus. I set my phone alarm with a fun dance song and make updated "time till we leave" announcements. After each announcement, I ask each kid to respond to "What happens after the alarm goes off?"

My children now chorally say, "We leave."

When the alarm goes off, I announce, "Dance party." We dance for a second and then I ask, "Which animal are you going to be?" Early on, I gave them a limited choice of two different kinds of animals, but now my children love choosing their own animals. Off we go, tantrum free, my daughter as a cheetah, my oldest son as a train (who am I to limit his imagination for trains to be alive?), and my youngest son as a dog.

This has worked brilliantly over and over. Now that I have used this technique for so many years, I have had countless other moms ask me where I got these strategies. Eagerly I give them my greatest secret: the Positive Discipline books.

—Kari Franco

TOOL TIPS

1. Remember that offering a choice invites your child to feel capable in his or her cognitive abilities.

2. When a child wants something other than the choices offered, say, "That isn't one of the choices," and repeat the choices. Remember the importance of adding "You decide."

3. If the child still won't accept one of the choices, say, "I'll have to decide until you are ready." Then decide what you will do and allow your child to have his or her feelings.

4. The key is keeping a kind and firm tone of voice, even in the midst of a temper tantrum. Don't join your child with your own temper tantrum.

CHAPTER SEVEN

PRACTICAL SKILLS

ALLOWANCES

It is often worthwhile to support children in a faulty suggestion [assumption] and let them experience the result.

—*Rudolf Dreikurs*

Allowances can be a great way to teach children about money.

1. Avoid connecting allowances to chores (although children may choose to earn money from selected special jobs).
2. Allowance amount depends on your budget and what you expect children to do with the money.
3. Let children learn from their mistakes in spending their money. Show empathy and avoid rescuing.

Jane

Have you figured out what Dreikurs means in the quote at the beginning of the chapter about supporting children in a faulty assumption?
Let me explain.

As soon as my children were old enough to be more interested in
putting coins in a piggy bank than in their mouths, they received an
allowance of a few pennies, nickels, dimes, and quarters. Their first
lesson in money management involved the musical ice cream truck
that drove by our house every day in the summer. We explained that
they had enough allowance to buy three treats a week—a concept they
could understand only through experience.

I'm sure they assumed they would be able to purchase a treat every day. However, by Thursday, their money was gone and the tears would spill.

The only way to allow them to learn from the results of their faulty assumption was to validate their feelings, wait for them to calm down, and then ask some questions to help them understand what happens when there are seven days in the week and they have enough money for only three days.

The next step was to find some solutions. We gave each a big calendar, showed them how many squares represented a week, and invited them to choose three days in each week that they would purchase an ice cream and which days they would go without.

They weren't too happy about the days they would go without, so we came up with a solution: we could make fruit juice popsicles in the freezer for the other days.

As our children grew older, the amount of their allowance got larger. However, we always used allowances to teach about money management. Once or twice a year we would discuss the amount of allowance they would receive, based on what they were expected to use the money for. We taught the "envelope system" that Mary still uses. They would have an envelope for charity (10 percent), an envelope for weekly expenses, such as movies and a few incidentals, and an envelope for savings. We agreed to pay half if they wanted to purchase big items such as a car. Once they had saved half, we would pay our half.

Twice a year they would get a clothing allowance. If they spent it all at once, they had to get creative until their next clothing allowance. One year Mary formed a "trading" system with her friends to vary her wardrobe.

One of my favorite things about our allowance system was the arguments and temper tantrums that were avoided. When we were shopping and my kids wanted some frivolous toy, I would say, "Do you have enough money saved to purchase it? If not, how long do you think it will take for you to save enough?" They hardly ever wanted the toy enough to spend their own money. Even if they thought they wanted something badly enough to save for it, they usually changed their minds within days, if not hours.

Brad

We have a system in place for my kids to make money. When my son turned thirteen, I stopped paying for a babysitter and instead paid my son to "babysit" and my daughter to be "good." Still, it is not uncommon for my kids to come up to me and ask, "Dad . . . when are you going out again? I need a new video game."

I like the idea of allowances for a few reasons:

1. My daughter started to take an interest in fashion, and those adorable fashion choices at Justice Just for Girls can add up. I like the idea of allowing my daughter to start budgeting for her wardrobe using an allowance.
2. When kids have their own money, you can start teaching them about investing. I wish someone had taught me about investing when I was young. I would have bought five thousand shares of Apple in 1980 and would be celebrating my early retirement right now.
3. Paying my children an allowance spared me the lemonade stand experience. Any of you who have ever had your children beg you to help them with a lemonade stand know what I am talking about. It's kind of like Play-Doh. It's fun for kids, but parents have to do all the work of cleaning up.
4. College fund!
5. Car. By the time my kids get their driver's license, they will be used to budgeting and paying for things themselves. So they will probably want to start working to earn their own money.

Mary

I can't remember for sure how old I was when I received my first allowance, but what I do remember is that it was a quarter, a dime, a nickel, and a penny; and how much I loved putting them in my piggy bank, taking them out, and then putting them back.

As we grew older, my parents would give us our allowance once a week. I always looked forward to the day—usually Friday. I also remember that I was the only one of my friends that had an allowance, and they thought I was so lucky.

I also thought I was lucky, until I realized that every time I wanted my parents to buy me something, they would say, "Did you bring your allowance?" Or "How long do you need to save until you can afford it?" I didn't realize until I had my own kids how easy this made it for my parents to say no without having to actually say no.

I started giving my oldest son, Greyson, his allowance when he was 4 years old. I started a few months earlier with my second son, Reid, because he quickly caught on about Greyson's allowance and naturally he wants to be just like his big brother, and Mommy wants to be fair.

My husband wasn't too sure about giving a 4-year-old four dollars a week. He believed that it was too much money for a 4-year-old. I reminded him how much we spend on all the little stuff every time we go somewhere, and that by giving him an allowance, it would save us money. Also, I explained to him all the values of receiving an allowance.

1. Teaches children to save their money
2. Delayed gratification
3. The value of a dollar
4. That you receive an allowance because you're a part of the family (you can always earn extra by working for it by doing specific jobs around the house)
5. Counting, addition, and subtraction
6. Loans (if your children forget their wallets) that have to be paid back

A few days ago we were at Legoland and Greyson was asking for a Star Wars Lego set. I asked him if he had enough money. After figuring out how much it cost, he was able to understand that if he saved last week's and this week's allowance, then he would have enough money next time we went, in a few weeks.

A few days later he saw a toy that he wanted at Target, and I asked him if he preferred to have that instead of his Star Wars Legos. He thought about it and decided that he would rather save his money. The most amazing moment of this story was that when we were in both places he was able to quickly agree that he could wait until the following week. I loved seeing him practice patience, and I loved even more that I didn't have to battle a full meltdown temper tantrum the way I had anticipated.

The Positive Discipline tool for allowances is beneficial not only for the child but also just as much for the parent.

SUCCESS STORY FROM SAN DIEGO, CALIFORNIA

The Parent's Story

We had a family meeting where we discussed allowances for our two girls. We came up with a sum after looking at our expenses for clothing, gifts, and many other things they would need to purchase.

They were now empowered to purchase their own clothing and buy gifts or cute things from the store. If they ran out of their allowance earlier than the next allowance was offered, then they could either wait or borrow more money with an interest rate.

One of my girls decided to open a bank account and start placing some of the money in the bank, after we offered to double the cash they had to buy a car when they were older. My youngest daughter chose to make us things like painted red and green rocks for our anniversary, rather than buy us a gift. When asked what the colors represented, she replied, "The red rock at the front door meant that we were not home and the green rock meant that we are home." When we asked about the allowance we had set up, which included $15 for a gift, she said, "I put it in the bank because you always say that homemade gifts are worth more." Both of the girls were able to purchase a car with the money they saved over the years.

The Child's Story

My parents have truly succeeded in teaching me the value of money. Ever since I was 6 years old, I've had a weekly allowance that eventually stopped in high school. It started with $5 and was eventually increased to $25 over the years.

I was allowed to spend it on anything I wanted, within reason. Candy, for example, was only permitted on Saturdays when my dad would take us to the store to pick out any candy we wanted! This was also how they started teaching us about our health and what goes into our bodies. Anything that wasn't a "life necessity" had to come out of our allowance.

I saved up when I wanted a nicer pair of jeans and had to plan for what I wanted to buy. I learned a lot about budgeting and tracking my spending. My parents had also opened up a bank account for me. I loved (and still love) depositing money into the account and watching it grow.

On some occasions, my parents would see that my sister and I really wanted something and would get it for us "just because." We appreciated the gesture and how they had to work for their money to give it to us. My sister and I never felt deprived and we did feel more grown-up when we were able to do these things and make our own decisions. Today I'm in college and can definitely say that I am so thankful for the skills they've taught me.

—Nikita Patel

TOOL TIPS

1. It is up to parents to decide the amount of the allowance based on what they can afford and what they expect their children to purchase on their own.

2. Validate feelings when your kids run out of money, but do not bail them out. Keep in mind there are exceptions to every rule. Just be aware of what your children might be learning from every bailout.

3. Do not combine allowances and chores (jobs). Children do chores because they are part of the family and get allowances for the same reason.

4. Have a list of paying jobs such as washing your car, extra weeding, or anything that isn't part of regular chores.

5. When your children want a raise, encourage them to present their case for how much they need and for what purposes.

JOBS

Never do for a child what he can do for himself.

—Rudolf Dreikurs

Children learn life skills, develop social interest, and feel capable by helping out at home.

1. Brainstorm a family job list together.
2. Create fun ways to rotate jobs, such as a job wheel with a spinner, job charts, or a job jar for fishing out two chores for the week.
3. Take time for job training—do chores with them the first six years.
4. Discuss all problems at a family meeting and focus on solutions.

Jane

How many times have you said, "It is easier to just do it myself," or "I'll just do it myself so it will be done right"? Perhaps you have told yourself, "I'll wait until my child is older, and then get him involved in jobs." The first two comments are true. It is easier to do it yourself. It will get done better and faster if you do it. But if you wait until later to get your child involved in jobs, it may be too late.

Remember what we said in the Introduction about children creating "beliefs" that are the motivation for their behavior. These beliefs can become deeply embedded and difficult to change, especially when they are formed at a preverbal and pre-rational stage of life. These beliefs can have an effect on the rest of your child's life. What kind of beliefs do you hope your children develop about contributing to household jobs? What kind of beliefs might they be creating about themselves and their abilities if everything is done for them? If you've read through the majority of this book, I think you might know the answer.

Now for the challenge. Except for 2-year-olds at the "me do it" stage, your children will resist taking responsibility for jobs. Why? Because jobs (chores) are not on their top-100 list of important things to do, and that is why they still need parents to teach them the skills that will serve them well all their lives. So use as many Positive Discipline tools as you can to keep them involved, even when they resist, and avoid giving rewards as an enticement. Make it clear that we all do jobs because we are part of the family, and we all get an allowance because we are part of the family. The two are not connected.

The detriment of rewards is mentioned many times in this book (along with the research that illustrates the negative effects on children to develop social interest and risk taking). Children are born with an innate desire to contribute. Felix Warneken and Michael Tomasello called it altruism and demonstrated this very concept. The researchers had mothers bring their 18-month-old toddlers into a room. The toddler would watch as the researcher hung things on a clothesline and then deliberately dropped one of the clothespins. The toddler would look at the clothespin, and then at the perplexed look on the researcher's face, and then pick up the clothespin and "help" by handing it to the researcher.[19]

Yes, kids love rewards (just like they love candy and screens and praise), but rewards are addictive and lead to the demand for more and bigger rewards, or refusal to do the task if the reward isn't big enough. This destroys the development of the trait children are born with—the desire to contribute.

Mary

I grew up brainstorming during our family meetings for different ways to decide who was responsible for what chores. I especially appreciated this tool with my first college roommates. Most of them weren't used to participating in chores (unless they received rewards from their parents), and it began to create resentment between those who did and those who didn't. When we had our family/roommate meeting we agreed to create a chore wheel. This wheel was created with two paper plates. The smaller plate had our names on it and the larger plate had the basic weekly chores. Every week the wheel was rotated. It was a fair idea, one that we all agreed on and were excited to participate in. Having these job descriptions created peace and cooperation as well as satisfaction with our clean house and appreciation for each other.

Since my boys are so young, in our house jobs have become something that they have more or less volunteered to do with enthusiasm. A few examples include:

- Greyson helping Reid in and out of his car seat.
- Cracking the eggs and then stirring the pancake mix. (They take turns.)
- Putting the laundry detergent in the washing machine.
- Washing each other's hair.
- Draining the bathtub water while the other puts all the bath toys in bucket.
- Opening doors (especially for ladies).
- Making sure all lights are turned off.

These jobs are fun for my boys, and it helps them feel capable and to identify different parts of their role in our family. As they get older, I'm sure I will use some of the systems I grew up with.

Brad

On the last day of school, I got the kids involved in creating a job wheel for the summer. Gibson created the wheel and Emma colored the pictures. We decided to have a daily job and a weekly job, which rotate every week.

I think we can all agree that it is important to teach kids the value of work. Contributing to the family will instill a sense of purpose and belonging for children. But let's face it—when kids help out, it sometimes creates *more* work for parents!

For example, feeding the dog is one of the chores in our household. It would take me all of thirty seconds to feed the dog, but I'm trying to find ways for my children to contribute. So Emma had the chore of feeding the dog one week. The dog food is in the garage, which meant my daughter had to navigate two doors in the process of feeding the dog. First she scooped a cup full of dog food and spilled half of it on the garage floor. Then she spilled some more while opening the door to the laundry room. Then she spilled even more while opening the door to the backyard. And then again while pouring the dog food into Gracie's dish.

So now instead of just having a dog to feed, I have ants in the garage and a mess to clean up in the laundry room. Not to mention a very thin dog who only receives a small portion of the original cup of dog food.

My son had the chore of trimming the shrubs with an electric trimmer. So he grudgingly started trimming the shrubs, but failed to realize that an electric trimmer has a power cord. So about five minutes into the job he trimmed the extension cord along with the shrubs, destroying the extension cord and blowing out half the electricity in the house!

It is always with a bit of anxiety that I venture into the kitchen to spin the job wheel.

SUCCESS STORY FROM RIYADH, SAUDI ARABIA

I am very busy these days because I'm working on a research paper, which takes more than four hours each day. My 4-year-old daughter tries to get my attention by crying, not eating her meals, and breaking her toys and then asking me to fix them.

I was feeling guilty because I feel I am not giving her enough time and annoyed because I cannot finish my work quietly.

Because I was so busy I tended to do things for her, even when she could do it herself (like fixing her toys), just to calm her down. She would stop her annoying behavior for a while, but when I started to work again, she would find new ways to get my attention.

It was so helpful to learn about the mistaken goal of undue attention and that her belief was "I belong only when I'm being noticed or getting special service. I'm important only when I'm keeping you busy with me."

The coded message on the Mistaken Goal Chart is "Notice me. Involve me usefully." I chose to involve her by giving her useful responsibility to help me with my work, like sorting my pens and arranging my papers.

Her response was much greater than I expected. She is excited and happy and she hasn't continued her annoying behavior in the past few days. I feel happy too and I am not feeling guilty. Also, I think she is now changing her belief about how to feel belonging and significance—by getting attention in useful ways.

—Khulod Muhammad Al Assaf, Certified Positive Discipline Parent Educator

TOOL TIPS

1. Be constantly aware of the beliefs your children might be forming based on the experiences you provide for them.

2. Don't expect kids to love doing jobs. Be kind and firm and creative in your training and motivation methods.

3. During a family meeting, your kids might decide on a job plan that will work for a whole week. Instead of feeling discouraged when they lose interest in the plan, put "jobs" on the agenda again and let them come up with a new plan.

4. Avoid rewards so your children can develop the inner rewards of contribution.

LIMIT SCREEN TIME

Screen time is addictive and interferes with relationships.

1. For young children, be careful about using the TV as a babysitter.
2. Do not allow computers, TVs, or cell phones in children's rooms.
3. Make agreements with children about how much TV, video games, texting, and Internet time is reasonable.
4. Brainstorm fun alternative activities that can bring family members together.

Jane

There was once a segment on *Oprah* in which families were challenged to give up electronics for a week, including TV. It was interesting to watch how difficult it was for the parents, as well as their children, to give up all of their screens. One scene was particularly difficult to watch. A 5-year-old boy could hardly stand to give up playing video games and had frequent dramatic temper tantrums. His mother shared that she was embarrassed when she realized he had been playing video games for five hours a day. The good news was that after the whole family went through "media withdrawal," they discovered how to replace screen time with family activities that increased their family closeness and enjoyment.

The excessive use of screens is a hot topic. Many believe screens are addictive. There are hundreds of rehabilitation centers in China and Korea to help addicted teenagers. A Kaiser Family Foundation study in 2010 found that the average 8- to 10-year-old spends nearly eight hours a day in front of a screen, and for teenagers it is more than eleven hours per day.[20] Others claim there is no proof behind the claim that screens are addictive, and they argue that children have to be familiar with technology to get a good job.

In any case, we hear again and again from parents who are in daily power struggles with their children over the issue of excessive screen use—as they sheepishly admit their own overuse of their phones and computers. What to do?

Most of the Positive Discipline tools discussed in this book can apply to dealing with screen time—except for having faith in your children's ability to work this one out on their own. They need parental guidance (and modeling). They need rules. Of course it is best if they help create the rules, but it is up to parents to make sure those rules are followed. This is one case where parents should intervene with logical consequences: if the kids don't want to follow the established rules, they lose the privilege of using screens.

The American Academy of Pediatrics also recognizes the growing problem of increased media use among children. Take a look at the following recommendations the AAP has provided for parents regarding the regular use of electronic media at home:

1. Limit your child or teen's entertainment media time to one to two hours per day.
2. Remove TVs from your child's bedroom (all ages).
3. For children under age 2, forgo all digital entertainment in favor of interactive activities that promote healthy brain development, such as talking, playing, singing, or reading together.
4. Monitor your child's TV shows to ensure they are informational, educational, and nonviolent.
5. Watch TV with your child and discuss the content.

6. Use controversial topics in entertainment media to initiate discussions about family values, violence, sex, sexuality, and drugs.

7. Record your child's shows to encourage mindful viewing habits.

8. Support efforts for media education in schools.

9. Encourage a variety of entertainment for your children, including reading, sports, hobbies and creative play.

10. Establish screen-free zones at home.

11. Enforce a ban on media during mealtimes and after bedtime.

12. Create a comprehensive family media use plan covering the use of Internet, social media, cell phones, and texting.

Remember the importance of kindness and firmness at the same time. Putting *kind* and *firm* together can be a challenge for parents who have a habit of going to one extreme or the other, but especially when you are setting boundaries around screen time, it becomes important to focus on the *and* of kindness and firmness.

- [*Make a connection.*] I love you, **and** the answer is no iPad right now.

- [*Empathize and set a limit.*] I know you don't want to stop playing video games, **and** it is time to turn them off.

- [*Show understanding.*] I know you would rather watch TV than do your homework, **and** homework needs to be done first.

- [*Put everyone in the same boat.*] You don't want to turn your phone off for dinner, **and** it's time to eat. We'll all turn our phones off.

- [*Empathy and curiosity question.*] I know you want to watch TV, **and** what was our agreement? (Wait kindly and quietly for the answer—assuming you decided together on an agreement in advance.)

- [*Provide a choice.*] You want to watch a movie, **and** it is almost bedtime. Do you want to watch only thirty minutes tonight or the whole movie tomorrow?

- [*A choice, then follow through by deciding what you will do.*] I know you want to keep playing games, **and** your computer time is up. You can turn it off now, or I will.

Sometimes the energy of firmness needs to be a little stronger. It can still be respectful. Remember that kids know when you mean it and when you don't. Notice that there is no "piggybacking" (adding lectures of blame and shame) on these statements.

When kids behave provocatively, imagine a fishhook dangling in your face. Don't take the bait. Be smart enough to avoid biting and swim in a different direction. You have stated the limit kindly, now hold it firmly; kindness and firmness together provide the supportive environment necessary for setting effective limits.

Brad

Did you hear that? It was me, having a panic attack after reading this tool!

It's not that I disagree with the concept. On the contrary, I wholeheartedly agree that limiting screen time for my children would be better for their mental and physical health. But it's *my* mental and physical health that I'm concerned about!

Let me explain the situation in our house. When my children are not doing their homework or practicing their instruments, they are in front of a screen, whether it's a TV screen, a computer screen, or a video game screen. Even when we leave the house, they get in the backseat of the minivan and watch a DVD.

To add to the difficulty, my job requires that I spend a fair amount of time in front of *my* computer screen. So it's hard for me to set a good example for my children. Can you see why I had a panic attack?

I'm not proud of this fact. But you have to understand that when my kids aren't staring at a screen, they are staring at each other . . . and arguing, bugging each other, and yelling, "Daaaaaaad!" Then I have to referee the current squabble. So, in the interest of peace and quiet, I not only allow my kids to have their screen time, I encourage it. Yikes!

But since I believe in the concept of limiting screen time and I am committed to improving my parenting skills each week, I was going to make every effort to implement the concepts of this tool.

When we had our family meeting about limiting screen time, my kids decided that during the school week one hour of TV each day should be enough. We also agreed that there will be no TV until homework is done and music practice is complete. Half an hour of recreational computer time and half an hour of video game time would be enough each day. And if the kids need the computer for homework, that doesn't count.

So if you add it all up, that would be two hours of screen time each day during the school week. We decided to leave the weekends open because it's best to take baby steps . . . and football season wasn't over yet.

My biggest concern was how I would monitor the children's screen time. To start out I would have to just use the honor system because I didn't have time to run around with a stopwatch. I was sure that the kids would help by tattling on each other if one of them watched too much TV. Especially if that child was waiting for their turn. And I would just have to take away the handheld devices if they became a problem.

Limit Screen Time: Day One

The first day of limiting screen time was marginally successful. As predicted, there was no way for me to monitor the amount of time the kids spent watching television or playing video games. My kids get home from school by about 3:00 p.m. and I need to be working until at least 5:00 p.m. The kids did get their homework done before turning on any screens, so that was a good thing.

However, I was beginning to realize that it is nearly impossible to limit screen time to any specific amount of time. The only really effective method is to turn off the power switch. So for the second day, we tried to have a time of day when everything was off . . . TV, computer, video games, and phones. From six to eight in the evening we were screen free.

My teenage son was skeptical at first. He was convinced that keeping track of screen time was working great. But when we discussed our screen time on Monday, he soon realized that we were way over the limits we had set for ourselves. And my daughter probably quadrupled her allotted screen time.

At 5:45 p.m. we were eating dinner and my son said, "But this isn't fair. By the time we finish dinner it will be 6:00 p.m. and we'll have to turn everything off."

I said, "So?"

He replied, "So I should be able to use the computer right now."

I said, "But we are eating dinner."

He said, "Exactly."

So I tried to explain to him that he was completely missing the point. The goal was not to sit in front of a screen for every possible second until it was time to turn everything off. The goal was to reduce our screen time, so trying to make up for the lost screen time was completely counterproductive. He still wasn't buying it, but I persevered.

The clock struck 6:00 p.m. and I turned off all the screens in the house. After a moment of uncomfortable silence, we looked at each other and my son said, "So now what do we do?"

I said, "Well, what are some of the things on our list?" (We have a list of screen-free activities on the refrigerator.) "How about if we take the dog for a walk?"

My daughter hadn't felt well that day, so she stayed home and read a book while my son and I took the dog for a walk. We both really enjoyed the time together and the chance to get out of the house for some fresh air.

When we returned, we decided to play a card game, and then my son showed my daughter and me a couple of card tricks. Then we sat down and played a game of Pictionary with much laughter and enjoyment. By now it was 7:30 p.m. and I told my daughter it was time for a bath. While she was taking a bath, I sat down and played my guitar, something I hadn't done in months.

When 8:00 p.m. rolled around, we all sat down together and watched *American Idol*. And we were able to watch it without commercials because my son had recorded the program during our screen-free time.

So all in all, the plan worked quite well. And I didn't anticipate how much I would enjoy turning everything off for two hours. Since I run a business from home, I am constantly using every spare moment to catch up on some project. The reason they call it "running a business" is because you are always running, and you never catch up, so there is always something to do. Turning off the computer and cell phone allowed me to relax and decompress a bit.

Mary

Thank goodness I didn't test the limit-screen-time tool during my boys' spring break. Holy cow—that would have been a long week. No TV means less free time for me. If I attempt to leave the room where they are playing, it isn't long before I'm called to play referee over some argument.

Don't get me wrong. We are a very active family and engage in many outdoor activities, so my kids are not constantly glued to a screen. However, there are times when I depend on the TV to entertain my children and buy me some time to clean the house, do laundry, or have some computer time. I'm guilty of using the TV as my babysitter. Although I've always been mindful and very aware that TV isn't good for kids, I found myself justifying the screen time by saying that the program they were watching was educational or that it was only for an hour.

This tool prompted me to challenge my children and myself to go without TV for one day. The next day happened to be a Tuesday, when my oldest son would be in school until 3:00. My 3½-year-old would be home with me all day, but he wasn't fazed for a moment—he never noticed or cared. He was easily entertained playing with his toys and became completely absorbed in his make-believe world.

My oldest son, on the other hand, felt challenged five minutes after he walked in the door. His favorite thing to do after being at school all day is to watch a show. I totally get it! After I've had a long day—especially after school or learning—I too just want to check out. I also feel more entitled and deserving of the reward of TV. Even though he was feeling angry and resentful and didn't fully understand why, I know he appreciated the quality time we spent together.

My boys and I had fun, but at the end of the day we were all exhausted because of the nonstop interaction. Although it forced us to be creative, it also made me grateful that I wasn't completely opposed to TV. I've always believed that most things should be enjoyed in moderation. To me, "limited" means balance instead of abstinence.

Still, I was reminded that limited screen time is good for everyone. We spent more active and quality time together. I just have to remember to balance screen time with plenty of active together time.

SUCCESS STORY FROM XIAMEN, CHINA

Niuniu is a concert pianist studying at Juilliard. People have often asked if I encouraged him to practice the piano.

He has always liked watching cartoons, especially before the age of 4, when his grandpa and grandma lived with us. He would even watch TV while eating.

We all thought watching too much TV was bad for him, so I said, "I know you like to watch Altman. I will buy a full set of Altman DVDs for you, but you can only watch it Saturday night. Can you do it?"

He was happy about having a whole set of Altman, but he didn't immediately promise.

I continued, "You can still choose any episode you like from the set, and watch it as many times as you'd like on Saturdays. What do you think?"

He agreed brightly.

After that, I bought the cartoons he liked and followed through with our verbal agreement that he could watch on Saturdays.

After entering school, Niuniu liked playing video games—just like his classmates.

Again we established an agreement that he could play only once a week. When we were making the agreement, I asked him how long he wanted to play. His answer: "Half an hour."

I asked again and offered more time. "Is forty minutes enough?"

He liked that. So he had fun doing other things when the time was up. I think he learned how to consistently practice the piano because we limited his screen time early on in his development.

—Zhili Shi, Certified Positive Discipline Parent Educator

SUCCESS STORY FROM SYDNEY, AUSTRALIA

As a self-confessed technology junkie myself, I have to be very careful where I tread on this one. Many times I have broken screen time "rules"—not sending inappropriate stuff, I hasten to clarify, but certainly checking for messages and emails constantly when with my family (yes, even in restaurants), which I know sends the wrong message. It's something I am constantly trying to improve on. So how can I expect my 12-year-old to do better than a 50-year-old? Food for thought. But then again, I can always say sorry and use my mistakes as great learning opportunities!

We are halfway through our long summer holidays here, and in a family meeting we held before the start, we all agreed, myself included, to have tech-free nights on Monday, Wednesday, and Friday. No phones, TV, or Internet. I have to say it's been fantastic. We play board games and card games (including Cards Against Humanity, which always gets us in hysterics). Those tech-free nights, I think, have been the best thing we have done to strengthen our family values and connection these holidays.

—Freddie Liger, Certified Positive Discipline Parent Educator

TOOL TIPS

1. Screens are here to stay, and they are addictive. Guidelines are imperative for the development of healthy minds and habits.

2. The tool is to limit, not eliminate. Take the time to create plans that limit screen time.

3. One of the best ways to limit screen time is to plan plenty of activities that do not include screens.

4. Stick to plans even when children cry and scream in protest. Let everyone have his or her feelings and then do it anyway.

5. Be a good role model by limiting your own screen time.

ROUTINES

We use our minds and our bodies, our thoughts and our emotions, every part of our beings, for the purposes that we have set for ourselves.

—Rudolf Dreikurs

Help children create routine charts to encourage self-discipline.

1. Create routine charts *with* your child.
2. Brainstorm tasks that need to be done (bedtime, morning, homework, and so on).
3. Take pictures of child doing each task.
4. Let the routine chart be the boss: "What is next on your routine chart?"
5. Do not take away from feelings of capability by adding rewards.

Jane

During one of my workshops, a mom asked a question about her 6-year-old daughter, who refuses to go to sleep unless her mom stays in her room with her. If Mom leaves, her daughter will come find her and insist that she can't go to sleep on her own. Now her 3-year-old son is starting to mimic this behavior, and Mom is exhausted and has no time to herself. Since so many parents experience this challenge, I share here the advice I gave her:

In your attempt to wean your daughter off having you stay in her room while she falls asleep, she has learned manipulation skills, and your son is a quick learner. You probably have a sensitive guilt button that they can push regularly. Have faith in yourself that changing this habit is ultimately good for your children as well as for you. Think of the long-term results of teaching them self-reliance instead of manipulation.

I had the same problem with my first five children because I allowed frustrating bedtime habits to develop. I would fall asleep with them, and my evening was suddenly gone. No time for myself.

Fortunately, I learned new methods and wrote *Positive Discipline* before my last two children were born, so they experienced a consistent bedtime routine from the beginning. Here are some suggestions based on what helped me.

First, sit down with your 6-year-old and admit you made a mistake. Tell your daughter that you have allowed her to form some bedtime habits that are not respectful to either of you, and that you have faith in her ability to fall asleep on her own. This is a good time to start teaching that mistakes are wonderful opportunities to learn.

Get her involved in creating a bedtime routine chart. Your 3-year-old can watch. Later, you can both help your son create his own bedtime routine chart. It is very important that your children do as much as they can so it is *their* routine charts. They are motivated to follow routine charts when they are involved in creating them.

Ask your daughter to make a list of all the things she needs to do before she goes to bed. Let her write them down, or you can take dictation. Her list might include a bath, putting on her pajamas, having a healthful snack, and story time. If she doesn't mention some important things, you can ask, "What about brushing your teeth and choosing your clothes for the next day?" You might want to add the tradition of asking her to share her saddest time and happiest time of the day. Let her do most of the work creating a chart with pictures for each task. When it is bedtime, let her check her routine chart to see what is next. This way the chart becomes the boss instead of you.

Allowing her to create her routine chart is the first step. The second step is to decide what you will do and let her know in advance. Let her know that if she gets out of bed after her routine is complete, you will kindly and firmly take her back to bed—no matter how many times it takes.

One way to be kind and firm is to take her back to her bed and give her a kiss without saying a word. Another way is to say a very few words, such as "It's bedtime. I have faith in your ability to handle it." You may have to do this several times, and it is important to remain kind AND firm.

Children know when you mean it and when you don't. If you are kind and firm and consistent, it usually takes about three days for them to know you mean it and to quit testing you. Rudolf Dreikurs taught that children who "misbehave" at night are more likely to misbehave during the day. Many parents do not understand that their children actually feel more capable and confident when they learn to have faith in themselves instead of manipulating others, so when bedtime hassles are eliminated, daytime behavior improves.

If your 3-year-old is old enough to engage in creating his routine chart, follow the same procedure. If not, it is okay to simply change your energy from annoyance to kindness and firmness while taking him back to his bed every time he gets up.

I'm not saying it will be easy (weening is just as difficult for the weanor and the weanee), but if you are consistent, it won't take long for your children to know you mean what you say. One of my children was 3 years old when I learned these Positive Discipline tools. She had the habit of continually coming out of her room at bedtime. I walked her back, kicking and screaming, for several nights. It took an hour the first night till she fell asleep exhausted in her doorway. The second night she cried for a half hour. The third and fourth nights, her crying lasted only ten minutes. After that, bedtime became enjoyable. I'm sure the process would have been easier if I had known then to help her create a routine chart.

Recently I was asked why children need routine charts when adults don't need them. I pointed out that many adults create lists to help them keep track of what they want to do during the day, week, or month—and feel such a sense of accomplishment when they cross things off their lists. Many create goals and write them down to increase the effectiveness of their resolve. Others carry day planners to keep track of their appointments (and lists and goals).

Creating routine charts is great training for children to learn time and life management skills. Parents help their children by guiding them in the creation of their routine charts instead of creating charts for them. Parents add to the effectiveness of routine charts when they allow their children to experience the satisfaction of following their charts because it feels good (a sense of accomplishment) instead of giving them stickers and rewards (which takes away from their inner sense of accomplishment). Also, we have to wonder if rewarding children with toys and treats fosters more materialistic behavior.

Many parents ask why we discourage rewards when children love them so much. Children love a lot of things that aren't good for their long-term mental and physical health, such as sugar and video games. A little of these things is not harmful, but too much creates dependence and encourages addiction.

Rewards teach kids to do things for the reward instead of enhancing the good feeling of contribution. Eventually they may not do things that are good for them because they don't care about the reward, or they may bargain for a bigger reward. This is an external locus of control—dependence on external motivators to control their behavior.

Instead, invite your kids to share with you how they felt while accomplishing something, such as attaining a goal they have set for themselves. This teaches them to understand and trust their own feelings and to enjoy their own capabilities. This is an internal locus of control—doing the right thing when no one is looking.

Some parents forget that their most important task is to make their job obsolete. Their job is to help their children be self-sufficient instead of dependent. Teaching children to create routine charts is a great step toward that end. Does this mean that routine charts are magical and will prevent all future resistance and challenges from children? No. Testing their power is part of their individuation process. However, working *with* children to help them learn skills will make your job easier much more quickly and effectively than thinking it is your job to be in charge of everything they do.

Remember that the goal of routines is to help children feel capable and encouraged. A nice fringe benefit is that you will be able to stop nagging and will experience more peaceful mornings and bedtimes when children follow their routine charts.

Brad

I have to confess that I have attempted this process of creating routine charts in the past without much success. Most of that, however, is due to my lack of follow-through. When the kids were much younger, I took pictures of all their morning routines. We created the routine charts, put them up on their bedroom walls, and then completely forgot about them. Next thing I knew, I was back to my usual morning routine of reminding them to do every little task: "Have you brushed your teeth? Did you make a lunch? What about your library book?" Not only was I reminding them to do every little thing, but several times a week I would receive a phone call from the school: "Dad, I forgot my lunch."

As my children and I sat down to discuss this tool, the most important step seemed to be brainstorming tasks that need to be done. This really got the kids thinking about what they needed to do every day. They came up with things I hadn't even thought of.

So after the brainstorming I set them free to create their routine charts. I didn't interfere too much in this process. They seemed to be excited about taking ownership for their own routine charts. My daughter was very interested in typewriters, so she decided to type her routine chart. My son opened up Microsoft Word and started creating his routine chart using clip art files. I didn't even know Word had clip art files, so I learned something.

After a few minutes they were both finished and hung their new routine charts on their doors.

EMMA'S ROUTINE CHART

6:30: Wake up, get dressed and eat breakfast, brush teeth

7:00: Make lunch, make sure you fixed your backpack

7:45: Be ready/go to school

2:30: Go home/get homework done

3:30: Clean room/make bed

4:00: Free time/practice violin

5:30: Eat dinner

6:30: Bath or shower

7:00: Get PJs on/brush teeth & read

9:00: Go to sleep

GIBSON'S ROUTINE CHART

Shower

Clean bathroom/room

Brush teeth

Homework

Piano

Feed Sally (the fish)

Relaxation

My daughter, who was 10 at the time, thrived with this new routine chart system. She was diligent about following her routine and had a very positive attitude. She didn't forget to make her lunch or miss any school assignments. Emma even took it a step further and started focusing more on nutrition and fitness. I didn't even discuss those things with her, but she added push-ups and sit-ups to her daily routine. She also started asking me to cut up some carrots and broccoli for her after-school snack. The whole thing seemed very empowering to her.

My 13-year-old was not quite as enthusiastic about the whole process, although there was improvement, and I think when it comes to teenagers any improvement is a big step. What I've noticed is that teenagers are in the middle of that individuation process and they really hate being told what to do by their parents. So with Gibson, I couldn't even remind him to check his routine chart. As soon as I got involved, he became a bit passive-aggressive and started leaving things off his morning routine. For example, he would pick up his pajamas in the bathroom but wouldn't hang up the towel. One day I suggested that he might want to add turning out all the lights downstairs to his routine chart because that would be a big help to me. After I dropped the kids off at school, I went downstairs and found that all the lights were blazing as a passive-aggressive gesture. I figured it was probably best to wait until we had our weekly family meeting before making any new suggestions.

Mary

Many people miss the point of this tool. The operative word is "with"—we have to work *with* our kids to help them feel capable, to teach them skills, and to invite more cooperation. They are empowered by being respectfully involved.

One of my favorite stories about routine charts is the bedtime routine chart created with my son Greyson when he was 3 years old. I prepared him for a few days in advance simply by discussing it and telling him about it. He got excited when I told him we would go to Michael's craft store to pick up some items, and then we would take pictures of him doing all the tasks he does before bedtime. He was more than ready when we finally sat down at the table with all our supplies.

First I asked him to tell me about all the things he needed to do before he went to bed. I explained to him that I would write them all down and then he would be able to pick the order that he wanted to do them. Luckily for his dad and me, he picked the order that he was used to doing—like bath before pajamas and teeth before books.

After we made our list I told him we were going to take pictures of him doing everything. He was so enthusiastic and happy to pose for a photo doing each task. Then Greyson (with just a little help from me) stapled each photo to the ribbon we had purchased at the craft store. I made a number for each photo. Greyson was just learning his numbers and he got to stick the numbers on the photos.

He loved running to his chart to check out what to do next. If and when he got sidetracked, I'd simply say, "Greyson, what's next on your routine chart?" He would run to the back of his door where it was hung and then run to do the next task.

Now bedtimes are peaceful and stress free, and I can say I enjoy our bedtime routine!

SUCCESS STORY FROM BURNABY, BRITISH COLUMBIA, CANADA

My daughter had just started kindergarten and was having a difficult time in the mornings. She was really poky and it drove me and my husband nuts trying to coax her through every activity.

I read one of the Positive Discipline books and decided that we would try making a morning routine chart to help our daughter know what to expect next in order to get out the door in the morning.

We had a blast together doing the photo shoot. We talked about the order each activity should be done in, then printed the pictures off and pasted them onto some cardboard. She helped me with the numbering and I wrote the activities.

It worked immediately! She would run to the routine chart without any coaxing and scamper off to do the next activity. After about two weeks, she had the routine down pat, so she didn't even have to refer to the chart anymore. (My 3-year-old son found it helpful and wanted his own chart!) And if she did get off course, instead of barking orders at her about what she should be doing, we would positively ask her, "What's next on your routine chart?"

I have managed to implement many Positive Discipline tools in the home, and I can't believe how much happier our family is. The kids love our family meetings, which are followed by watching an episode of *America's Funniest Videos* as a family. And my two kids barely fight anymore (not 100 percent gone, but much improved!), and they are much more likely to work together on things, which has been the biggest improvement for me. Now our interactions are so much more positive and my husband and I can help coach the kids in solving their own problems instead of just telling them what to do.

—Shelley Buchi

SUCCESS STORY FROM SAN DIEGO, CALIFORNIA

I remember having a hard time getting my youngest out the door in the morning. We would always be late, forget something, and leave the house feeling frustrated. It was *not* a good way to start the day!

I decided to try one of the Positive Discipline tools I had recently learned. My son and I created a small routine chart so that he could be in charge of his own schedule and I could stop nagging him. What a relief it was to let go of having to remind or coax!

When done right, even young children can learn to be responsible and feel successful.

—Jeanne-Marie Paynel, Certified Positive Discipline Parent Educator

TOOL TIPS

1. Remember it is your child's chart, not yours.

2. Don't do any part of the routine chart that your child can do. Ownership increases effectiveness.

3. If the novelty wears off, do it again—maybe with new photos.

CHAPTER EIGHT

LESS IS MORE

LISTEN

One should never talk to a child unless one is sure that he wants to listen. That eliminates 90 percent of all parental "talk."

—*Rudolf Dreikurs*

Children will listen to you *after* they feel listened to.

1. Notice how often you interrupt, explain, defend your position, lecture, or give a command when your child tries to talk to you.
2. Stop and just listen. It is okay to ask questions such as "Can you give me an example? Is there anything else?"
3. When your child is finished, ask if he or she is willing to hear you.
4. After sharing, focus on a solution that works for both of you.

Jane

Many parents complain that their children don't listen, yet few parents really listen to their children. Instead they tend to:

- **React and correct.** "Don't talk to me that way." "Why can't you be more positive [or grateful, or respectful]?" "You shouldn't feel that way." "Why can't you be different—more like your sister or brother?"
- **Fix or rescue.** "Maybe if you would do ____, then ____" (for example, "Maybe if you would be friendlier, then you would have

more friends"). "I'll talk to your teacher [or your friend's mother]." "Don't feel bad."

At an even deeper level, many parents don't listen between the lines to the belief behind the behavior. For instance, perhaps a child is feeling "dethroned" by the birth of a new baby. Parents don't listen to hear if their children are feeling powerless or discouraged. Children will react to too much control by rebelling in order to regain some of their power.

They don't listen from an understanding of age-appropriateness or brain development. For instance, toddlers don't understand "No" the way most parents assume they do. They assume their toddlers know they shouldn't touch something (or run into the street) because they have been told not to. The truth is that they are developmentally programmed to explore and experiment more than to obey commands. In addition, they do not have the maturity and judgment to handle the responsibility of not running into the street. That is why they need parents.

Example is the best teacher. Learn to be a better listener and someday, when all their growing catches up to them, your children will learn what they live—to listen because they have been listened to.

Brad

First, let me say that I have always thought I was a good listener. But then I asked my kids and they said, "No way, Dad. You're a lousy listener!"

What? So I asked my mom and she confirmed the fact that I am a lousy listener. Apparently I really need this parenting tool.

I have two very different teenagers. My daughter likes to talk a lot! My son can go all day without saying more than two words to me. I don't count grunting as words. So listening to my daughter involves great focus, while listening to my son involves a little bit of mind reading and interpretation.

With my daughter I have been practicing closing my laptop and giving her my full attention. I've learned a lot by listening to her. I learned that she got a perfect score on her history test. I learned that YouTube has a lot of hilarious videos. I learned a new magic trick. I learned that she doesn't like Chick-fil-A for dinner. I learned that the kids in her school swear a lot, and she doesn't like that. I learned a joke about a foreign guy who practiced English by watching commercials.

I didn't learn quite as much from my son. But I did try to observe him a little more closely this week. You can learn a lot from teenagers by observing their body language. For example, if my son sighs, slumps his shoulders, and starts cooking a hot dog, that means he is not pleased with our choice of dinner. If he comes into the living room and sits on the couch, that means he needs a little time with Dad. If he comes home and goes downstairs without saying a word, it was a long day at school and he needs to unwind. And if he rewashes his hair three times, that means he needs a haircut.

Mary

While practicing the listening tool, I quickly found out that I am not as good at listening as I thought. Too many times when one of my boys gets loud (yelling, pouting, back-talking, whining) or I feel disrespected or ignored, I flip my lid and react irrationally instead of acting thoughtfully by just listening.

I was driving with my mom once when Greyson was acting obnoxious—or, in other words, like a typical 5-year-old. He was demanding that his 3-year-old brother, Reid, share the toy he was playing with. Back and forth they were yelling and saying mean things to each other. I looked at my mom and said, "I am so annoyed right now. What should I do?"

She said, "Stay out of it."

Did I listen to her advice? Of course not! Before I could even think about it, I reacted and said, "If you don't share with your brother and give him back his toy, I'm going to take it away from both of you and then neither one of you will have it."

Naturally, Greyson gave me attitude by sticking out his tongue and rolling his eyes. Hmmm, I wonder why. Could it be that he was mirroring my model of disrespectful behavior?

After I dropped my mom off, I got out of the car to take a few deep breaths and confront my mistakes. Right then I had my aha moment, when the learning clicked. Greyson wasn't listening to me because I wasn't listening to him. I wonder what would have happened if I had just validated his feelings and then listened.

The good thing about my mom is that she is always supportive and nonjudgmental. She is constantly reminding me that everything I am feeling and doing (mistakes and all) was also part of her learning process. She followed with encouragement by reminding me that the times I listen to my children outnumber the times I lose it.

But when I slip and fall (which I often do), I get to keep learning that mistakes are opportunities to learn.

SUCCESS STORY FROM SEATTLE, WASHINGTON

Just today, J. was having a meltdown after school because we are having a sitter come over for curriculum night. Normally I would have just said something like, "This is the sitter we have been using for three years. You'll be fine when she gets here . . . we have to go to curriculum night, it's important, yada yada . . ."

Instead I followed what we learned in class and tried to connect with him with a hug. Then I told him we could talk about it after we got out of the car.

He was still stewing when we got inside. I invited him to the couch and cuddled him for a couple of minutes until he started to relax a bit.

He said, "L. is the worst. I hate L."

Instead of saying, "That's not a very nice thing to say; she's a nice person," I said, "Can you tell me more about that?"

He said, "She never gives us enough snacks."

I thought, "Aha! I can do something about that!" So I said, "How about if I leave out extra snacks for you guys before I go?"

He said, "Yeah, that sounds good."

He perked right up. Unbelievable! No drama!

—Student of Julietta Skoog, Certified Positive Discipline Parent Educator

TOOL TIPS

1. Ask curiosity questions: "What happened? Do you want to talk about it?"

2. Invite deeper sharing: "Anything else? Is there more? Anything else?"

3. Listen with your lips closed: "Hmmm."

4. Have faith in your child. Know that, in most cases, your child simply needs a supportive, listening ear as part of the process of venting before coming up with his or her solution. Through this process your child learns resiliency and capability.

PAY ATTENTION

If we are to have better children, parents must become better educators.

—*Rudolf Dreikurs*

Are your children getting the impression that they are not important?

1. Put down whatever you are doing and focus on your child as though he or she is more important than anything else you could do.
2. Don't forget to schedule special time (Chapter 4).
3. Remember what Toni Morrison said: "Do your eyes light up when they walk into the room?"

Jane

Ever since the Industrial Revolution, we have become a sped-up world—and are quickly becoming speedier and speedier. We all claim that our children are more important than anything in the world. One way to test how true that statement is would be to notice what takes up most of your attention during each day.

We claim, "But I'm so busy," as though we have no choice in the matter.

As Adler cautions in his quote that starts this section, we do have choices. The first step is awareness.

The paying attention tool says, "Put down whatever you are doing and focus on your child as though he or she is more important than anything else you could do." But what about those times when there really is something that needs your full attention? That's when you can combine this tool with special time. When you and your child have worked together to create the time and pace for your special time, and your child is demanding time when you are too busy, you can say, "I can't right now, but I am looking forward to our special time."

Or you could combine it with asking for help. "You can see how busy I am right now. Would you be willing to help me with this task so I can then give you my full attention?"

This tool is not meant to make you feel guilty and think that you must always give your full attention whenever it is demanded. In fact, there is a name for parents who give their children too much attention: "helicopter parents." Constant attention can be smothering, or it can invite children to believe they should always be the center of attention. Children need enough quality attention to help them feel a strong sense of belonging, but not so much attention that they lose their ability to be self-confident and self-sufficient.

Brad

All of these Positive Discipline tools are valuable, but some of them seem to resonate a little bit more with me. When I read about paying attention, it had a profound impact on me. Maybe that is because I see myself in that picture above. Instead of reading the newspaper, I am usually working on my computer. My children may not have a teardrop running down their cheek, but I know they are hurting inside when I continue working while they are talking to me.

This situation occurs more often in the summer, when my kids are home every day. I try to keep them occupied so they don't spend all day staring at screens. But I also have to make a living, and so I am usually busy with work when they come up to me and need my attention.

Just the other day my son came into my office and sat down. He started talking to me as I continued to type away on my computer. I was listening to what he was saying, but I wasn't paying attention to him. I don't even think he knew what he wanted to talk about; I could just tell he needed some time and attention. But I had deadlines and a hundred other things to do, so I kept going at a frantic pace and left him sitting in my office with a dejected look on his face.

Now, I'm not advocating that we all quit our jobs and pay attention to our children 24/7. Our children wouldn't want that anyway. But when your child approaches you, it's usually a signal that he needs your attention. My children avoid me most of the time, because they are afraid I am going to give them a chore. So the fact that my son came into my office and sat down with me was a clear signal that he needed some attention.

Even though I was busy, I could have taken a minute to stop what I was doing and pay attention to him. Then, if he needed more time than I could give him, I could have explained that I was very busy right now and I could have asked him if we could plan some time after work to talk. Then I could have ended the conversation by giving him a hug and telling him that I love him. He would have left feeling so much better about himself and our relationship. Chances are he wouldn't even need to talk later because all he really wanted was a little love and attention.

Mary

I asked my boys, "Does Mommy pay attention to you when you're talking or trying to show me something?"

Reid, who was 7 at the time, quickly said, "No."

Here I thought I was really good at paying attention, because I know how disrespectful it can be when you're trying to talk to someone and they're on their phone, watching TV, working on the computer, or trying to multitask with something else. Even if that distracted individual hears what you're saying, they're not really engaged. I can imagine how discrediting this is for children.

Another night I was lying on the bed with two of my boys. Reid was reading to me, and Greyson and I were silently playing a word scramble game.

Reid slammed his book shut and said, "You're not even paying attention to the story."

Busted! Here I thought I was being a thoughtful mom by multitasking and giving them both my attention. Oops, not so much.

Greyson, on the other hand, was thrilled to have my attention and to not have to sit through another one of Reid's "boring" books. Reid was obviously annoyed and he quickly realized I wasn't fully involved in his story.

We went through the process of problem solving together and came up with a solution. We decided each of my boys would have ten uninterrupted, fully present mommy minutes. Each agreed to read silently as the other was getting 100 percent attention.

I get it, because my husband, Mark, and I both agree that when one of us is on our smartphone checking social media, it feels like a total disconnect. I have made a commitment to my boys to keep my phone in my bedroom on the charger when we're home unless I actually need to make a call. Hopefully, this will be setting a good example and modeling for them the good behavior I hope they emulate when they're teenagers.

SUCCESS STORY FROM SHENZHEN, CHINA

I needed to take my 4-year-old daughter, Serenity, with me to my Positive Discipline parenting class in the morning. There was not a babysitter available. That means she would need to play by herself for three hours.

I asked her: "Three hours? Do you think you will be bored?"

She nodded.

"So what can you do when you are bored?"

"I can play with that!" She pointed to her Dora game.

"Great! Let's write all the ideas down. I'll get a piece of paper." We have done this revised version of the wheel of choice before: the cards of choice.

She came up with eight ideas of what she could do in the three hours, including listening to music with her earphones, drawing, playing with her animal toys, learning piano, lying on the couch, sitting with Mommy, playing with her Dora game, and eating sunflower seeds.

In the morning, with those eight cards of choice, Serenity played by herself for two hours in my class. That is a long time for a 4-year-old.

She started feeling "bored" when there was about one hour left, "because Mommy didn't play with me."

I pointed to the clock on the wall: "When the long arm goes to twelve, I will play with you."

After thirty minutes she came to me again. I asked if she would like to sit on my lap or on the chair next to me. I could feel all the student moms looking at me intently. I kept calm. She sat on my lap, but only for one minute before beginning to sob and covering my mouth with her hand.

I stopped the class for a moment and held her tight, put her head on my chest, kissed her, and said, "I know you are bored and sad, because it's been a long time, and Mommy is still not playing with you. You wish I could stop the class right now and play with you." She nodded.

"I can play rock paper scissors game with you. Two or three times?"

"Five times!"

"Hmmm, how about not three, not five, but four times!"

"Okay."

"After the game, do you have any good ideas so you won't feel bored and Mommy could continue the class?"

She said, "I can go out and play the Dora game without earphones."

"Would you like to play the rock paper scissors game before going out or after the class is over?"

"After the class is over."

After our conversation, she was able to entertain herself for the rest of class. There is no better role-play than a real-life experience in class. All my class members later told me how much they learned by watching us in action.

—Elly Zhen, Certified Positive Discipline Trainer

TOOL TIPS

1. Paying attention is one of the greatest gifts you can give your children.

2. Ask yourself, "What will I remember ten years from now? Getting these important things done, or the times I gave my child my full attention?"

3. Don't go overboard. Full-time attention invites children to develop the belief that they are not okay unless someone makes them the center of their universe.

4. A few moments of quality attention prevents children from seeking "undue attention."

ACT WITHOUT WORDS

Life happens at the level of events, not words.

—*Alfred Adler*

At times the most effective thing to do is keep your mouth shut and act.

1. Let kids know in advance what you are going to do.
2. Check that they understand by asking: "What is your understanding of what I am going to do?"
3. Follow through by acting kindly and firmly without saying a word. For example, pull over if kids fight while you are driving, and read a book until they let you know they are ready for you to start driving again.

Jane

Have you found yourself raising your voice, only to feel guilty because that isn't the kind of parent you want to be? Have you found yourself feeling extremely frustrated when your children don't seem to hear a word you say—until you do raise your voice? Have you noticed how awful it sounds when you hear other parents yelling at their children?

Diane promised she would never be like her friend Sara, who was always yelling (often screaming) at her kids, "Don't do that! Do this! I'm sick and tired of telling you!" On and on! It was difficult for Diane to be around Sara, and she felt so sorry for the kids.

One day Diane found herself telling 3-year-old Seth, "Don't do that! Come here right now! Pick up your toys! Get dressed!" Fortunately she heard herself and said to her husband, "Oh, my—I sound just like Sara." Gently he said, "I didn't want to say anything, but yes, you do."

Diane remembered the Positive Discipline tool act without words, and decided to try it for one whole day. When Diane wanted Seth to stop doing something, she walked over to him, took him by the hand, and removed him. When she wanted him to come to her, she got off the couch and went to him to show him what needed to be done. When he started hitting his little brother, Diane gently separated them without saying a word.

During a calm time, Diane sat down with Seth and said, "Let's play a game. When I want you to do something, I'll keep my lips closed tight and will point to what needs to be done and you can see if you know what I want without me saying a word. Okay?" Seth smiled and agreed.

When it was time to pick up his toys, Diane went to him, grinned, and pointed to the toys while making a sign with her hands for him to pick them up, and then helped him, knowing that it is encouraging and effective to help children with tasks until they are at least 6 years old and can "graduate" to doing tasks by themselves. When it was time for him to get dressed, she took him by the hand, made a zipping-her-lips sign, and pointed to his clothes. Seth grinned and let Diane help him get dressed without a struggle—doing most of it by himself.

Later Diane shared with her husband how much more peaceful her day had been, and how much she enjoyed her interactions with Seth. Diane added, "I know actions without words won't work all the time, but this day sure helped me realize how important it is to at least get close enough to see the white in his eyes before I talk, and then to use more action and fewer words."

Putting a challenge on the family meeting agenda is one way to act without words. The words can come later, during the family meeting, when everyone is focusing on solutions. Make sure your actions are both kind and firm at the same time. Mean silence can be devastating to kids. If you can't be silently kind and firm, try another tool such as "One Word."

Brad

Act without words is a tool I use often when my children are arguing about what to watch on TV. We decided in advance during our family meetings that when the kids are arguing about what to watch, I will turn off the television until they can stop arguing and agree on something to watch together.

The amazing result has been less time in front of the TV. When I hear my kids arguing about what to watch, I simply walk into the room and turn off the TV. They both look at me, and then they get up and walk away—without saying a word. Usually the child who didn't want to watch that particular program will have a satisfied, smug look on his or her face, but both kids seem relieved to have a quick solution to the problem.

Once I did this when Gibson and Emma were arguing about what to watch on television. Ten minutes later I found them both in their rooms, reading a book!

Mary

We've all heard the saying "Actions speak louder than words." One of the reasons I love to use this tool so much is because it eliminates any regret or guilt on my part.

I recently downsized my car and lost my third row of seats. I knew it would be advantageous, in that it would save gas—and a total disadvantage, in that the three boys would be sitting so close together. My boys would argue and bicker about pretty much anything: "He's looking at me!" "He's touching me!" "He's bugging me!" Most parents can understand how annoying and distracting it can be when your kids are fighting in the backseat.

I knew that with a smaller car and a long daily commute, I had to teach and then practice this tool of acting without words. During a calm time, I had fun teaching this tool. My husband, Mark, and I love to practice role-playing as a way of helping the kids understand our perspective. It's also a fun way to bring a sense of humor into a situation and truly engage our children in learning.

The two most important rules to role-playing are to exaggerate and have fun. I promise your kids will love this style of learning. To set up our role-play we placed four chairs in the living room (to set the scene for a pretend car) and asked, "Who would like to play Mommy?" My two older boys both wanted to play me—which was perfect, because then they were able to take turns being in the role and observing.

We said we were going to role-play two scenes. Scene one would be what happens in the car when Mommy isn't practicing Positive Discipline. My oldest son, Greyson, played me first. My husband and I started fighting in the backseat (our chairs). My two younger boys were laughing hysterically. Of course, Greyson did a great job of playing me—it was embarrassing and humbling at the same time.

What I realized, as my husband and I were role-playing our kids, was that we didn't even hear what Greyson was saying as the mom. We noticed he was trying to get our attention, but my husband and I were having way too much fun. (What an insight. My mom has told me that fighting kids are like bear cubs having fun, but I had to experience it to believe it.)

After we role-played, we processed as a family what we were each thinking, feeling, and deciding. Greyson's aha moment was the greatest—he said, "You guys are crazy and it didn't matter what I said or how loud I got, you wouldn't stop fighting." He continued by saying, "I can see why this is so frustrating and annoying for parents."

Back in the role of Mom for scene two, I spoke with the boys and said, "As you just witnessed, it's not effective, respectful, or safe for me to try to play referee while I'm driving. From now on, if you boys decide to fight while I'm driving, I will pull over to a safe parking lot and get out of the car, and you can fight for as long and as loud as you want. I will calmly wait outside until you knock on the window. When

I get back into the car, I will need to hear from each one of you that you're done fighting and it's safe for us to go." I then asked, "How will I know it's time to start driving again?"

They repeated back, "When we each say we're done fighting."

I replied, "Great! I'm happy we've come up with a plan that is respectful and safe for everyone."

We began the role-play of me driving, and Reid and Greyson joyfully acted the part of fighting. I pulled my chair (car) over to the side. They soon stopped fighting, but it took a few minutes for them to remember that they both needed to tell me they were done fighting and that it was safe to go. Greyson kindly reminded his younger brother by saying, "We both need to say it." I thanked them and started driving again.

We had fun laughing and talking about what we had learned from this role-playing. Now let's fast-forward to real life. The kids started fighting, and I made the mistake of asking them, "Do I need to pull over?"

Of course they said no, but they continued to fight. I then found a safe place to pull over and got out of the car. It was like magic—honestly, they stopped fighting before the car was even in park. I think they were both so shocked by the fact that we were in a parking lot and I wasn't threatening and yelling at them.

Acting without words is a powerful, guilt-free, and respectful way to parent. It's amazing how much less I need to apologize and repair when I can just shut my mouth and act. I often remind parents that our kids will test the limits. My advice is to expect this and be prepared to leave early the first time you try this.

SUCCESS STORY FROM WASHINGTON, D.C.

Act without words is a Positive Discipline tool that has truly saved my sanity—especially in the car. My kids, like all kids, love to stir things up on long car rides. And, sibling rivalry seems to be at its height when we're stuck in traffic.

Taking the time to explain that I planned to pull the car over and stay on the side of the road (or wherever I can find to park safely when there is fighting) changed things forever. It only took one time of pulling over and stopping before my kids got the message. I didn't say a word.

Because of all I had read about Positive Discipline, I knew to tell my kids ahead of time what to expect. Then acting without words got their attention. No one wants to sit on the side of the road going nowhere. Like magic, they were working together to assure me that I could get back on the road and there would be no more fighting.

—Anonymous

TOOL TIPS

1. Don't expect your children to control their behavior when you don't control your own. This is a tip that will serve you well in many situations.

2. Having an advance plan for how you will act without words (and letting your kids know of that plan) makes it easier to follow through.

3. Acting instead of talking is a great way to get the attention of children who may have learned to tune out lectures.

SILENT SIGNALS

Talking is one of the most ineffective things to do.

—Rudolf Dreikurs

Parents often talk too much. A silent signal could speak louder than words.

1. Smile and point to the shoes that need to be picked up.
2. Decide with your child on signals that would work better than words during a conflict or as a reminder of manners.
3. When you feel upset, try putting your hand on your heart to signal "I love you." You'll both feel better.

Jane

If it's difficult for you to act without words, it might be a helpful step for you to pretend you have lost your voice and have to use some kind of sign language. This is especially fun and effective when you get your kids involved in helping you create some silent signals.

Mrs. Beal was frustrated because it irritated her so much when the children would come home from school and dump their books on the couch. Constant nagging was not producing any change.

During a family meeting she told her children she didn't want to yell and nag anymore about this problem. She suggested the silent signal of putting a pillowcase over the television as a reminder that there were books on the couch. The children agreed to this plan, and it worked very well. Mother no longer got involved beyond the signal. When the children saw the pillowcase, they either picked up their own books or reminded someone else to.

Several weeks later, Mrs. Beal wanted to watch her favorite TV program after the children had gone to school. She was surprised to find a pillowcase on the television. She looked at the couch and saw the packages she had left there the night before, when she was in a hurry to fix dinner. The whole family had a good laugh over this turn of events. They enjoyed this method, and from then on the children thought of many silent signals as solutions to problems.

The silent signal illustrated at the top of this section is to point to your watch when you have agreed (together) on a specific time that something should be done. Remember to smile while you are pointing.

Silent signals can help solve problems, help children follow through, and help parents avoid constant nagging and reminding. Mary shares an example of a silent (secret) signal. Kids love the secret part—especially when they have helped create it.

Mary

I started using silent signals when my oldest son was almost 3 years old. It began when I would get frustrated with him, raise my voice, and get really stern. Then I would feel horrible and guilty for raising my voice. I knew there was a better way to handle this.

I'm always talking about how important it is to model the behavior we expect from our children. Once again, easier said than done. The absolute worst feeling is when I hear my oldest son yelling at his younger brother. It's ridiculous and embarrassing knowing that he is speaking that way because of how I spoke to him.

Thank goodness for my Positive Discipline tools. I started with an apology and explained to Greyson that I didn't want to be a screaming meany mommy. I asked him if we could come up with a silent signal to help me remember to take deep breaths and calm down. I shared with him that I always wanted to be able to speak to him in the same respectful tone that I expect from him.

Greyson came up with the idea that he would touch his nose to remind me that I needed to calm down and take some deep breaths. I assured him that it was a brilliant signal and then asked him if I could do the same if and when he wasn't speaking in a calm tone.

It was only a few days later that Greyson had the opportunity to use his silent signal with me, and of course it worked like a charm. I immediately stopped to take a few deep breaths, gave him a hug, and then sat down to speak to him at eye level.

When Greyson was 4 years old we created another signal about interrupting. We took time to practice by role-playing. (Remember, that time for training takes place during calm times—not at the time of conflict.) When I am talking to someone else, Greyson squeezes my hand to let me know he wants to say something. I put my hand on his shoulder to let him know I'll finish as soon as I can so I can listen to him. Greyson seldom interrupted after that. It was obvious that he felt pleased about our secret signal.

We have adopted another silent signal from my dad (their grandpa). He would put his hand over his heart as a signal that he was having a "love flash." I always felt so special every time he did this—which was often.

My boys loved the idea that we were using a signal in our family that had been used in my family when I was a little girl. It is a great way to make a connection, and I hope they will pass this tradition on in their families.

SUCCESS STORY FROM BRITISH COLUMBIA, CANADA

My 4-year-old was whining and interrupting a lot. It was helpful to realize that her mistaken goal was undue attention. We decided to create a silent signal.

We now have a secret arm squeeze that my daughter can use when I'm talking to someone else to let me know she has something to say to me. I give her a little arm squeeze back to let her know I understood her squeeze and will let her know when I'm ready to listen to her.

At first, when she interrupted, I would stop talking and explain to her that it's rude to interrupt and remind her to use the arm squeeze instead. Now I simply give her arm a squeeze and continue my conversation. It works so well. She stops talking and waits her turn.

—Sarah Joseph, Certified Positive Discipline Parent Educator

SUCCESS STORY FROM ATLANTA, GEORGIA

When my kids were little, it seemed that every time I got on the phone one of them needed something. Okay, my kids are teenagers and this still happens. But it is not a problem because the silent signal tool really works.

My kids and I have developed all kinds of silent signals, which have been especially helpful when I need to make work calls from home. If I am on the phone and they want to know how much longer, they point to their wrist or watch, and I hold up fingers to show them how many more minutes. We also have a silent signal as code for a work call.

Agreeing on silent signals ahead of time is super important, and I have noticed that when my kids come up with the signal, even if it seems ridiculous, they use it with even more success.

—Kelly Gfroerer, Certified Positive Discipline Trainer

TOOL TIPS

1. Have a brainstorming session with your kids to get their ideas for the silent signals that will work for them.

2. Encourage your children to come up with silent signals they could use to remind you of things you need to change, such as talking too much or flipping your lid.

3. Be sure to take time for training about how to use the signal during a calm time.

ONE WORD

To reestablish language as a means of communication within the family would require the avoidance of talk whenever conflict arises.

—Rudolf Dreikurs

Avoid lecturing and nagging. Use one word as a kind reminder.

1. For the towel left on the floor: "Towel."
2. When the dog has not been fed: "Dog."
3. "Dishes."
4. "Bedtime."
5. When agreements are made together in advance, one word is often all that needs to be said.

Jane

If acting without any words is too difficult, try keeping your reminders to just one word. The illustration at the beginning of this section depicts what often happens when parents talk too much. Children may not actually put their fingers in their ears, but they often tune out just the same. Rudolf Dreikurs reminds us that we would be wise to stop talking when conflict arises. We believe he means until you have calmed down and can be rational and encouraging. And it is wise to know when talking too much actually creates conflict.

Why just one word? There are many reasons:

1. It will be a reminder to you to avoid lectures.
2. It can be a reminder to control your own behavior.

3. Depending on your tone, one word can be kind and firm.

4. One word doesn't give your kids enough time to tune you out.

If you really can't stand saying just one word, try using just a few more by adding, "I notice _____." For example:

1. "I notice a wet bath towel on your bed."
2. "I see art supplies on the dining table and it is almost dinner-time."
3. "I see your bike outside and it's starting to rain."

Simply observing, without a single word or very few words, shows faith in their ability to figure out what needs to be done.

Mary

One morning my oldest son, Greyson, who was almost 7 at the time, said to me, "I can't wait until I'm grown up so I can boss my kids around."

I was amused, surprised, and hurt at the same time. Amused because he thought that being older means being the "boss." Surprised because we were having a cuddle moment on the rocking chair and I was sharing with him that I didn't want him to grow up. And hurt because I didn't like that he perceived me that way.

I asked him, "What does being a boss sound like?"

He said, "Go clean your room . . . *now*."

Ugh. I knew that wasn't how I speak to him all the time, but I also knew I was guilty of it sometimes.

I asked him, "What if we came up with an agreement where all I said was one word?"

He said, "I'd like that!"

I said, "I know that you are aware of all the chores and expectations we have of you as a member of this family."

He sighed, "But sometimes I do need reminding."

We agreed that I could skip the lectures, and one word would be enough.

Later that morning he left his bowl on the counter, I said, "Greyson, bowl."

He said, "Mom, that was two words."

I smiled, gave him a big hug, laughed, and said, "Okay, maybe it will be two words if your name is going to count."

This tool continued to work throughout the day with one-word reminders such as "hands," "teeth," "shoes," and "hug."

What would I do without these Positive Discipline Tools?

Brad

My son has a tendency to be a bit negative (especially toward his sister). So we discussed the problem in our family meeting and we all came up with the word "sunshine" as a reminder to not be so negative.

I think he likes that a lot better than getting a lecture from me on the finer points of being positive. It can also be fun. When you say the one-word reminder, you might get a little grin from your children when the lightbulb goes on and they remember what they need to do.

You also may have to revisit the topic at your next family meeting. That's what happened in this case. We tried "sunshine" for a week, but it was more fun for Emma than it was for Gibson. Emma and I would smile and say "sunshine" and Gibson would just get more irritated.

So at the next family meeting, we discussed the topic again. I asked Gibson if there was another word that would work better. He said no. So I asked him if he could think of something else that would work. He mentioned that he really liked the hug tool. So we agreed to give Gibson a hug if he was being negative. That worked a lot better the following week.

Remember that there are a lot of parenting tools to choose from. Not every tool works for every child. Use your intuition and ask your children what will work.

My kids tune me out immediately anytime I use too many words. When they were 1, 3, and 5 years old, my pediatrician (who, thank goodness, knew Positive Discipline) advised me to remember that when it comes to being a parent, "more words mean less." He encouraged me to use just one word anytime I started getting frustrated or found my kids not following multistep directions—which can be pretty difficult for most young kids.

Even a simple "please go upstairs and get your shoes so we can go to the park," involves multiple steps. This seems simple enough, but to a preschooler, these two steps can be a challenge—at least they were at my house. Using one word, "shoes," when my kids would inevitably return back downstairs empty-handed helped every time.

One word helps bring focus for action. Even now that my kids are teenagers, I still find that using just one word brings quick results and definitely helps me avoid becoming a nag.

—Kelly Gfroerer, Certified Positive Discipline Trainer

TOOL TIPS

1. Tone of voice is important. Disgust and/or sarcasm are not encouraging or helpful.

2. Remember that children don't have the same priorities you have.

3. Make it a game. Put a dollar in a secret jar every time you remember to say just one word.

4. Make it a joke. Tell your kids they can start counting on their fingers when you start using too many words.

5. Use your intuition to know when one word might be the most effective.

6. If you have created an agreement with your child, you may ask, "What was our agreement?"

7. If your child doesn't respond to one word or to "What was our agreement?" put the problem on the family meeting agenda to allow for some calming-down time.

CHAPTER NINE

CONSEQUENCES

LOGICAL CONSEQUENCES

It is better to be wrong in figuring out the meaning of a situation than to overlook it.

—Rudolf Dreikurs

Too often logical consequences are poorly disguised punishments.

1. Use consequences rarely. Instead, focus on solutions.
2. When appropriate, follow the 3 R's and an H of logical consequences. Does the consequence have all four characteristics?
   - Related
   - Respectful
   - Reasonable
   - Helpful
3. If any of these characteristics are missing, it is not a logical consequence.

Jane

It is almost funny to watch the faces of parents when I announce, "No more logical consequences—at least hardly ever. Focus on solutions." Especially since I have already shared so many other no-no's: "No punishment, no rewards, no praise, no punitive time-out, no taking away privileges." They wonder, "What else is there?" Positive Discipline answers that question by providing so many nonpunitive discipline tools.

For years I advocated the use of logical consequences. After all, Rudolf Dreikurs was the first to teach about logical consequences. However, I kept noticing that what most parents called a logical consequence was really a poorly disguised punishment. When I pointed this out, they agreed. However, they still reverted to punitive logical consequences when they were upset, frustrated, and didn't know what else to do.

So I created the 3 R's and an H of logical consequences:

1. **Related** means the consequence must be related to the behavior.
2. **Respectful** means the consequence must not involve blame, shame, or pain and should be kindly and firmly enforced. Also, it must be respectful to everyone involved.
3. **Reasonable** means the consequence must not include piggybacking (adding lectures or any kind of blame, shame, or pain) and is reasonable from the child's point of view as well as the adult's.
4. **Helpful** means it will encourage change for everyone involved.

If any of the 3 R's or the H is missing, it can no longer be called a logical consequence. And if the consequence is not related, respectful, reasonable, and helpful, children may experience the 4 R's of punishment:

1. Resentment ("This is unfair. I can't trust adults")
2. Revenge ("They are winning now, but I'll get even")
3. Rebellion ("I'll show them that I can do whatever I want")
4. Retreat, in the form of sneakiness ("I won't get caught next time") or reduced self-esteem ("I am a bad person")

It can be very difficult for parents to give up the idea that you have to "make children feel bad in order to teach them to do better." Science has proven what we have taught in Positive Discipline for years: children do better when they feel better. Years ago, I saw a cartoon that illustrated this very belief. It showed a mother watching her husband chase their child with a stick. In the caption the mother is calling,

"Wait! Give him another chance." The father replies, "But he might not ever do it again."

Suffering is not a necessary characteristic of logical consequences. For example, a child might enjoy cleaning up his mess. This is fine, since the purpose of a logical consequence is to change the misbehavior and find a solution, not to get revenge by causing suffering. Wanting the child to suffer is what turns a logical consequence into a punishment.

There are other methods that would be more effective, such as holding a family meeting, focusing on solutions instead of consequences, creating routines, offering limited choices, asking for help, dealing with the belief behind the behavior, deciding what you will do instead of what you will make your child do, following through with dignity and respect, hugging, or any other Positive Discipline tool that seems appropriate for the situation. Instead of *imposing* consequences on your child, it is always encouraging and empowering to help your child *explore* the consequences of her choices through curiosity questions.

Exploring is very different from imposing. Curiosity questions help your child explore the consequences of his or her choices in a way that leads to solutions: "What happened? What do you think caused it to happen? How do you feel about it? How do you think others feel? What have you learned from this? How can you use what you have learned in the future? What ideas do you have to solve the problem now?" These are just examples, not to be used as a script. Be in the now and be curious about getting into the child's world.

Even though logical consequences would be close to the bottom of my tool list in nine out of ten cases, when properly used they can be an effective and encouraging method. In fact, we've shared several tools that could be called a logical consequence by another name—for example, decide what you will do, shut your mouth and act, follow through, use mistakes as opportunities to learn, let go, and allow children to experience consequences (which is very different from imposing consequences).

The litmus test to determine whether or not a logical consequence is effective is the question "Does this consequence make my child 'pay' for something he or she did in the past, or does it help my child feel encouraged to learn for the future?"

Mary

One thing that really pushes my buttons is the fighting and bickering between my two oldest sons at bedtime. They share a room and they tend to be more energetic five minutes before it's time to fall asleep. Either they want to wrestle or they try their best to annoy each other (and me, of course).

I try to stay calm and patient by asking them nicely to stop. Of course, this doesn't work. This is where my parenting could get really ugly if I didn't go searching through my Positive Discipline toolbox.

First, I remember that their actions are normal, age-appropriate, and definitely not meant to get me irritated. Then I think, "Now what was it that my mom said reduced the fighting between me and my brother when I was growing up? Oh, yes—family meetings."

At one family meeting we discussed the agenda item of fighting at bedtime. We were all able to focus on solutions that were also logical consequences of fighting at bedtime.

We decided to allow one hour for our bedtime routine. We all agreed that they needed about fifteen minutes of downtime to lie on the ground, wrestle, and goof around. Once we completed our final bedtime book reading and back scratches, it was lights out. "Lights out" was the code word my boys came up with to mean no more talking.

If they continued fighting after "lights out," we would start the bedtime routine thirty minutes earlier the next night. We kindly reminded them that this might involve leaving baseball practice early. Greyson hated that idea, and Reid (who was not currently playing baseball) smirked.

Greyson made a valid point when he said, "What if I'm ignoring Reid and he continues to annoy me?" So we came up with the related consequence of having Reid go to bed by himself fifteen minutes earlier than Greyson. This would allow Reid time alone with no one to bug.

Reid didn't like that idea, but agreed it was fair. Having Reid go to bed fifteen minutes early felt a little punitive, but I realized it was actually a logical consequence because it was related and reasonable (especially since they agreed to it). It would be up to me to make sure it was enforced respectfully. We could then check back at our next family meeting to see if it had been helpful. If not, we could brainstorm for more solutions. And we had all agreed in advance.

The first night we tried the "lights out" strategy, it worked!

Note to self once again: family meetings work, and having the kids focus on solutions, even if they're logical consequences, is so effective.

Brad

When I heard, "No more logical consequences—at least hardly ever. Focus on solutions," my only thought was, "Well, that makes sense." I always get mixed up on the difference between natural and logical consequences anyway, and would much prefer to focus on solutions.

I've used logical consequences most often with toys that are left out. There is a very logical consequence for that. The children pick up their toys (related, reasonable, and respectful) or I pick them up and put them away for a week (again: related, reasonable, and respectful). My children may not always agree with the logical consequence, but they would say that it is fair, so long as I am kind and firm in my delivery.

I love focusing on solutions, which also require kindness and firmness at the same time. When I come home to find that my daughter has left all of her belongings spread out on the kitchen table, I don't get upset. I simply ask her to please clean up her things so we can have dinner, which Emma is happy to do. When she was getting a bad grade in math, I kindly suggested the solution of her staying after school to do her homework in the math lab, where she could get help with the concepts she didn't understand. That seemed like a logical and helpful solution to her.

I have heard others ask, "What would be the logical consequence for this behavior?" as though it is really hard to think of one. I have noticed that thinking of a solution is much easier than trying to come up with a logical consequence, especially if I ask my children what they think. They are even better at thinking of solutions than I am.

SUCCESS STORY FROM MARSEILLE, FRANCE

We agreed with our two older sons on how long they could use their iPod or computer (an hour and a half on Wednesdays and two hours on weekends) and, in case of noncompliance, on the logical consequence (taking the device away for a while). This method worked well . . . before going wrong in early July.

It irritated me to see Léon still glued to his screen. I snatched the iPod from his hands, and he reacted by kicking me.

I was shocked. How could he be so violent with me? Then I realized that in my own way I had been violent too, and I should have been more patient to make him give me the device instead of taking it from him. My main mistake was forgetting to review the agreement before the school vacation.

After having stressed that it was unacceptable, I followed the 3 R's of recovery from mistakes: I apologized (recognizing my mistake), I showed interest in his video games (reconciliation), and I offered to work with him on a new agreement for the summer and on another way to express our frustrations (resolution).

He was very surprised by my sudden interest. He detailed his universe with passion. This conversation allowed me to see my son as a bright child, not an apathetic geek, and gave me the idea to ask him to download music on my phone (validation). I experienced how much it meant to him for me to value his contribution, and how much it helped him feel belonging and significance.

—Marie de Ménibus Le Marois

TOOL TIPS

1. Consider your immediate goals. Do you want to make your child pay for the past or to learn for the future?

2. Consider your long-term goal. Do you want your child to feel guilt and shame or empowered and capable?

3. When in doubt, forget about logical consequences and use the same 3 R's and an H for solutions.

NATURAL CONSEQUENCES

We need to recognize the tremendous power which lies in all of us and which we cannot use as long as we feel victimized.

—Rudolf Dreikurs

Children develop resiliency and capability by experiencing the natural consequences of their choices.

1. Avoid lectures or saying "I told you so."
2. Show empathy: "You're soaking wet, it must be uncomfortable."
3. Be comforting without rescuing: "A warm shower might help."
4. Validate feelings: "Sounds like that was very embarrassing."

Jane

A natural consequence is anything that happens naturally, with no adult interference. When you stand in the rain, you get wet. When you don't eat, you get hungry. When you forget your coat, you get cold. No piggybacking allowed. Adults piggyback when they lecture, scold, say "I told you so," or do anything else that adds more blame, shame, or pain than the child might experience naturally.

Children usually feel bad or guilty when they make a mistake. Lectures lessen the learning that can occur from experiencing a natural consequence because the child stops processing the experience and focuses on absorbing or defending against the blame, shame, and pain. Instead of lecturing, show empathy and understanding for what the child is experiencing: "I'll bet it was hard to go hungry [or get wet, get that bad grade, lose your bicycle]." It can be difficult for parents to be supportive without rescuing or overprotecting, but it is one of the most encouraging things you can do to help your children develop a sense of capability.

Even though natural consequences often help children learn responsibility, there are times when natural consequences are not practical:

1. When a child is in danger. Adults cannot allow a child to experience the natural consequences of playing in the street, for example.

2. When natural consequences interfere with the rights of others. Adults cannot allow the natural consequences of allowing a child to throw rocks at another person.

3. When the results of children's behavior do not seem like a problem to them and the natural consequences will adversely affect their health and well-being. For example, it does not seem like a problem to some children if they don't take a bath, don't brush their teeth, don't do their homework, or eat tons of junk food.

In these cases, there are many other tools that could be more effective.

Mary

A few weeks ago, my son and I were running errands and he discovered a yogurt in his snack pack. He was sitting in his stroller and I knew if he ate it there rather than at a table, it would most likely spill and make a huge mess.

I tried to reason with him by explaining my theory, and because he's 3, he didn't care. The more I tried to convince him, the more he insisted he didn't need my help. Several times he said, "Me do it."

I quickly realized we were in a power struggle. In the moment I was trying to avoid a huge mess and a possible meltdown. Then I remembered that it would be more important for him to experience the natural consequences of eating his yogurt in his stroller rather than at a table. Sure enough, he spilled it, and it made a huge mess. It took everything in me not to say, "See, I told you that you were going to spill it."

Instead I said, "Uh-oh, you made a mess, let's clean it up." There was no shame or blame. We both stayed calm and even laughed at the mess he made. Thank goodness I had an extra change of clothes in the car.

Once again Parker insisted on getting in the car by himself. Luckily I had extra time and patience that day. In the end we were connected, he felt empowered, he experienced the natural consequences of his actions, and his confidence increased.

Brad

As a single parent, sometimes your only choice is to allow your children to experience natural consequences. Especially when you go out of town.

First of all, I often get calls from my kids when I leave town. Sometimes if I can't get to my cell phone right away, my children will leave an elaborate message that lasts about three minutes. Once when I was on a golf trip, my son called and left a message that went something like this.

"Dad, I can't get into the house because me and my friend came back from his house and I forgot my key. So we tried to pick the lock with a twig, but the twig broke off and now the key won't work. So we went around to the backyard and tried to get in through one of the windows, but the window was locked and now the screen is broken. But we finally found an open window, and you know those big blue barrels in the backyard? We climbed on one of those to get in the window. So I was able to feed the cat and get out through the front door, but now we can't lock the door. Hope you're having fun on your golf trip!"

Are you starting to get the picture?

I arrived home from one of these trips and found:

1. The cat used the basement carpet as her own personal litter box.
2. The kids fell asleep and forgot to let the dog out and so she peed in my son's room.

3. The cat coughed up a hairball in my daughter's room.

4. The kids left some food out and the dog decided to do a version of the Irish River Dance on our new kitchen table.

5. The kids (who know there are no drinks allowed in my office) spilled chocolate milk on the carpet.

6. Nobody did the dishes while I was gone, and so when I served chicken noodle soup for dinner, I realized that there were no clean spoons and I had already started the dishwasher. So I got creative and had my daughter eat with a large serving spoon and my son eat with an ice cream scoop. My daughter was so amused by the sight of my son eating with an ice cream scoop that she burst into laughter, spitting her chicken noodle soup across the table in my son's face and causing a reaction not unlike what you would expect if he had been hit by sulfuric acid.

Ahh . . . there's nothing like a nice little vacation from home to unwind and relax.

There is a happy ending to all of these experiences of natural consequences. My kids are now teenagers and have learned from all of their previous mistakes. Now when I leave town, they are quite capable of taking care of themselves. They plan meals together, take the dog for walks, and keep the kitchen clean. And I learned to hide a house key outside in one of those fake sprinklers, so if they do forget their key, they can get back in the house without using a twig.

SUCCESS STORY FROM MONTERREY, MEXICO

I have an 11-year-old son whom I label as "distracted" because he always forgets to write his homework down or bring everything he needs to do it. The problem is, we've changed him to another school with different rules and every time he misses a homework assignment he gets a "homework report."

He was not used to that and he seemed not to care, but reports are something serious at this school. They take points from his grades (which are excellent, by the way). So every time he came home with a report I was super angry with him. I yelled, I grounded him, but nothing seemed to work. He couldn't care less (or so I thought).

So after a meeting with his teacher, who told me that he was about to be suspended, I was very angry with him. I felt he was not capable of keeping up with the school. And then it happened—I ran into a person who heard my story and told me about the Positive Discipline workshop. I decided to sign up immediately.

As I attended the workshop, every single tool was an eye opener for me. I understood that I was not listening to my son; that I was making him feel inadequate; that I rescued him every time I thought he was not going to be able to succeed. So I decided to try natural consequence—letting the reports affect his grades.

He didn't like it. So he came up with a plan to double-check his homework notebook and check if he had everything written down and in his backpack. We started using family meetings to talk about school and home issues, and it worked perfectly. I used the Mistaken Goal Chart and started empowering him and noticing what he did right. I let him do his homework by himself—with incredible results. I started listening to what he said.

It has now been a year and I can say that he is more confident, he is more responsible with school issues, and he is more involved in family activities. The best of all is that I am enjoying motherhood. I feel less stressed. I can show myself more as an understanding mother and enjoy every moment I spend with my son.

—Samantha Garcia, Certified Positive Discipline Parent Educator

SUCCESS STORY FROM PARIS, FRANCE

Starting when my son was 3½, I spent one year repeating every night, at least five to ten times, that it was eight o'clock and time for him to go to bed so that he would have sufficient energy for the next day. This part of the day was painful; I was often angry or stressed. I tried everything I could think of—punishment, even blackmail—but it was always the same story.

One day I discovered natural consequences in the Positive Discipline book. I committed myself to never use punishment or blackmail again, and said to myself, "Why not try natural consequences?"

On that day my son asked me to continue playing when it was time to go to bed. I answered in a kind manner: "I can see that you really want to continue playing instead of going to bed. I am okay with that, but I just want to let you know that tomorrow is a school day and you need to get up early. By going to bed later than usual, please note that you will probably be tired tomorrow. If you commit to get up on time no matter how tired you are tomorrow, you can continue playing. It is your choice and your responsibility."

He was so happy and chose to continue playing. I felt relieved because I could go on with my activities without stressing about him having enough sleep. And he went to bed around 10:00 p.m. The next day he looked very tired, but he woke up. I helped him get dressed without a word about him being tired. On the way to school he told me, "Mum, I am tired."

I said, "Oh, you are tired. It's difficult. Personally I prefer being full of energy in the morning."

He added, "So do I."

This gave me the opportunity to ask him what solution he could put in place to be full of energy in the morning. His answer was: "To wake up later." I wanted to laugh but I didn't, and just explained that it was not possible on school days if he wanted to be on time. So I asked him if he could think of another solution, and he answered, "Go to bed earlier?"

I looked at him with a smile and confirmed to him that he had found a very good solution. Then I asked him what would be the ideal time for him and he said very seriously, "How about 1:00 a.m.?"

I wanted to laugh again, but refrained. I simply told him, "Well, 1:00 a.m. is later than the time you went to bed last night. Would you like me to suggest an hour that is earlier?"

He agreed.

I said, "How about eight p.m.? That's earlier than yesterday. Does it suit you?"

Yes, he said.

I asked him, "When you come home from school, would you like me to show you the eight on the clock so you can be responsible for going to bed on time?"

He answered yes, with enthusiasm.

When he got back from school, I showed him the eight on the clock and told him that now he was responsible for getting to bed on time. I added that if he was in bed at eight, we would still have time to read a story.

For a month, every night he came to me when it was close to eight to tell me that it was almost time to go to bed. What a relief for me and my son!

After that month, he needed to reexperience the natural consequences of going to bed late. That was all it took to reinforce what he had learned before.

This happened one year ago. Since then I have learned to be more flexible about bedtime on weekends and holidays. I trust his capacity to wake up early enough on school days even though he goes to bed later on some weekends and wakes up later too. And I am really impressed because he manages the rhythm changes very well. Thank you so much for this inestimable gift!

—Tarisayi de Cugnac, Certified Positive Discipline Parent Educator

TOOL TIPS

1. Several other tools are necessary for natural consequences to be effective, such as: taking time for training, showing faith, and seeing mistakes as opportunities to learn.

2. After allowing your child to experience the natural consequence of a choice (such as being cold because he didn't want to wear a coat), you can ask conversational curiosity questions to help him be more aware of how he has more control over what happens based on his choices.

3. Don't stand by and allow natural consequences when they might be hurtful to your child or someone else now or in the future.

4. Another possibility is to ask your child if he or she would like to put a challenge on the family meeting agenda to help brainstorm solutions.

PUT KIDS IN THE SAME BOAT

Accusations do not promote cooperation.

—Rudolf Dreikurs

Instead of taking sides when children fight, treat them the same.

1. Give the same choice: "Kids, would you like to go to the peace bench (if you have all created one together) or the wheel of choice?"
2. Show faith: "Let me know when you have identified the problem and have ideas for solutions."
3. Leave. Fighting will diminish significantly when you stop taking sides—so long as you are having regular family meetings to teach problem-solving skills.

Jane

Most parents are lousy detectives when it comes to solving the puzzle of who started the squabble. After all, the one who is crying must be the innocent victim of a bullying sibling, right? Wrong!

Rewind the scene and you will almost always spot a younger sibling provoking a very easily provoked older sibling. Why? It can be so much fun to be the victim. The punch of an older sibling is a small price to pay for all the love and attention as Mom rushes in to protect and soothe.

Watching this scene played out can seem quite funny—until you investigate the long-term effects. The youngest child is developing a "victim mentality," deciding that the best way to get love and attention is to be a victim. Not a good plan for successful living. Again, it's important to consider the long-term results of our behavior.

Do not take sides or try to decide who is at fault. Chances are you are not right, because you never see everything that goes on. What seems right to you will surely seem unfair from at least one child's point of view.

Instead, treat them the same. Instead of focusing on one child as the instigator, say something like, "Kids, which one of you would like to put this problem on the agenda?" or "Kids, do you need to go to your feel-good places for a while, or can you find a solution now?" or "Kids, do you want to go to separate rooms?" You can use these words even when a 6-month-old or an 18-month-old is involved and you are sure the youngest is totally blameless. Of course, the baby or toddler won't understand the words, but the older child will understand that he or she is not being blamed for everything. Also, the younger child will not have the opportunity to catch on to how much fun it can be to provoke the older one when Mom isn't looking so he or she can get a lot of attention for being a victim.

Give up on trying to eliminate all sibling rivalry. Some of it just isn't as bad as parents think it is. When I went through the bedtime routine of asking my children about their saddest and happiest times of the day, they seldom mentioned their fights (even though their fights were always my saddest). Also, children can learn a lot from a little sibling rivalry, especially when they learn alternatives during regular family meetings where they have weekly practice giving each other compliments.

Mary

It's so easy to get caught up in my boys' fights and defend my youngest son. I find myself feeling sorry for him and angry at my oldest for hurting him.

Since I'm the youngest child in my family, I know that the younger child usually provokes the older sibling. Remembering this helped me feel comfortable putting them in the same boat.

When I remind them that I will not be involved and that they can come find me when they're done, they handle it and solve the problem better than I could if I chose to be involved. By putting my boys in the same boat, I eliminate one of them learning to get attention by being the victim while the other gets lots of training in being the bully. Treating my kids the same way when they fight actually results in more peace for all of us.

One week when my boys started fighting, I told them, "It looks like you guys are fighting, and I don't want to be involved. I'll be downstairs. Let me know when you are done so we can finish our bedtime routine." I added, "I hope you can resolve it quickly so that we still have time for books and sharing happiest and saddest times."

I hadn't reached the bottom of the stairs when I heard Greyson calmly explaining to Reid, "The reason I took that toy from you and hit you with it was because you weren't letting me have a turn."

Reid then said, "But I wasn't done playing with it."

Greyson said, "How long until I can have a turn?"

Reid replied, "Let's play a game where we can both use it."

Greyson then told Reid he was sorry and asked him if he could have a hug.

I couldn't have been more pleased. I know the results would not have been that good had I been involved. I was proud and amazed at the same time.

I know it helps when my boys are involved in learning problem-solving skills during family meetings. They also love quoting me: "Are you looking for blame or are you looking for solutions?"

This tool has provided more peace in my home when I'm not in the middle taking sides and/or defending one of them. Even more amazing is how quickly they resolve their problems when I stay out of it.

Brad

This tool is very difficult for me. Of course, I am coming from the perspective of a younger child with a mean older brother. On the bright side, my older brother did help me improve my athletic ability because

I was always trying to outrun him. In fact, when I was 10 years old I won the local Junior Olympics pentathlon.

My brother grew up to be a good, law-abiding member of society and I managed to survive my childhood. But I think it is still in the back of my mind when I'm dealing with my kids. I'm always assuming that the older brother is the instigator.

Then something happened that completely changed my perspective. My children were invited by their cousins to go to our local amusement park while I stayed home to recuperate from knee surgery. I was obviously concerned how they would behave without my supervision. My kids are constantly bickering and fighting around me, but I crossed my fingers and sent them on their way.

When they returned I was pleasantly surprised to learn that Gibson had been the model older brother, taking care of his younger sister and making sure she had a good time and didn't get lost in the crowds. Their aunt reported back how impressed she was, how great my kids were together, and how they seemed to be best friends.

It warms my heart to know that while my children do experience the typical sibling rivalry, deep down they also love each other and are best friends.

As I reflected on this experience, I realized that perhaps my children were fighting and bickering for my benefit. Having me as an audience and knowing that I would jump in and take sides only added fuel to the fire. When I was not around to interfere, my kids were quite capable of resolving their own conflicts.

SUCCESS STORY FROM OAKLAND, CALIFORNIA

I want to tell you my success story from this morning. I feel like one of the examples from the book; I was so surprised at its effectiveness!

This morning my 5½-year-old son, Eden, left his favorite Transformer toys on the floor, and his 1½-year-old sister, Lulu, ran to them and started playing. He saw that, ran over, and pushed her backward, so her head banged the floor.

I calmly went over and said, "Do you two need some help? Lulu doesn't know why you pushed her. Use your words to tell her. I know you two can work this out. I'm going in the kitchen now so you can work it out."

I walked away as Lulu whimpered a few times, just sitting next to her brother, probably unsure why I hadn't defended her better.

Only five to ten seconds after I walked away, Eden said, "Hey, Louie, do you want another one? I'll get you one!" and jumped up to get her the one Transformer he wasn't playing with. He gave it to her, she happily accepted, and she scooted away a few inches to play with it in her own space.

I couldn't believe it! Even though it worked so well, I did feel a bit guilty about seemingly abandoning Lulu to her big brother in a moment of distress. But I get that their relationship benefited from his problem solving so much more than if I had stepped in.

If we can be consistent with this kind of conflict resolution, both kids won't feel abandoned, but empowered.

—Rachel, participant in Lisa Fuller's Positive Discipline class

TOOL TIPS

1. You may think you know who started it. In most cases, you don't.

2. There is more to the story than just treating kids "the same." You need to supplement with regular family meetings where kids are learning other skills for solving conflicts.

3. Fights are greatly diminished when you have weekly family meetings because kids learn problem-solving skills.

4. Invite your kids to create their own wheels of choice (see Chapter 5) and review them periodically.

5. See the section on sense of humor in Chapter 10 for more creative ideas on how to deal with sibling fights.

CHAPTER TEN

MODEL BEHAVIOR

CONTROL YOUR OWN BEHAVIOR

We can change our whole life and the attitude of people around us simply by changing ourselves.

—Rudolf Dreikurs

Example is the best teacher.

1. Don't expect your children to control their behavior when you can't control your own.
2. Create your own special time-out area and let your children know when you need to use it.
3. If you can't leave the scene, count to ten or take deep breaths.
4. When you make mistakes, apologize to your children.

Jane

It is nearly impossible to solve problems at the time of conflict when both the child and the parent have flipped their lids. The result is distance and hurt feelings, usually followed by guilt.

Why not let your children know that you are taking a time-out? Remove yourself from the situation and get centered before attempting to solve the problem. How you take your time-out is up to you. Maybe you will go to your room. Maybe you will go for a walk. Maybe call a close friend and discuss the problem. Whatever you decide, the important thing is to take time to cool off before addressing the problem.

If you can't leave the scene, count to ten or take deep breaths. This solution is very helpful when you have younger children or the situation requires your presence.

It is okay to share what you are feeling: "I'm so angry right now; I need to calm down before we talk." Kids need to know that what they feel is always okay, but what they do is not always okay. You model this by sharing your feelings. Avoid saying, "You make me so angry." Take responsibility for your reactive feelings instead of blaming your children.

When you make mistakes, apologize to your children. As we have said many times, children are wonderfully forgiving when we take time to sincerely apologize when we lose control. During lectures I ask, "How many of you have apologized to a child?" Every hand goes up. I then ask, "What do they say?" The universal response is, "That's okay."

By apologizing, you have created a connection (closeness and trust). In this atmosphere you can work together for a solution. Once again you have demonstrated that mistakes are opportunities to learn and that you can then focus on solutions.

Controlling your own behavior is imperative if you want to create a cooperative atmosphere in your home.

Brad

Before focusing on this tool, I had a discussion with my mom about my difficulty communicating with my teenager. In my mind, it seemed like Gibson was just trying to stir up controversy and start arguments. I even went as far as to suggest that Gibson join the debate team at school so he could get all that arguing out of his system.

But then my mom said something to me that really hit home: "It takes two to argue."

Hmmm . . . That was a pretty good point. In fact, I didn't have a response. Talk about a debate-ending statement. Then she suggested that I just use questions to allow Gibson to explore his ideas without engaging in an argument.

I was fixing breakfast one morning and Gibson announced that we needed to replace the banister on the stairs, because it didn't seem too sturdy and he was worried that it would break when he leaned on it. Since my kids not only lean on the banister but often practice gymnastics moves on it, my immediate thought was, "Then don't lean on it!"

Now, just because that was my initial thought, it doesn't mean I have to say that. Right? But often I don't have much of a filter between my thoughts and my mouth, so I said, "Then don't lean on it!"

Gibson said, "But what if I forget and just lean on it like this?" And he demonstrated, leaning on the banister.

"Don't lean on it!" I said once more.

By that time Gibson was in full debate mode and was about to argue the Pythagorean theorem as it relates to banisters. But I didn't even let him get that far. "D-O-N-apostrophe-T lean on it!"

Now let's rewind a bit and see how that discussion could have gone if I had just taken a deep breath, pushed my initial thoughts aside, and simply explored the possibilities with my son.

GIBSON: Dad, we need to replace this banister because I am worried it will break when I lean on it.

DAD: Oh, tell me more about that.

GIBSON: Well, it doesn't seem very sturdy.

DAD: What do you think we could do about it?

GIBSON: We should replace it.

DAD: How much do you think that would cost?

GIBSON: I don't know.

DAD: Well, maybe you could check into that for me.

This may or may not put an end to the topic of replacing the banister. It depends on how much Gibson was invested in this notion. My guess is that he probably would have let the topic drop and would not have brought it up again.

But let's also explore the possibility that Gibson was really invested in his idea of replacing the banister and followed through finding out how much it would cost. Maybe he found out it would be $1,000. That's when I could say, "Wow, that's a lot of money. I can't afford that."

An important tip: over the past thirteen years of single parenting, I have learned that a key to controlling my behavior is taking care of myself. Parenting can be stressful, and we need to take breaks to fill our emotional buckets. Not only do we parents need breaks from our children, but our children need breaks from us. In the long run, when you take care of yourself, you will be a better, more patient parent.

Mary

I sometimes have to be reminded how silly it is to expect my boys to control their behavior when I don't always control my own. Controlling my behavior can be challenging at times. Maybe it's because I have three young boys!

There have been times when all three push my buttons on a given day, such as when my 3-year-old was having temper tantrums, my 7-year-old was giving me grief because he wanted everything right away and couldn't stand to wait patiently for anything, and my 9-year-old was sassing me because he was feeling rushed.

I know it's hypocritical of me to expect my three young boys to stop yelling when I'm shouting at them, "We don't yell!" And it's unfair for me to demand that they practice the tools of walking away, ignoring, focusing on solutions, or taking deep breaths when I'm not modeling any of those.

So one day when my children were inviting me to lose control and react to their behavior, I simply did not accept their invitation. I caught myself and remembered the value of modeling control of my own behavior. I remembered to first shut my mouth while I counted to ten, took deep breaths, and actually thought about what I wanted to say and the impact it would have.

A little later the deep breaths didn't work to help me feel calm, so I walked away to another part of the house until I could calm down.

When my 3-year-old followed, screaming for my attention, I jumped into the shower. I knew I couldn't give him the attention he needed until I had calmed down.

After I calmed down I was able to help defuse the situation, saying to one child, "I don't like it when you use hitting hands and I wish you would touch nice." To another I said, "Your tone is disrespectful and I'm realizing that's how I spoke to you. Let's start over. I'd like to ask again in a respectful way."

I try to practice these behaviors after every altercation. As soon as I calm down and take responsibility for my behavior, I say I'm sorry. I am specific in stating how I lost control of my behavior and how unfair it was for me to expect different behavior from them. I then follow up with a plan or solution that we come up with together.

If there's anything I'm learning daily throughout this parenting journey, it is that being a parent is about improvement, not perfection. These tools help me improve my behavior as well as the behavior of my children.

SUCCESS STORY FROM MARSEILLE, FRANCE

As parents of four boys, the oldest two being 13 and 15 years old, we have to face constant conflicts. How can we successfully talk to them without shouting and how can we maintain a respectful dialogue? In 2012, concerned about the behavior of Léon, our second son, my husband and I met with a family therapist (unsuccessfully) before turning to Positive Discipline. Initially we felt that it robbed us of our authority, but we also felt happy that it emphasized kindness. Initially we tended to forget about the firmness component and were too permissive. But after three Positive Discipline classes, we managed to integrate the approach into our daily lives, and for the next year we worked on repairing relations with our second son. However, without regular practice or coaching, we eventually resumed our bad habits.

The publication in September 2014 of the book *Positive Discipline for Teenagers* brought us a second wind. Positive Discipline is not a quick-fix formula, but there are several tools that we found very helpful. One example is controlling our own behavior.

Jules, our eldest, often comes back from school quite aggressive. He is obnoxious, rude, and insults his brothers. I get very annoyed and angry with him; I cut short his dinner and I don't wish him good night.

After sleeping on it, I realized that his aggressive behavior indicates his mistaken goal. We are in a power struggle. I thought about how I have contributed to the power struggle.

I invited him to lunch the next day (special time), which allowed him to put words to his feelings and tell me how he suffers from being teased by his classmates (connection before correction). I suggested we find a solution together in order for him to find his place in the group. We brainstormed several ideas. I'm not sure any of them have worked yet, but we feel more connected because I was able to control my behavior.

—Marie de Ménibus Le Marois

TOOL TIPS

1. Take a look at what you are doing (or not doing) to create what you want.

2. Make a list of what you need to stop doing and what you need to do.

3. Follow your plan.

4. Don't expect perfection. You can start over and over and over.

TONE OF VOICE

We ourselves so many times instigate misbehavior on the part
of the child because of the tone we use.

—*Rudolf Dreikurs*

The energy conveyed by your tone of voice can make all the difference.

1. When you are upset, try to think about how much you
   love your child.
2. Take some time out, if needed, until you can speak
   respectfully.
3. When you catch yourself using a disrespectful tone,
   apologize.
4. Forgive yourself.

Jane

Have you noticed how terrible it feels to listen to another parent scold a
child? Because you are not emotionally involved, you notice the shrinking posture of the child and empathize with the shame and discouragement he or she must be feeling.

During our Positive Discipline classes and workshops, we do an
experiential activity called "The Competent Giant." Participants pair
up and take turns being a parent who stands on a chair and scolds the
other person who is role-playing the child. Then they switch roles.
We then process what they are thinking and feeling in the role of

the child. I'm sure you can imagine the words they share: "scared," "shamed," "hurt," "not good enough," "wanting to shrink away and disappear."

Then we ask what they were thinking and feeling in the role of the parent. They share words such as "angry," "frustrated," "out of control" (even though they are acting controlling). Then they have to admit that they are not thinking rationally. They are not looking into the eyes of the child, and they are not aware of the effect they are having on the child.

Once out of the role, they also share how hard it was to even pretend they were scolding when they are not really upset. They are too aware of the effect they are having on the child. It shows how unlikely it is for parents to really yell at their children if they're thinking rationally.

This tool is to remind us how important it is to remember our tone of voice and the effect it has on our children—and then to use a tone that is encouraging and empowering.

Mary

How many of us have attempted to teach our children to treat others the way they want to be treated? And how many of us have spoken to our children in a tone we would not appreciate?

For example, yesterday I told my oldest son, "Get your protein shake out of my car or it will be disgusting tomorrow." Surprisingly, he didn't give me any grief or attitude and did what I told him to do.

Once I had clocked out from "Mommy duty," I realized how disrespectful my tone was. I replayed in my head how I could've, should've, would've "asked" instead of "told."

I spoke to Greyson the next day and apologized for my tone of voice about his protein shake. He looked at me, confused. Maybe my tone hadn't been as bad as I'd thought. Or maybe he's just learned to tune me out and not take it personally.

I repeated how I spoke to him the day before and acknowledged that I wasn't proud of myself for speaking to him with that tone. I followed up by practicing how I should have spoken to him. "Greyson, what do you think will happen if you leave your protein shake in the car overnight?"

He grinned and said, "Oh, I get it."

I followed up by acknowledging that sometimes I use a tone with him because I'm feeling annoyed, irritated, impatient, or mad that he's not reading my mind and is instead thinking like a 9-year-old. He laughed.

I said, "Mommy doesn't want to use that tone; and because I'm imperfect I can guarantee I will again. Would you be willing to use a code word and remind me when you hear that tone?"

Greyson said, "Of course, Mom."

My two older boys are familiar with using silent signals and code words, so this concept wasn't new to him. He also knows how much I appreciate it when he reminds me.

I once had a parent in one of my parenting workshops say, "Don't you feel disrespected when your son calls you out?"

I replied, "Not at all. We have made an agreement that we can do this. I might not have liked it if we hadn't agreed in advance during a calm time."

I want to model for him that sometimes I need reminders—and he will too. My hope is that I will model being human and humble. I believe that having him remind me can be a valuable skill for his future—if he sees me being appreciative of his helpful reminders (after setting up an agreement in advance) without getting defensive or angry, it may teach him a skill he can use with his brothers, teachers, friends, future wife, and future coworkers.

Brad

This tool is about tone of voice, but it could just as easily be about sarcasm. In case you haven't noticed, I have a bit of a sarcastic streak in my personality. Unfortunately, my children don't always appreciate my sarcasm and it has backfired on me many times.

When my children were younger, I could get away with sarcasm a lot more. But as soon as they became teenagers, they completely lost all appreciation for my sarcastic humor. This is what I hear from my teenagers: "Dad, you're not funny!" "Dad, stop! You're embarrassing me!" Or sometimes they don't say anything at all. I just get the eye roll.

I've learned to bite my tongue when I'm around my teenagers. This is great, because tone of voice only applies when you are talking.

SUCCESS STORY FROM ALABAMA

I believe my house is the loudest on the block. Remembering to use a quiet voice when I want my kids' attention can be a struggle, especially when we are trying to get out the door.

Just a few days ago we were packing for vacation. Everyone seemed to be procrastinating. When I got frustrated about lack of packing progress, I focused on getting myself organized rather than shouting orders.

Eventually each of the kids came to check in and asked what they could do to help. I wish it could go this well all the time—and it probably would if I would remember to get quiet whenever I'm tempted to raise my voice. My kids often "step in" when I "step out." This reminds me of two other tools: letting go and showing faith. I really appreciate how all the Positive Discipline tools work to support each other.

—Kiley Granger

TOOL TIPS

1. Your tone of voice speaks much louder than your words.

2. Model controlling your tone of voice before expecting your children to control theirs.

3. Take a deep breath, and remember: connection before correction.

4. Since you are an imperfect parent, you will lose it many times, so practice apologizing.

5. Put challenges on the family meeting agenda to give yourself time to calm down and speak respectfully.

DON'T BACK-TALK BACK

Words are as often used to conceal the meaning of our action as to convey it.

—Rudolf Dreikurs

Don't back-talk back. This creates a power struggle or a revenge cycle.

1. Validate feelings: "Sounds like you are really angry."
2. Take responsibility for your part: "I realize I talked disrespectfully to you by sounding bossy or critical."
3. "Let's take some time to calm down until we can be respectful."
4. "Do you know I really love you?"

Jane

Mrs. Henderson told her son, Jon, for the third time that evening, "You had better do your homework before it gets too late."

Jon shot back, "If it's so important to you, why don't you do it?"

Mrs. Henderson was shocked. After all, she was only trying to help. She reacted by saying, "Don't talk to me that way, young man. I'm your mother."

Jon reacted right back: "Well, don't talk to me that way. I'm your son."

At this point Mr. Henderson stepped in and shouted, "Go to your room right now. You are grounded until you can learn to be respectful."

Jon shouted back, "Fine," as he stomped off to his room and slammed the door.

What creates a scene like this? Mom was modeling the opposite of what she was trying to teach by back-talking to her son. How could the above scene be changed?

MOM: I notice you haven't done your homework. I'm wondering how you will feel when your teacher gives you a bad grade.

JON (WHO IS USED TO HIS MOM NAGGING): I'll feel just fine. It is my business.

MOM: You are so right. I was just curious. And if you will feel just fine by not having it done, I'm glad you aren't doing it.

JON: Are you being sarcastic?

MOM: No. I hope you will always think ahead about how you will feel when it comes time to experience the consequences of your choices. You think you'll feel fine when you don't have it done, so don't do it.

JON (AS HE AMBLES OFF TO DO HIS HOMEWORK): Sheesh!

Jon didn't seem too happy about doing his homework, but by avoiding back talk Mom invited Jon to think about the long-term consequences of his choice. Since he decided to do his homework, even though reluctantly, he must have decided he wouldn't like the consequences of not doing his homework.

Here are some typical parental reactions to back talk:

"Don't talk to me that way, young lady!"
"How can you talk to me that way after all I have done for you?"
"You just lost all your privileges."
"How far do you think that smart mouth is going to take you?"

If you were a child listening to these responses, what would you be learning, and what would you be decide to do? If you look at the characteristics and life skills list in the Introduction, would you be learning anything on that list? Would you be tempted to react by engaging in some of the behaviors on the challenges list?

Next are some responses from a Positive Discipline parent who avoids talking back to a back-talking child, which effectively defuses the situation instead of exacerbating it. Again, listen to these responses from a child's viewpoint.

"Wow. You are really angry."

"I wonder what I did to upset you so much."

"I can hear that you are really angry right now. Do you feel like telling me more about it?"

"Do you know that I really love you?"

Now look at the two lists again. As a child, what would you be learning from these statements? This is another reminder to keep the long-term results in mind.

Brad

When I mentioned this tool at a family meeting, my daughter said, "Hey, Dad, that sounds like you and Gibson."

Guilty as charged! I have to admit that I tend to get into some heated discussions with my son. To me, it seems like my son thrives on debating with me. It doesn't really matter what the topic is—he seems to enjoy taking the opposite point of view. But I am sure from his perspective I am just trying to create a power struggle to prove that I am in charge.

Take this example. We were doing back-to-school shopping, and I had to return something at Costco, so I said, "Hey, kids, let's see if they have any good back-to-school stuff at Costco." You would have thought that I just asked Gibson if he would like to restock the shelves in the entire store.

GIBSON: Daaaaad . . . I hate it when you do this.

DAD: Do what?

GIBSON: You always add extra errands when we leave the house.

DAD: Gibson, if walking into Costco is the toughest thing you have to do today, then I would say you have a pretty easy life. Maybe we need to send you to a third-world country where you actually have to do something for your survival. [Please note: this is not a Positive Discipline method of communication.]

GIBSON: Whatever!

DAD: Why do you have to be so negative all the time, Gibson? It's not very much fun doing things with you, because you are always so negative.

GIBSON: I'm not negative.

DAD: You are totally negative.

GIBSON: No, I'm not!

You get the picture. I definitely needed to use the don't back-talk back tool with my son that day. I think the key for me is just validating my son's point of view: "I understand that you don't like running all of these errands. We still need to go into Costco to return something, so I need to you come with me."

I don't need to get caught up in the negativity. I probably would feel the same way if I was a teenager running errands with my family, even if I didn't have anything better to do.

Mary

I had an aha moment when practicing the don't back-talk back tool. It happened early in the week when, once again, we were rushed to get out the door. I had snapped at my son for doing something that he could've waited and done in the car. (He was putting his new spy gear together.) When I took a disrespectful tone with him, he immediately snapped back at me in the same tone.

That had happened before; the only difference this time was that I was able to recognize it right away. I got down to his level and said, "You just raised your voice at me and spoke disrespectfully because I just raised my voice with you and was disrespectful to you. I'm sorry for not realizing that what you were doing was important to you. I was expecting you to value my sense of urgency for getting out the door on time."

Can you guess what he said? "That's okay, Mom."

Once again I learned that how my days go is not about how my children act or behave but about how I, as a parent, act or behave.

Children mirror what we do. We cannot expect our children to control their behavior when we don't control our own. In other words if you want to know why your children are speaking to you disrespectfully or back-talking, then rewind or replay how you just spoke to them.

For the rest of the week I was extra mindful of my tone of voice. The next time Greyson was dawdling, I gently touched him on the shoulder and said, "I'm worried about being late and I need your help." He immediately stopped dawdling and got ready so we could leave on time.

Every time I use a tool like this, I have to wonder why I ever forget. It may take a few more seconds to get down to the level of my boys when I speak to them, instead of snapping with irritation; but it saves me from a lot of irritation and stress, and I enjoy a more peaceful and respectful time with them.

SUCCESS STORY FROM MICHIGAN

The Positive Discipline tool about not back-talking back has helped me to avoid so many power struggles. One of my biggest parenting dilemmas has been how to refrain from micromanaging my kids' schoolwork. I've found when I want to react, it helps so much to validate feelings instead.

Last year, when one of my sons was adjusting to the demands of middle school, we started to get into a power struggle when he would procrastinate (which was often). Curiosity questions went out the window, and I started telling him what I thought he should do, which is not at all helpful or effective.

Fortunately, because of Positive Discipline, I caught myself immediately and used this tool when things weren't going well. It helped me remember to validate his feelings and acknowledge that school was really hard and different this year.

When I took responsibility for meddling in his business and I simply walked away, it helped him build his own sense of resourcefulness and kept us from fighting.

—Kristine Gallagher

TOOL TIPS

1. Be aware of what you are modeling—and model the behavior you want to teach.

2. Review the section "Control Your Own Behavior" earlier in this chapter.

3. Be prepared to "act" thoughtfully instead of "reacting"—just like your child.

4. Remember connection before correction.

SENSE OF HUMOR

The chief danger in life is that you may take too many precautions.

—Alfred Adler

Humor can help parents and children lighten up.

1. Remember to laugh and have fun.
2. Use games to help make chores fun: "Here comes the tickle monster to get kids who don't pick up toys."
3. When kids are fighting, gently tackle them and say, "Pig pile."
4. Be sensitive to times when humor is not appropriate.

Jane

What on earth is "pig pile"? My husband, Barry, invented this game. When the kids would start fighting he would wrestle them to the ground, calling, "Pig pile!" Then he would grab them and roll around on the floor. Soon they were all laughing as the kids would join together trying to get on top of their dad.

One father shared with me how he would stick his thumb in front of his fighting children and say, "I'm a reporter for CNN. Who would like to be the first to speak into my microphone and give me your version of what is happening here?" Sometimes his children would just laugh, and sometimes they would each take a turn telling their version. When they told their versions of the fight, the father would turn to an imaginary audience and say, "Well, folks, you heard it here first.

Tune in tomorrow to see how these brilliant children solve this problem." If the problem wasn't resolved by then, the father would say, "Are you going to put the problem on the family meeting agenda so the whole family can help with suggestions? Or can I meet you here tomorrow—same time, same station—for a report to our audience?"

A word about sensitivity: have you noticed that when someone tickles you, you can't help but laugh even though it isn't fun? Kids aren't really having fun when they are being tickled—at least not all the time.

Be sensitive to the fact that children may not have a highly developed sense of humor; so be careful about using humor that isn't funny to them. Children can have their feelings hurt by something a parent says in the name of humor, and then be teased for not thinking it is funny.

Brad

A sense of humor is absolutely invaluable in parenting. We need to be able to have a sense of humor with our children and also have a sense of humor with ourselves. I don't know how I would survive this crazy world of single parenting without a sense of humor.

One day I picked my daughter up from school and on the way home she was telling me all about the game they played in class called Hinky Pinky (it can also be called Hink Pink or Hinkety Pinkety). Here is how it works. You think of two rhyming words that describe something else, then ask people to guess. Emma had a list of Hinky Pinky riddles for me on the way home from school. Then at dinner she explained the game to Gibson and we all had fun taking turns thinking of Hinky Pinky rhymes.

Here is a list of some of my favorites from dinner last night.

A rabbit comedian: funny bunny
When Einstein passes gas: smart fart
A chubby feline: fat cat
Complimenting a power source: battery flattery

A pregnant reptile: fertile turtle
A cruel vegetable: mean bean
A vehicle that is good at golf: par car

Try it with your kids. It's guaranteed to entertain!

Mary

When I think back to why I wanted to have children, the first thought that comes to mind is, "Because I want to have a joyful life with lots of fun and loving memories." Sounds lovely, right? Then my boys do something so annoying, such as fighting, that it is all I can do to keep from reacting and getting frustrated.

Once I made the decision to practice the sense of humor tool every chance I could, I found that every time I did, the many challenges of temper tantrums, whining, back talk, not listening, fighting with siblings would stop immediately. Like magic.

One day Greyson was upset and was saying things such as "I hate you," "Worst day ever!" or my favorite, "You wish I wasn't even in this family." Instead of telling him that what he was saying was totally ridiculous and untrue, I started tickling him and singing, "You don't think I love you?" And then I completely overwhelmed him with "I love you's" and some playful tickles and kisses. It wasn't long before we were both laughing.

Just the other day, when they were supposed to be in the garage cleaning up the mess of toys, Greyson and Reid were fighting over who had to pick up what or who made what mess. I was feeling irritated that they were fighting once again. Then I remembered about sense of humor. I turned the car radio on and said, "Dance party." We instantly started laughing and being silly. We were putting things away together as a team, totally connected and having fun. Not only did the garage get cleaned up, but we created a great memory while doing so.

Anyone who loves cooking knows: it's very discouraging when a recipe doesn't turn out the way you'd hoped. As an experienced cook, I still feel deflated when I create a dish that flops.

My daughter, Claire, has been cooking since she could walk. Now 8 years old, she loves to prepare dishes completely on her own. She understands the value in following a tested recipe, but she prefers to make up her own. While I admire her enthusiasm for creating something from scratch, it sometimes means her concoctions are less than delicious! In fact, some have been downright awful. The Positive Discipline tools Sense of Humor and Show Faith have helped her through the disappointments.

Last summer Claire watched a kids' cooking show where the chef prepared turkey roll-ups. It involved deli turkey layered with cheese and veggies, rolled up and sliced into pinwheels. Claire was immediately inspired to make her own version of this recipe, all by herself. (Translation: "Mom, don't offer any suggestions this time, I know what I'm doing!")

That night, Claire placed two slices of turkey on a plate. Then she got to work on the filling. I must admit, it was hard not to interject (or gag). In a bowl, she combined mayonnaise, barbecue sauce, cracker crumbs, dried basil, and sliced cherry tomatoes. She spooned thick blobs of the filling on each slice of turkey and tried to roll them up. Not surprisingly, it didn't work. The turkey was overstuffed with the goopy, gummy filling. Undeterred, Claire squashed the turkey around the filling and pinched it together at the top. She renamed them "turkey bags." They really did look like little satchels on a plate! I certainly admired her ingenuity.

Did I mention that Claire insisted on preparing these as a special meal for her daddy? As soon as my husband, John, walked in the door, Claire proudly handed him the plate of turkey bags. John and I exchanged glances and he took a bite. He choked it down, and finally I couldn't take it anymore. I exploded with laughter. John said wryly, "Well, Claire, the cracker crumbs certainly are . . . surprising."

Thanks to Claire's great sense of humor, she found it funny that her dad could barely swallow his bite. Naturally, she was also disappointed that her dish hadn't worked. We discussed how lousy it feels when your recipe fizzles. I reminded her that the same thing had happened to me earlier that week when I cooked a new dish. We also discussed how she could improve her dish the next time. Claire suggested using the original recipe as a guide to the quantities and ingredients, while improvising with other ingredients to make it her own.

Instead of rescuing Claire by telling her the recipe would flop, I showed faith that she could muddle through the disappointment when it happened. I also validated her feelings by sharing my own story.

One of the best results of showing faith is seeing Claire's resiliency grow. Experimenting in the kitchen, while working through the occasional disappointment, has given her confidence both in the kitchen and out in the world. Claire is not afraid to make mistakes, because she knows we will be there showing faith that she can handle the outcome.

—Amy Knobler, Certified Positive Discipline Parent Educator

TOOL TIPS

1. Get your kids involved in creating funny and ridiculous signals that they agree on in advance.

2. Model having a sense of humor often by finding the funny part of situations and laughing a lot.

3. Never use sarcasm as an excuse for humor.

4. What is funny to you might not be funny to someone else.

5. In other words, use this tool with caution.

EMPOWER YOUR KIDS

To see with the eyes of another, to hear with the ears of
another, to feel with the heart of another. For the time being,
this seems to me an admissible definition of what we call social
feeling.

—*Alfred Adler*

Share control with young people so they can develop the skills needed to have power over their own lives.

1. Teach life skills.
2. Focus on solutions together.
3. Have faith in your children
4. Let go (in small steps).
5. Increase self-awareness: "How do you feel? What do you think? How does this affect what you want in your life?"

Jane

A friend asked me if Positive Discipline was a program to teach parents to manage their children. I said, "No, it is a program to help parents *empower* their children to manage themselves." And there you have it—the primary goal of Positive Discipline. It is so important to provide parents with the tools to empower their children.

We previously stated that Positive Discipline is an encouragement model. Encouragement is the essence of empowerment. Our definition of encouragement is "turning control over to young people as soon as possible, equipping them with the skills they need and empowering them to live their own lives as happy, contributing members of society."

Our definition of discouragement is "inserting excessive control in the lives of young people (usually in the name of love) to save them from experiencing the consequences of their choices."

In this chapter we want to clarify the difference between discouraging statements that are disempowering, and empowering statements. We will start with the discouraging statements to get them out of the way.

DISCOURAGING STATEMENTS FOR CHILDREN AGES 2–5
1. "No. No. You can't pour the milk into your glass. You might hurt yourself or make a big mess."
2. "Pick up the toys now or you will sit in the naughty chair."
3. "Other children pick up their toys. I wonder if you are a baby or a big girl."
4. "I'm going to set the timer for three minutes and these toys better be picked up when it dings!"
5. "You are too little. Mommy will do it for you."
6. "We go through this every day. I'm tired of it."
7. "If you don't want your toys thrown away, you'd better pick them up right now!"
8. "Why can't you just listen to me and do what I ask?"
9. "It's okay. Your grandma or I will do it."
10. "Don't ever ask me to do anything for you."

EMPOWERING STATEMENTS FOR CHILDREN AGES 2–5
1. Show faith and provide safe exploring environment: "I know you can do it. This pitcher of milk is just your size."
2. Acknowledge feelings first: "You are so excited to try. Show me how you can do it."
3. Check the child's understanding: "What do we need to do with the toys before story time?"
4. Invite cooperation and then a choice: "I need your help. Do you want to clean up while singing or silently?"
5. Share power: "Here is the timer. See how many toys you can pick up before it rings."

6. Offer limited choices: "Do you want to put the big blocks away first or the small blocks?"

7. Get down to child's level and say what you want (and mean it): "Sweetie, it's time to put the blocks away now."

8. Ask a curiosity question: "Where does this toy go?"

9. Connect and redirect: "It is more fun if we work together. What would you like me to do to help, and what will you do?"

10. As soon as ____, then ____: "As soon as the toys are picked up, it will be story time."

DISCOURAGING STATEMENTS FOR CHILDREN AGES 6–12

1. "How many times do I have to tell you not to leave your bicycle in the driveway?"

2. "You act like this every day! What is wrong with you?"

3. "I don't care what you want. Do it now."

4. "Never mind. I'm sure you'll do it later."

5. "If you can't be more responsible, you are grounded."

6. "I am going to set the timer for ten minutes and your chores better be done when it dings."

7. "I am so tired of nagging at you."

8. "It's okay. I can do it for you this time."

9. "Why can't you just listen to me and do what I ask?"

10. "If you don't want your things thrown away, you'd better pick them up right now!"

11. "Why do you expect me to do everything for you when you don't do anything for me?"

EMPOWERING STATEMENTS FOR CHILDREN AGES 6–12

1. Show faith with a reminder of what the child can do: "I know you know where your bike goes. Thanks for taking care of that now."

2. Curiosity questions: "What do you need to do to keep your sports equipment safe?"

3. Acknowledge feelings first: "It is hard to remember things that are not on your list of priorities. I'm happy to remind you once."

4. As soon as _____, then _____: "As soon as your chores are done, I'll give you a ride to your game."

5. Check the child's knowledge or understanding: "What is supposed to be happening now?"

6. Invite cooperation and then a choice: "I need your help. Do you want to do your chores now or in thirty minutes?"

7. Connection before correction: "I don't know what I would do without your help. Anything you can do will be appreciated."

8. "I love you, and _____ [say what you want/mean]": "I love you, and this needs to be done now."

9. Use nonverbal language: Put a gentle hand on his or her shoulder and then take the child by the hand, point at what needs to be done, and smile with a knowing look.

10. Give power: "Do you want to set the timer for how much time you think it will take to get it done?"

11. Connect and redirect: "It is more fun if we work together. What would you like me to do to help, and what will you do?"

DISCOURAGING STATEMENTS FOR TEENS

1. "I can't believe you're procrastinating again. What will become of you? Okay, I'll do it this time, but next time you'll just have to suffer the consequences."

2. "Honey, I thought you would do your homework after I bought you a car and a cell phone and gave you a big allowance."

3. "Honey, you hurry and do as much as you can now while I pick out your clothes and warm up the car so you won't be cold when I drive you to school."

4. "I just don't understand. I excused you from chores. I woke you up early. I drove you everywhere so you would have more time. I made your lunches. How could this be?"

5. "Okay, I'll write a note to the teacher that you were sick this morning, but you'll need to be sure and catch up."

6. "You are grounded and you lose all your privileges—no car, no video games, no friends—until it is done."

7. "No wonder. I saw you wasting your time on video games and spending too much time with your friends and sleeping in."

8. "You should feel ashamed of yourself. You'd better shape up or you'll be living on the streets like a bum."

9. "How many times have I told you to get your homework done early? Why can't you be more responsible like your brother?"

EMPOWERING STATEMENTS FOR TEENS

1. Curiosity questions: "What is your picture of what is going on regarding your homework? Would you be willing to hear my concerns? Could we brainstorm together on some possible solutions?"

2. Show faith: "I can see that you feel bad about getting that poor grade. I have faith in your ability to learn from this and figure out what you need to do to get the grade you want."

3. Decide what you will do and inform in advance: "I'm not willing to bail you out. When your teacher calls, I'll hand the phone to you so she can discuss it with you."

4. Listen: "I would like to hear what this means for you."

5. Decide what you will do and follow through: "I'm willing to be available for an hour two nights a week when we agree in advance on a convenient time, but I'm not willing to get involved at the last minute."

6. Share what you want and listen: "I hope you'll go to college, but I'm not sure it's important to you. I'm happy to talk with you about your thoughts or plans."

7. Share your feelings, use positive time-out, and have family meetings: "I'm feeling too upset to talk about this right now. Let's put it on the family meeting agenda so we can talk about it when I'm not so emotional."

8. Joint problem solving: "Could we sit down and see if we can work on a plan regarding homework that we both can live with?"

9. Unconditional love and acceptance: "I love you just the way you are and respect your decisions."

Discouraging behavior from adults may invite rebellion *or* an unhealthy dependence in children, preventing them from feeling capable. Discouraging behavior includes rescuing, overprotecting, and controlling.

Empowering behavior from adults invites children to learn the life skills they need to have power over their own lives and experience the joy of contributing to others. Empowering behavior means having faith in their ability to learn and recover from their mistakes in a supportive environment.

If you are used to employing short-term solutions of control and rescuing, you might not realize how powerful these empowering statements are. Empowering statements and actions are important because they give your kids power over their own lives. This power often leads to mistakes and failure. When you understand and trust that learning from mistakes and failure is an important part of a successful life process, you may find it easier to use the empowering statements. If what you are currently doing isn't working, take a leap of faith and work on using empowering statements with your kids.

Brad

You never really know for sure the impact your parenting is having on your children. My mom says that a true sign of good parenting is how your children act when you are not around. I don't take credit for the accomplishments of my children, but I try my best to provide an encouraging environment of love and support that will allow them to succeed. And, I have to admit that I hear nothing but compliments about my children from other people.

Mary

The one tool that was consistent in my childhood, and even into my adult years, is empowerment. I have so many vivid memories of my mom using empowerment to teach me so many of the life skills and characteristics she wanted me to have.

One great example comes from a time in my life when I was 16 years old and went through a short-term rebellious stage. I tried out for the cheer squad and didn't make it. I was in honors English and hated my teacher. I had a boyfriend one year older than me. My older brother had left the house for college. I had a car, a driver's license, and a desire to test independence and limits. I even considered taking my GED so that I didn't have to go to school ever again.

As I sit back, now as a mom, and think of all the ways I pushed buttons and lots of limits, I honestly cannot remember one time that my mom threatened, lectured, bribed, shamed, or even took away privileges (as a consequence that wasn't related, reasonable, or respectful). Instead she asked a *lot* of questions and really invited me to think about what my life would look like over the long term with the decisions I was making. She was always there to encourage, support, and help solve problems, while truly inviting me to come up with the answers.

Looking back at my adolescence and even into my early twenties, I can recognize so many of the poor decisions and mistakes I made. As a mother, I can only imagine how difficult and tempting it may have been for my mom to want to step in and "tell" me how I was making the wrong decision, or to want to rescue and help me avoid making mistakes. Thank goodness she didn't! Instead she practiced what she preached and let me live my life (mistakes and all).

I decided to complete high school while working two jobs, and went on to college and finished with my master's degree in counseling marriage and family therapy. I studied abroad and was always employed, with at least one job—usually two. I lived my twenties to the fullest and had my first son when I was thirty-one years old. I honestly believe that my life would not have turned out the way it did had my mom not empowered me and shown total faith in me.

Today I have used all of my mistakes and unconditional support from my parents to teach others through Positive Discipline Parenting Workshops, presentations, working with clients as a marriage and family therapist, and, more important, raising my three boys.

I honestly have no regrets because once again I live by my mom's words of wisdom and know that "everything is perfect—exactly how it's supposed to be."

I remember when I was a new mom and was struggling with a challenge with one of my sons. I thought, "Who better to call than my mom, the expert?" Instead of giving me the tools or advice I wanted, she asked, "What does your heart tell you?"

FINAL TOOL TIPS

1. Empower your children to discover how capable they are by allowing them to experience their capability.

2. Their suffering is likely to be harder on you than on them. Keep the long-term results in mind.

3. Understand that the principle behind all of the Positive Discipline tools is to empower your children—and yourself—in the process.

ACKNOWLEDGMENTS

From Brad: My son, Gibson, has provided a great deal of comic relief in this book. I love how he always challenged the status quo and forced me to look deeper at my parenting. In between our many power struggles, Gibson and I have developed a close father-son bond. He has grown up to be a responsible and respectful young gentleman. He is even nice to his younger sister, Emma, and has become a great role model for her. Gibson is now in college studying computer science.

When my youngest daughter, Emma, was finishing the sixth grade, I attended the ceremony at the school district offices where she was given the Outstanding Student of the Year Award. I was so proud of her!

Below is a letter from her teacher that was read to the audience when she was presented with her award.

Emma is an outstanding girl. She is one of the kindest people you will meet and is always seen including kids who don't have anyone else to play with. She tries her absolute hardest at any task she is given, and usually goes above and beyond surprising her teachers with her extra effort. She has a wonderful combination of intelligence mixed with creativity and curiosity.

But what really sets Emma apart, is her dedication to issues that are beyond the thoughts of most sixth-grade students. She is wholly dedicated to the environment and the misuse of our natural resources. She has started her own business that sells school supplies made of mostly recycled materials, and has even donated a portion of her profits to the school.

Emma is a wonderful person and will make a fantastic citizen of our country. No one who knows Emma will be surprised to see her succeed at whatever she sets her sights on. We are proud to have her as a student in our school!

Emma is now a junior in high school and will be leaving the nest soon. I don't mention my oldest daughter, Kelsie, in this book. She was already in college when I started blogging about the Positive Discipline tools. But I never felt like she needed much parenting anyway. In fact, she was a big help as an older sister to her two younger siblings. She has such a loving personality that everything is always better when Kelsie is around. If anything, she made my job as a single parent much easier. Kelsie graduated from high school with honors and attended college. She has taken breaks from her college studies a few times: once to work as a nanny in Germany, another time to serve as a missionary, and the most recent time to get married. She is now back in school and finishing her college degree.

From Mary: Many of my siblings did not have the benefit of my mom being a more available grandma to their children, because she was still raising some of her own. When my first child was born she moved close to me, intending to stay for a month. She still lives close and has had a huge influence on me, and thus on my children. I had no idea I would become an advocate of Positive Discipline, but how could I escape? She has been a constant encourager, and thus helped me discover how much I love encouraging others to use these wonderful tools.

From all of us: We are most grateful for our roots, and that is why we start every chapter with a quote from Alfred Adler or Rudolf Dreikurs. Their philosophy has changed our lives and the lives of millions. It pleases us greatly to "share it forward" through our books, workshops, and classes. And round and round it goes. Many of these parents, from all over the world, now share their success stories in this book. We know they will inspire many others by sharing the practical application of Positive Discipline tools with their children.

It has been so gratifying to receive the many Positive Discipline success stories from all over the world that will inspire our readers.

Our thanks goes to the Positive Discipline Association (www.positivediscipline.org), a not-for-profit organization that is responsible for the certification and quality assurance of hundreds (quickly growing to thousands) of Certified Positive Discipline Parent and Teacher Educators and Certified Positive Discipline Trainers of Trainers. These certified trainers are conducting Positive Discipline classes and workshops all over the world.

Our thanks again for the illustrations of Paula Gray and Diane Durand that have appeared in many of the Positive Discipline books. We love how their illustrations often say more than words.

Thanks to Dr. Kelly Gfroerer for the research we have quoted in this book. Kelly is the coauthor of the soon-to-be-published *Positive Discipline Tools for Teachers*. Because Kelly loves research so much, this new book will include research to validate every teacher tool we present.

We rave to everyone about our editor, Michele Eniclerico. We feel blessed for having the privilege of working with someone as talented and encouraging as Michele. Her contributions in both editing and organization have made this a book we want to read over and over. Thank you so much.

All of our children know how many mistakes we make; and love us anyway. (Did we mention that Positive Discipline doesn't make you a perfect parent?) We are grateful that our children don't have the burden of living up to perfection. Smile.

CONTRIBUTORS

Many people have contibuted success stories to this book. The following contributors are also Certified Positive Discipline Parent Educators and/or Trainers who regularly conduct Positive Discipline classes and training:

Khulod Muhammad Al Assaf

Melissa Bugeja, Malta www.breastfeedingmatters.net

Joel Devyn Carter

Tarisayi de Cugnac, France

Cheryl Erwin, www.cherylerwin.com

Lisa Fuller, www.lisafullercoaching.com

Samantha Garcia

Kelly Gfroerer, www.positivedisciplineatlanta.com

Dimitrios Giouzepis, www.positiveparentingguy.com

Gina Graham and Mariella Vega, Peru, www.crianzapositiva.org

Georgina Gurdian, Costa Rica, www.facebook.com/
    noalmaltratoinfantilcr

Saleha Hafiz, www.parentingfortomorrow.com

Monica Holliday

Lois Ingber, www.AdlerianConsulting.com

Julie Iraninejad, Certified Positive Discipline Trainer,
    www.parentingforabetterworld.com

Sarah Joseph, www.prenataltoparenting.com

Seonghwan Kim, www.pd-korea.net

Amy Knobler, www.connectandrespect.com

Freddie Liger, www.relationshiphelp.net.au

Nisha Maggon, www.newlifeparenting.com

Flora McCormick, www.justastayathomemom.com

Casey O'Roarty, www.joyfulcourage.com

Yogi Patel, www.kinderhousemontessori.com

Jeanne-Marie Paynel, www.voilamontessori.com

Aisha Pope, www.RootsAndWingsConsulting.com

Joy Sacco, www.positivedisciplinesocal.com

Shaza A. S. Salaheldin

Christine Salo-Sokolowski, www.internallymotivatedkids.com

Julietta Skoog, www.juliettaskoog.com

Marcilie Smith Boyle, www.workingparenting.com

Elly Zhen, www.pd-china.org

REFERENCES

1. Baumrind, D. (1966). Effects of authoritative parental control on child behavior. *Child Development, 37,* 887–907.

2. Baumrind, D. (1967). Childcare practices anteceding three patterns of preschool behavior. *Genetic Psychology Monograph, 75,* 43–88.

3. Baumrind, D. (1971). Current patterns of parental authority. *Developmental Psychology, 4(1, Pt.2),* 1–103. doi: 10.1037/h0030372.

4. Baumrind, D. (1996). The discipline controversy revisited. *Family Relations, 45,* 405–414.

5. Bower, B. (1989). Teenagers reap broad benefits from authoritative parents. *Science News, 136,* 117–118.

6. Gershoff, E., & Larzelere, R. (2002). Is corporal punishment an effective means of discipline? American Psychological Association.

7. Adler, A. (1927). *Understanding human nature.* (W. B. Wolfe, Trans.). New York: World.

8. Furnham, A., & Cheng, H. (2000). Perceived parenting behavior, self-esteem, and happiness. *Social Psychiatry Psychiatric Epidemiology, 35,* 463–470.

9. Maccoby, E. E., & Martin, J. A. (1983). Socialization in the context of the family: Parent-child interaction. In P. H. Mussen (Ed.), *Handbook of child psychology: Vol. 4: Socialization, personality, and social development* (4th ed., 1–101). New York: Wiley.

10. Masud, H., Thurasamy, R., & Ahmad, M. (2015). Parenting styles and academic achievement of young adolescents: A systematic literature review. *Quality and Quantity, 46,* 2411–2433.

11. Milevsky, A., Schlechter, M., & Netter, S. (2007). Maternal and paternal parenting styles in adolescents: Associations with self-esteem, depression and life satisfaction. *Journal of Child and Family Studies, 16(1),* 39–47. doi: 10.1007/s10826-006-9066-5.

12. Newman, J, Gozu, H., Guan, S., Lee, J. E., Li, X., Sasaki, Y. (2015). Relationship between maternal parenting style and high school achievement and self-esteem in China, Turkey and U.S.A. *Journal of Comparative Family Studies, 46,* 265–288.

13. Ren, L., & Pope Edwards, C. (2015). Pathways of influence: Chinese parents' expectations, parenting styles, and child social competence. *Early Child Development & Care, 185,* 616–632.

14. Dinwiddie, S. (1999). Effective parenting styles: Why yesterday's models won't work today. Kidsource.com/better.world.press/parenting.

15. Adalbjarnardottir, S., & Hafsteinsson, L. G. (2001). Adolescents' perceived parenting styles and their substance use: Concurrent and longitudinal analysis. *Journal of Research on Adolescence, 11,* 401–423.

16. Burback, D. J., & Borduin, C. M. (1986). Parent-child relations and the etiology of depression: A review of methods and findings. *Clinical Psychology Review, 6,* 133–153.

17. Turkel, Y. D., & Tezer, E. (2008). Parenting styles and learned resourcefulness of Turkish adolescents. *Adolescence, 43(169),* 143–152.

18. Dweck, C. S. (2006). *Mindset: The New Psychology of Success.* New York: Random House.

19. Warneken, F., & Tomasello, M. (2006). Altruistic helping in human infants and young chimpanzees. *Science, 311,* 1301–1303.

20. Kaiser Family Foundation (2010). Generation M2: Media in the lives of 8- to 18-year-olds. http://kff.org/other/event/generation-m2-media-in-the-lives-of.

INDEX